Japanese Tourists:
Socio-Economic, Marketing
and Psychological Analysis

Japanese Tourists: Socio-Economic, Marketing and Psychological Analysis

K. S. (Kaye) Chon
Tsutomu Inagaki
Taiji Ohashi
Editors

Japanese Tourists: Socio-Economic, Marketing and Psychological Analysis has been co-published simultaneously as *Journal of Travel & Tourism Marketing*, Volume 9, Numbers 1/2 2000.

Routledge
Taylor & Francis Group
New York London

First published 2000 by Haworth Press, Inc

Published 2020 by Routledge
605 Third Avenue, New York, NY 10017
2 Park Square, Milton Park, Abingdon, Oxon OX14 4RN

Routledge is an imprint of Taylor & Francis Group, and informa business

© 2000 by Taylor & Francis

Cover design by Thomas J. Mayshock Jr.

Library of Congress Cataloging-in-Publication Data

Japanese tourists: socio-economic, marketing, and psychological analysis / K.S. (Kaye) Chon, Tustomu Inagaki, Taiji Ohashi, editors.
　　　　p.　cm.
"Co-published simultaneously as Journal of travel & tourism marketing, volume 9, numbers 1/2 2000"

　　　Includes bibliographical references.
　　　ISBN 0-7890-0970-6 (alk. paper) – ISBN 0-7890-0988-9 (alk. paper)
　　　1. Travelers–Japan. 2. Tourism–Social aspects–Japan. 3. Tourism–Economic aspects–Japan.
I. Chon, K.S. II. Inagaki, Tsutomu, 1951- III. Ohashi, Taiji, 1931-
G330 .J36 2000
338.4′791520449–dc21

00-036964
CIP

ISBN-13: 978-0-789-00970-8 (hbk)
ISBN-13: 978-0-789-00988-3 (pbk)
ISBN-13: 978-0-203-82398-9 (ebk)

ABOUT THE EDITORS

K. S. (Kaye) Chon is Professor and Director of the Tourism Industry Institute in the Conrad N. Hilton College of Hotel & Restaurant Management at the University of Houston. Dr. Chon, who in 1993 received the John Wiley & Sons Award presented by CHRIE (Council on Hotel, Restaurant and Institutional Education) for his lifetime contributions in hospitality and tourism research, has published over 200 papers and five books, including *The Management of Hotel Sales and Marketing* (HSMAI Foundation, 1991), *Welcome to Hospitality* (Delmar Publishing Co., 1995 and 2000), and *Tourism in Developing Countries* (International Thompson Business Press, 1997). A former hotel manager and industry consultant, his research interests lie in marketing and strategic management in tourism and hospitality.

Tsutomu Inagaki is Professor of Hospitality Marketing and Cultural Studies of The College of Tourism and Deputy Director of the Institute of Tourism at Rikkyo University in Tokyo. He has published many articles and has authored or co-authored several books focusing on tourism and hospitality issues in the Pacific Rim, including *Hospitality Industry and New Products Strategy* (Daiichi-Shorin: Tokyo, 1994) and *Foundation of Tourist Industry* (Nihon-Keizia-Shinbunsha: Tokyo, 1981). Professor Inagaki also has a forthcoming book about hill stations in Southeast Asia. Currently, his research interest lies in the area of post-colonized countries and how these locations influence tourism.

Taiji Ohashi is Dean and Professor of Tourism Management in the Cultural Information Resources at Surugadai University in Hannoh, Japan. Professor Ohashi has acted as Chair of the Tourism Department at Rikkyo University in Tokyo and Chief Technical Expert of the Government Official Development Assistance to Indonesia in Tourism Education. He has published over 120 papers and ten books, including *Tourism Management System* (BPLP Press, 1991), *Strategic Management for Tourism Development in Indonesia* (STPB, 1994), and *The New Socio-Economic Tourismology* (Naigai Shuppan, 1998). His research interests include strategic management in tourism and hospitality, human resource development in tourism and the impact of tourism on communities.

Japanese Tourists: Socio-Economic, Marketing and Psychological Analysis

Journal of Travel & Tourism Marketing
Volume 9, Numbers 1/2

CONTENTS

Preface

This book presents a collection of recent studies on socioeconomic, marketing, and psychosocial analysis of Japanese tourists. World's tourism industry has witnessed a significant increase of outbound tourism from Japan for the past decade and, in most recent years close to 16 million Japanese tourists traveled around the world, accounting for a significant portion of international tourism arrivals and receipts. This book seeks to provide a forum for the exchange of information and ideas among researchers around the world on the studies and the phenomenon of Japanese tourists. Up to this point, there has been no tourism literature that has systematically reviewed the phenomenon of the Japanese outbound tourism. It is hoped that the 12 research papers included in this volume will provide new directions for research on Japanese tourists in the future.

It is acknowledged that the chapters included in this volume were selected based on a double blind review process by an ad hoc manuscript review committee. The assistance and support by the following ad hoc manuscript review panel members are greatly acknowledged. Without their helpful suggestions, constructive criticisms, and timely review of the original submissions and revised manuscripts, this volume would not have been possible.

Dr. Jerome Agrusa, University of Louisiana at Lafayette
Dr. Mark A. Bonn, Florida State University
Dr. Liping Cai, Purdue University
Dr. Sukbin Cha, Sunchunhyang University, Korea
David Leong Choon Chiang, Nanyang Technological University, Singapore
Dr. David Christianson, University of Nevada, Las Vegas
Dr. Thomas Iverson, University of Guam
Dr. Bharath Josiam, University of Wisconsin-Stout
Seongseop Kim, Texas A&M University
Dr. Patrick Legoherel, University d'Angers, France
Dr. Connie Mok, University of Houston
Dr. Heung-Chul Oh, Kyungsung University, Korea
(Late) Dr. Martin Oppermann, Griffith University, Australia

[Haworth indexing entry note]: "Preface." Chon, K. S., Taiji Ohashi, and Tsutomu Inagaki. Published in *Journal of Travel & Tourism Marketing* (The Haworth Hospitality Press, an imprint of The Haworth Press, Inc.) Vol. 9, Nos. 1/2, 2000, pp. xi-xii. Single or multiple copies of this article are available for a fee from The Haworth Document Delivery Service [1-800-342-9678, 9:00 a.m. - 5:00 p.m. (EST). E-mail address: getinfo@haworthpressinc.com].

Dr. Sungsoo Pyo, Kyonggi University, Korea
Dr. Wesley Roehl, University of Nevada-Las Vegas
Dr. Stowe Shoemaker, University of Nevada-Las Vegas
Heidi Sung, Purdue University
Dr. Fumiko Yokohama, Asia University, Japan
Dr. Jihwan Yoon, Kyungwon University, Korea
Dr. Larry Yu, The George Washington University
Dr. Zhongqing Zhou, Niagara University

K. S. (Kaye) Chon
Tsutomu Inagaki
Taiji Ohashi

Buyer Behavior
in the Japanese Travel Trade:
Advancements in Theoretical Frameworks

R. Bruce Money
John C. Crotts

SUMMARY. This paper offers insights on how social network activity operates in Japanese culture–as compared to the West–and why these differences must be appreciated for a Western tourism supplier to have any opportunity of achieving success in the Japanese market. More specifically, the influence of Japanese culture and location on social network activity and ultimately buyer behavior of both Japanese consumers and corporations is the focus of this paper. In addition, this paper puts forth a theoretical model that contends that social networks or 'ties' between individuals or between companies represent a basic unit of analysis in examining buyer-seller relationships in the international travel trade, particularly in vastly different national cultures such as Japan. *[Article copies available for a fee from The Haworth Document Delivery Service: 1-800-342-9678. E-mail address: <getinfo@haworthpressinc.com> Website:<http://www.haworthpressinc.com>]*

KEYWORDS. Social network activity, Japanese travel trade

When it comes to the global travel trade, few areas of the world are as complex as Japan. The Japan Airlines (JAL) Group, for example, has more

R. Bruce Money is affiliated with International Business Program Area, University of South Carolina. John C. Crotts is affiliated with Hospitality and Tourism Management, College of Charleston.

[Haworth co-indexing entry note]: "Buyer Behavior in the Japanese Travel Trade: Advancements in Theoretical Frameworks." Money, R. Bruce, and John C. Crotts. Co-published simultaneously in *Journal of Travel & Tourism Marketing* (The Haworth Hospitality Press, an imprint of The Haworth Press, Inc.) Vol. 9, No. 1/2, 2000, pp. 1-19; and: *Japanese Tourists: Socio-Economic, Marketing and Psychological Analysis* (ed: K. S. (Kaye) Chon, Tsutomu Inagaki, and Taiji Ohashi) The Haworth Hospitality Press, an imprint of The Haworth Press, Inc., 2000, pp. 1-19. Single or multiple copies of this article are available for a fee from The Haworth Document Delivery Service [1-800-342-9678, 9:00 a.m. - 5:00 p.m. (EST). E-mail address: getinfo@haworthpressinc.com].

1

than 200 companies strategically linked as a conglomerate ranging from air transport, hotels and resorts, tour companies and suppliers (Sullivan 1995). Western tourism suppliers desiring to do business with Japanese traveling abroad have often been advised to pursue buyer-supplier relationships with such conglomerates as JAL and the Japan Travel Bureau (JTB) (Crotts & Wilson 1995) since four out of five Japanese traveling abroad traditionally have done so under fully prepackaged tours (Japan Travel Bureau 1994). However, since the Gulf War there has been noticeable downsizing by these tourism conglomerates as well as a shift to more "free and independent" travel by Japanese travelers (Sullivan 1995). These circumstances create opportunities for non-Asian firms wishing to do business in what is the second largest economy of the world.

The Japanese way of doing business is significantly different from that of the West (Pascale and Athos 1981) and must be appreciated by Western firms to have any opportunity of achieving success. In fact, as Hall (1976) commented, "I can think of few countries Americans are likely to visit and work . . . where life is more filled with surprises than Japan" (p. 57). The purpose of this paper is to summarize recent research and suggest a theoretical framework of how Japanese make their travel purchase decisions as compared to the West. More specifically, the primary objectives are to: first, explore traits of Japan's national culture and other cultural dimensions in the literature as compared to those in the West (principally the U.S. in this case) second, and more importantly, examine the implication of these cultural traits on buyer behavior of Japanese consumers and corporations. Third, the research also addresses the issue of relative location (foreign or domestic) of Japanese buyers as a factor for choosing a travel service provider. Does the purchase behavior of Japanese firms operating in their domestic market differ from that of Japanese in a foreign market?

The implications of this paper are two-fold. First, for Western suppliers trying to sell travel and tourism services in Japan or to Japanese conglomerates, the task can be confusing and daunting (March 1997). The information on how to cultivate the right kinds of contacts in the right position is an important determinant of marketing success. Even with its lingering domestic recession, Japan in 1996 was the leading overseas tourist generating country to the U.S. (including Guam), representing 5,047,000 arrivals, nearly twice the visitors from the United Kingdom at 2,888,000 and Germany at 1,848,000. The focus on consumer, as well as business marketing, is necessitated since much of this travel should be dichotomized as free and independent versus group, or, on another dimension, leisure versus business, each of which requires a separate approach by travel and tourism suppliers to secure business from the respective target markets.

Second, travel researchers should find the discussion of social network theory and its dependent constructs useful in their buyer behavior studies within an international context. Since most of the research on the creation and management of marketing relationships has been focused within a single country (Kale 1986, Frazier et al. 1989)–that exhibits primarily Western culture (Frazier & Raymond 1991), we argue that these theoretical positions provide a better framework in which to examine buyer-seller relationships particularly in a vastly different national culture such as Japan. It is our contention that social networks or 'ties' represent a basic unit of analysis in the international travel trade, be they patterns of interactions between individuals or ties between companies as a result of the ties between the people who work for those companies. By providing an appropriate theoretical framework, the operational definitions of its constructs, and a list of hypotheses derived from the broader literature, this paper is intended to invite research into an area largely unexplored by travel researchers.

THEORETICAL BACKGROUND

In Figure 1 is proposed the conceptual framework for this paper. Within this framework, national culture and location of operation are posited to influence the observable outcomes of social network activity. These relationships have been empirically explored previously by Money, Gilly, and

FIGURE 1. Conceptual Framework

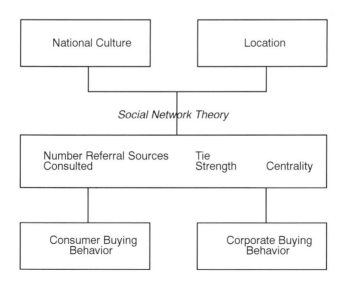

Graham (1998) on the basis of 10 commercial services. This paper extends that work by focusing exclusively on travel and tourism services. Furthermore, this paper expands the theoretical base to underscore the importance of social network activity in Japanese buyer behavior. That is, in the current research, social network activity is purported to have an influence on Japanese consumer buying behavior as well as corporate buying behavior (compared to that of Americans), since the decisions are made by Japanese employees.

NATIONAL CULTURE AND BUYER BEHAVIOR: JAPANESE VS. AMERICAN

Hundreds of definitions for culture have been advanced in the literature. Kluckhohn (1962) indicated that culture emanates from belonging to a group–it is learned and shared by others–"our social legacy, as contrasted to our organic heredity" (p. 25). National culture has been employed in developing a general theory of marketing (Clark 1990), advancing knowledge of the new product development process (Nakata and Sivakumar 1996), and the performance of global branding strategies (Roth 1995). National culture is important to the current study because word-of-mouth (hereafter WOM) referrals that generate new business for travel service providers would be expected to differ from country to country, at least in part because of cultural differences. Few would question that marked contrasts exist between the business and management practices of the U.S. and Japan (Drucker 1971; Ouchi 1981; Pascale and Athos 1981). In grouping countries into aggregate national cultural groups of similar characteristics (Norway and Sweden, for example), Hofstede (1980) found that Japan's national culture was the most difficult to group with any other.

According to previous research, Japan's national culture distinguishes itself from the U.S. on the following dimensions:

1. *Individualism/Collectivism*. Hofstede (1980, 1991) found that the national cultures of the U.S. and Japan differed in most of the five cultural dimensions that he and collaborators identified, particularly regarding individualism, where Japan's score was much lower than that of the U.S., indicating a high degree of collectivism. A wide range of phenomena in business and society demonstrate this, such as keiretsu industrial groupings (Gerlach 1992), comparatively long-term employment (Ouchi 1980), the education system of "no dropouts "(Glazer 1976) and closer cooperation between government and industry (Tyson 1992). Other researchers (Komiya, Okuno, and Suzumura, 1988) have shown how strategic industries have historically been nourished to globally competitive strength, emphasizing stability of operations over market share (Anterasian, Graham, and Money 1996).

2. *Uncertainty Avoidance.* This is basically a tolerance for risk. Hofstede found that Americans are much more risk-taking than the Japanese, with an uncertainty avoidance score almost half that of Japan. In a business setting, Japanese lower their risk of doing business with unfamiliar suppliers or customers by forming relatively long-term business relationships (Sullivan and Peterson 1988) and interacting extensively with those business contacts. For example, Japanese businesses spend six times more (as a percentage of GNP per capita) on business entertainment than do Americans or Europeans (Sakaiya 1993). *Keiretsu* member companies typically "get the business" from other members firms when considering potential channel members (Czinkota and Woronoff 1986). (Note: *Keiretsu* refer to long-standing, close-ly-knit industrial groups such as Mitsui or Sumitomo comprised of firms that refer each other business, share financial ties, and even exchange personnel.)

3. *Context.* Hall and Hall (1987) characterized Japan as a high "context" culture; defined as the degree to which social relations, innuendo, inference, and latent meanings shape the communications and value systems of a society (Hall 1976). On the other hand, in low-context cultures such as the U.S., meaning is communicated by explicit code in a more "cards-on-the table" approach. In Japan most of the meaning is not in the words that are spoken, but rather in the social context of what is said. Cateora (1996) ranked Japan and mainland China as the highest context countries while the U.S. and West Germany were ranked as the lowest. In these latter countries, candor, frankness, and a "face value" orientation are more valued. Tse, Francis and Walls (1994) theorized similar positions of high and low-context for Asian and Western cultures, respectively.

LOCATION OF OPERATION: FOREIGN VS. DOMESTIC

In a foreign market, a company would be expected to use more referral sources than in its domestic market. This is because managers deciding whom to use for travel services providers would naturally use informed intermediaries to source those services. The conceptual foundation for this proposition comes from three areas. The first is cognitive psychology in which Anderson (1983) argues that unfamiliar situations demand two types of knowledge to be developed: procedural knowledge (how to), and contextual knowledge (detailed and specific knowledge needed to implement the procedural knowledge). Of the second type, personal references would be extremely effective. The second arises from March and Simon's (1958) bounded rationality theory–people start with the known to proceed beyond the limits of their knowledge to the unknown. A referral source (known) in a foreign market (unknown) would be described by this theory. Third, transaction cost analysis (Williamson 1975) suggests that firms will seek to minimize their expense of either buying or building expertise in a foreign market. Utilizing an internal manager who uses external key market informants for sourcing quality travel service providers is an example of trying to keep transaction costs low. Therefore, in foreign markets, both Japanese and American companies will exhibit a greater degree of social network activity.

The following insights were gleaned as to differences in social network activity from a series of personal interviews conducted by one of the authors with 48 corporate buyers (in various lines of business) of several services, including travel. These 48 buyers were equally split between American and Japanese firms, and split again between the locations in Japan and the U.S. Therefore, 12 types of companies of each type (Japanese companies in Japan, American companies in Japan, Japanese companies in the U.S., American companies in the U.S) were interviewed. The nationality of the individual decision-maker interviewed paralleled the national culture of the company (i.e., only Japanese were interviewed in Japanese companies, not Americans working there). The buying companies were chosen from three broad types of industries: durables, nondurables and services. The industries within those categories were chosen by SIC codes at random. A 4-digit number was generated by a random number table, the SIC code that most closely matched that number was chosen, then categorized as one of the three types above (durables, nondurables, and services) until 4 industries in each type were selected. Companies were then contacted within those industries according to certain criteria, such as age and size. Table 1 shows the industries of all of the companies interviewed for the study. Individual company names are not disclosed for confidentiality purposes.

Japanese Companies in Japan. In explaining why they used some service suppliers and not others, some Japanese managers expressed general dissatis-faction in dealing with American companies as suppliers compared to Japa-nese companies. A Japanese executive gave very detailed accounts of how Japanese suppliers extend credit, much like a bank, in a way American suppliers have never understood in his industry. Another Japanese manager (who was in the food business) said that Americans must acquire more of a "smell" for Japanese business. These comments are consistent with a risk averse, highly collectivist business society that relies on established networks in transacting business rather than trusting newcomers, such as Americans. Probably the most common thread in the comments by Japanese managers in Japan was the reliance that small companies in Japan have on their banks. At least half of the managers mentioned that the bank plays an integral role in getting a company started by referring it business and service providers.

American Companies in Japan. American managers expressed frustration at trying to break into the Japanese service business circles, but once in, the business opportunities are many. Business is basically done with who knows

TABLE 1. Types of Company Industry by Location and Culture

JAPANESE IN JAPAN

Durables
- Measuring Sensory Equipment
- Toys
- Sensors and Guidance Components
- Radiation Equipment

Non-Durables
- Ceramics
- Agricultural Products
- Clothing, Art
- Cosmetics

Service
- Cold Storage
- Public Works Contractor
- Hotels, Resorts
- Software

AMERICAN IN JAPAN

Durables
- Appliances
- Medical Equipment
- Computers
- Retailing Equipment

Non-Durables
- Beverages
- Personal Care Products
- Tobacco Products
- Pigments

Service
- Cleaning and Pest Control
- Copying
- Relocation Services
- Public Relations

TABLE 1 (continued)

JAPANESE IN USA

Durables
- Auto Parts
- Cars
- Electronic Equipment
- Calculating Equipment

Non-Durables
- Bakery Products
- Paper and Pulp
- Chemicals and Plastics
- Foods

Service
- Advertising
- Construction
- Engineering
- Trucking

AMERICAN IN USA

Durables
- Furniture
- Filling and Packing Equipment
- Clean Room Piping
- Forged Aluminum

Non-Durables
- Reactive Chemical Agents
- Coated Fabrics–Industrial
- Women's Clothing
- Injected Rubber Molding

Service
- Health Care
- Linen Service
- Software Programing
- Management Consulting

whom, and "who needs the business these days." The American manager of a direct sales company indicated that because of the amount of obligation amongst the Japanese people, the first sale is easier than the second, after the obligation has been discharged. He was referring to the dealings of Japanese consumers with their Japanese friends in the network marketing sense. This stands in contrast to the difficult first sale that a non-Japanese supplier has in breaking into consumer and industrial circles. One American manager in Japan said that services are selected by American companies in Japan on the basis of who is reputed to be the best in the business. Because setting up an office is very expensive in Japan, paying extra for the blue-chip reputation of a service firm is not that much more in percentage terms. However, one manager cautioned against joining the network of too strong of a Japanese company, especially in a joint venture, since, according to the manager, the partner will "eventually keep the best business for itself while other companies won't touch you because you are in so-and-so's pocket."

In Japan where social networks are large and dense, competition for new service clients is intense, particularly for the accounts of a large, prestigious American firms' subsidiaries than for relatively smaller, less well-known firms. The manager of a Fortune 500 durable goods subsidiary recounted how, on the day he moved boxes into the company's new Tokyo office space, Japanese bankers were actually lined up at the door early in the morning to introduce themselves. The bankers even came from different branches of the same bank, competing vigorously for the new business. The bankers, losing their usual restraint, were literally tossing their business cards onto the top of the boxes he was carrying up the stairs. Alternatively, managers from smaller American firms in Japan recounted how they needed an introduction to their bank by a third party, such as a partner or customer.

Japanese Companies in the U.S. This type of company typically draws on strong ties back in Japan, sometimes hundreds of years old, mostly through banks, to set up their companies. One Japanese manager complained that American customers and sellers of services for his company do not understand the process of a Japanese company in the U.S. activating ties in Japan. Deals are constructed from the bottom up, but the top managers in the two companies most of the time know each other well, through sometimes decades of contact. That is why, when the buying decision gets to the top level, it is made rather quickly. In America, he perceived, firms doing business together allow the other party one major mistake. In network-intensive Japan, they give each other at least two.

American Companies in the U.S. These companies, for the most part, do not rely on referral networks, in contrast to the other three types in the study. Many company founders reported they found legal, CPA, and other important services in the Yellow Pages. In response to the question of how the company found its professional services such as accounting, surprising was how often an executive recounted merely seeing a provider's name on a sign while driving around and gave him/her a call.

SOCIAL NETWORKS THEORY

It was Granovetter's (1973) article on the "strength of weak ties" that was one of the first to prompt researchers to consider the characteristics of a relationship in studying communication patterns and information flow. The term "network" in this paper refers to the patterns of social business interaction that arise in relationships between individuals who work for companies. In addition to Granovetter's "tie strength" concept, the paper also considers the number of referral sources used, and "centrality," or how strategically a particular referral source is placed in a network. Although not specifically detailed as research propositions in this paper, these concepts of social network activity naturally influence the way both corporate and retail buyers of travel services go about making decisions, as shown in Figure 1. Those influences might be the scope of a future study. Rather, our propositions focus on the relationships between the independent variables of national culture and relative location vis-à-vis the social network dependent outcomes.

NUMBER OF WOM REFERRAL SOURCES CONSULTED

Word-of-mouth (WOM) is arguably the most influential source of information available to consumers (Crotts 1998; Mahajan, Muller, and Bass 1990) and WOM activity has been employed as a dependent construct in a social networks context in several marketing studies (Iacobucci and Hopkins 1993). For example, Reingen and Kernan (1986) exploration of social networks in piano tuner referrals was one of the first marketing studies to employ network analysis. Brown and Reingen (1987) used the context of a piano teacher's student population to measure the level of WOM referral activity among students and their parents. More recently, Frenzen and Nakamoto (1993) found that WOM information flow was restricted where divulging information might incur some kind of risk to the source. Several management studies have also used network analysis in explicating the differences in behavior among executives and organizations (Carroll and Teo 1996; Labianca, Brass, and Gray 1988).

Although network studies on an international scale have been few (for an exception, see Ruan, Freeman, Dai, Pan, and Zhang 1997), in a marketing setting Takada and Jain's (1991) study of innovation adoption rates indicated that Japanese use more WOM than do Americans. They found that WOM activity was positively influenced by the similarity of communication patterns in Pacific Rim countries compared to those of the more heterogeneous U.S. The Japanese may also use more WOM because of the difficulty of written communications in their character-based writing system (Pascale 1978). Thus, the present paper first hypothesizes that Japanese companies will employ more WOM referral sources to find sellers of commercial services than American companies. This is expected to hold true whether the companies are operating in Japan or the United States.

In addition to national culture, relative location of operation (foreign vs. domestic) is also proposed to have an effect on the number of WOM sources consulted. Foreign buyers (Japanese in the U.S. and Americans in Japan) are hypothesized to use referral sources more than domestic buyers (Japanese in Japan and Americans in the U.S.). Marketers wanting access to Japan have been advised to work with a contact in an existing distribution channel (Nairu and Flath 1993), or consult an expert insider in the desired line of business (Batzer and Laumer 1989). Those who are sent to Japan by American companies have been counseled to find a key source of information to help the manager establish the office (Gronhaug and Graham 1987). As in the discussion of procedural vs. contextual knowledge (Anderson 1983) and bounded rationality, (March and Simon 1958), buyers in a foreign culture will seek out referral sources more than they would in their own markets. The propositions that follow from the discussion are:

P1a. Japanese buyers of travel and tourism services will consult more WOM referral sources than American buyers.

P1b. Buyers of travel and tourism services in foreign markets will use more WOM referral sources than will buyers in domestic markets.

TIE STRENGTH

Reingen, Foster, Brown, and Seidman (1984) used tie strength to show that brand congruence (group members choosing the same brand) in a college sorority was higher for "private" products such as shampoo, than for "public" products such as pizza. In their study of piano tuner client referrals, Reingen and Kernan (1986) found that a strong tie in a subgroup was more likely to be activated for referral flow than a weak one. Brown and Reingen (1987) showed not only the importance of strong ties in networks, but also the function of weak ties as bridges between subgroups, consistent with Granovetter's (1973) work. Frenzen and Davis (1990) showed that tie strength affected positively the likelihood of purchases in home party direct sales. The measures of tie strength that have been employed in these studies are: *duration*: How long the seeker of the WOM referral and the source and have known each other (Ward and Reingen 1990); *frequency of contact*: How often (instances per year, for example) the referral source and seeker of information contact each other (Brown and Reingen 1987); and *social importance*: How "important" the seeker considers the referral source (Reingen, Foster, Brown and Seidman 1984, Brown and Reingen 1987, Frenzen and Nakamoto 1993).

Although the above measures have been used in the past in a consumer behavior, the present study expands the concept of tie strength to include corporate buying behavior as well. As a result, four other measures that would help capture the nature of the tie between buyer and seller in a business relationship were also added to the concept of tie strength: business importance, likability, trust, and perceived expertise. According to the social psychology literature, (McGuire 1985), three source characteristics are important in influencing attitudes of others: credibility (here "trust" and "perceived expertise"), attractiveness ("likability"), and power ("business importance," which can be very different from social importance, even between the same two people).

Several studies have indicated that the strength of ties will be greater in Japanese company referral networks than in America. Nakane (1970) suggests that U.S. society is characterized by impersonal ties, but that Japan is more relational in its social structure. The proposition that Japanese society is more collectivist, more risk-averse, and higher context than that of the U.S. would suggest that social ties are basically stronger in Japan, which leads to stronger ties in business settings as well. For example, Dore (1973) found that among British and Japanese factory workers, 32% of Hitachi's entry level workers found the position through a school friend; only 1% of British did so. Therefore, the level of tie strength is proposed to be higher in the referral networks of Japanese buyers than in those for American companies, whether in the U.S. or Japan. Relative location (foreign vs. domestic) is also proposed to have an effect, as explained in the discussion for P1a and P1b.

P2a. The ties between buyers and referral sources in referral networks used by Japanese buyers of travel and tourism services will be stronger than ties in networks used by American buyers.

P2b. The ties between buyers and referral sources in referral networks used by buyers of travel and tourism services in foreign markets will be stronger than ties in networks used by buyers in domestic markets.

CENTRALITY

Centrality implies how strategically placed a referral source is in the network (Bavelas 1950; Freeman, Roeder, and Mullholland 1980). The concept has three components, two of which are used in this study: *degree* (number of ties in the network between actors); and *betweenness* (how importantly or strategically the ties are placed). The third (*closeness*) is considered to have little explanatory power compared to the first two and is excluded from the study.

Management and marketing researchers have used the centrality concept to a limited extent. Ibarra and Andrews (1993) found that an employee's centrality in a network at the office affected perceptions of the company's environment for information access, job autonomy, and interdepartmental conflict. Ronchetto, Hutt, and Reingen (1989) used the centrality construct in an organizational buying system concept and found that influence within the system was dependent on centrality of workers in work-flow networks and communication networks.

It should be noted that the work of Freeman and his colleagues (1980) defined centrality for individuals, not companies. The centrality of an individual in a network is known as "point centrality." However, since the present paper also examines the ties between individuals that purchase, sell, or refer commercial services, the concept can shed light on the tourism marketing process, as has on the topics of other researchers (Ronchetto, Hutt, and Reingen 1989). Indeed, recent network research has defined centrality for "graphs," or groups of individuals (White and Borgatti 1994), which is applicable to the WOM referral network of both consumer and corporate buyers.

Centrality of referral sources in the marketing of travel services would indicate that one or more referral sources supplies critical information to buyers in their search for information. Such a person would be similar to Feick and Price's (1987) so-called "market maven," an opinion leader who influences the decisions of others through superior market, rather than product, information. In a travel services marketing setting, a "market maven" would be someone who influences the purchase decisions of commercial and retail buyers of services by virtue of his or her superior knowledge of the travel market.

"Ringi," or consensus decision making, is a well-known Japanese business practice. It is consistent with the Japanese values of long-term harmony in the organization (Hall and Hall 1987), where decisions are implemented by employees who will typically be with the company for a relatively longer time than Americans in their companies (Apasu, Ichikawa, and Graham 1987). There is little reason to believe that this type of decision making would not manifest itself in decisions made outside of the firm as well, particularly given the role of the all-important "shokaisha" (one who makes the introductions) in Japanese business (Graham and Sano 1989). Introductions by a trusted intermediary (e.g., banker, accountant), at the right level, is the way a business relationship is expected to begin (Van Zandt 1981). Cold-calling a sales prospect, especially by foreigners, without the help of an intermediary is a serious business blunder, word of which would spread to other potential clients or important vendors (Morgan and Morgan 1991).

In this research, "graph" centrality (in its components of degree and betweenness), is expected to be higher in Japanese companies than in American companies, in both the U.S. and Japan. That is, more ties will be present in the Japanese networks (degree) and the referral sources will be located more directly on the path of WOM information flow (betweenness). As discussed above, a relative location effect is also proposed in that networks of firms operating in foreign markets (Japanese in the U.S. and American firms in Japan) will exhibit higher levels of graph centrality because of the more strategically placed intermediaries they use. The research propositions that follow from this discussion are:

> P3a. Referral networks used by Japanese buyers of travel and tourism services will have higher levels of graph centrality (degree and betweenness) than will networks used by American buyers.

> P3b. Referral networks used by buyers of travel and tourism services in foreign markets will have higher levels of graph centrality than will networks used by buyers in domestic markets.

DISCUSSION AND IMPLICATIONS

This paper has attempted to summarize and integrate several streams of research in international marketing, industrial marketing of services, and social networks as to how cultural traits influence the buying behavior of Japanese consumers and corporations. Though it provides no evidence of its own drawn specifically from a travel and tourism context to support its inferences, we are unaware of any evidence that indicates national culture affects the marketing of tourism services differently from that of other commercial services. At the very least, this paper has laid the theoretical foundation and opportunity for others to follow in an area largely unexplored by travel researchers.

In spite of the above limitation, the synthesis of the research literature offers important insights into how social network activity operates in varying national cultures in different locations. Results of this review of the literature and interviews with managers indicate that culture and location influence aspects of social network behavior of consumer and corporate buyers. To adopt the popular saying, in Japan "it's not just who you know," but *where* that *who* is in the network. These insights have implications for tourism marketing professionals.

The effect of culture on WOM referral behavior in the marketing of services is an important consideration for managers attempting to sell their tourism services abroad. The existing relationships in a country and the way they operate in that country's business culture cannot be overlooked as a valuable resource or serious stumbling block in getting business done, especially in Japan. Specifically, a considerable amount of empirical evidence exists that indicates the business culture in Japan is vastly different than that of the U.S., and getting business done there requires a different approach than the "go it alone" business culture of the U.S. We can probably gather from reading of popular business press that the Japanese use more network activity than the U.S. But do they? For a wide variety of commercial services, Money, Gilly, and Graham (1998) found that Japanese indeed use significantly more referral sources than do Americans, regardless of location. The current study suggests developing full hypotheses and collecting further data to test those hypotheses to see whether the same holds true specifically for Japanese buying travel services, both on a corporate and consumer level, be they in Japan or in another country.

Finally, this summary of the literature and the interviews provide marketers with direction in formulating plans for cracking the Japanese travel and tourism market, both in Japan and with Japanese citizens and Japanese subsidiaries in the U.S. We conclude that Japanese use more referral sources than Americans, both in the U.S. and Japan. An American marketing manager should reasonably surmise that a program of cold calling prospects will meet with little success amongst these types of companies.

Both in the U.S. and Japan, American managers who want to sell travel services to the Japanese should be willing to exhibit patience in building solid relationships with well-placed intermediaries such as banks, trading companies, and insurance companies, which are key to Japan's industrial groupings (keiretsu). Joint venturing with a firm who is already well-entrenched in the market is one way to gain access to important Japanese markets. Success in Japan usually requires working with established companies (Brooks 1993) and systems rather than trying to work around them (Nariu and Flath 1993). One of the best ways to gain access to what some consider a "closed" Japanese market is patiently building relationships with strategically placed sources of WOM information.

REFERENCES

Anderson, John R. (1983), *The Architecture of Cognition*. Cambridge, MA: Harvard University Press.

Anterasian, Cathy, John L. Graham and R. Bruce Money (1996), "Are U.S. Managers Superstitious About Market Share?" *Sloan Management Review* 37 (Summer), 67-77.

Apasu, Yao, Shigeru Ichikawa, and John L. Graham (1987), "Corporate Culture and Sales Force Management in Japan and America," *Journal of Personal Selling & Sales Management*, 7 (November), 51-62.

Batzer, Erich and Helmut Laumer (1989), *Marketing Strategies and Distribution Channels for Foreign Companies in Japan*. Boulder, CO: Westview Press.

Bavelas, Alex (1950), "Communications Patterns in Task-Oriented Groups," *Journal of the Acoustical Society of America*, 22, 725-30.

Brooks, William (1993), "MITI's Distribution Policy and U.S.-Japan Structural Talks," in *The Japanese Distribution System, Opportunities and Obstacles, Structures and Practices*, Michael R. Czinkota and Masaaki Kotabe, eds. Chicago: Probus, 231-48.

Brown, Jacqueline Johnson and Peter H. Reingen (1987), "Social Ties and Word of Mouth Referral Behavior," *Journal of Consumer Research*, 14 (November), 350-62.

Carroll, Glenn R. and Albert C. Teo (1996), "On the Social Networks of Managers," *Academy of Management Journal*, 39 (April), 421-40.

Cateora, Philip R. (1996), *International Marketing*, ninth edition, Homewood, IL: Richard D. Irwin.

Clark, Terry (1990), "International Marketing and National Character: A Review and Proposal for an Integrative Theory," *Journal of Marketing*, 54 (October), 66-79.

Crotts, John C. (1998), Consumer Decision making and prepurchase information search. In Yoel Mansfield and Abe Pizam (eds.) *Consumer behavior in travel and tourism*. Binghamton, NY; The Haworth Press, Inc.

Crotts, John C. and David T. Wilson (1995). An integrated model of buyer-seller relationships in the international travel trade. *Progress in Tourism and Hospitality Research*, 1 (2), 125-39.

Czinkota, Michael R. and Jon Woronoff (1986), *Japan's Market: The Distribution System*, New York: Praeger, 1986.

Dore, Ronald (1976), *British Factory, Japanese Factory: The Origins of National Diversity in Industrial Relations*. Berkeley: The University of California Press.

Drucker, Peter F. (1971), "What We Can Learn From Japanese Management," in *How Japan Works*. Cambridge, MA: Harvard Business School Press, 3-10.

Feick, Lawrence F. and Linda L. Price (1987), "The Market Maven: A Diffuser of Marketplace Information," *Journal of Marketing*, 51 (January), 83-97.

Frazier, Gary L., James D. Gill, and Sudhir H. Kale (1989), "Dealer Dependence Levels and Reciprocal Actions in a Channel of Distribution in a Developing County," *Journal of Marketing*, 53 (January), 50-69.

Frazier, Gary L. and R. Raymond (1991), The use of influence strategies in interfirm relationships in industrial product channels. *Journal of Marketing*, 55 (1), 52-69.

Freeman, Linton C., Douglas Roeder and Robert R. Mullholland (1980), "Centrality in Social Networks: II. Experimental Results." *Social Networks* 2, 119-41.

Frenzen, Jonathan K. and Kent Nakamoto (1993), "Structure, Cooperation, and the Flow of Market Information," *Journal of Consumer Research*, 20 (December), 360-75.

Gerlach, Michael L. (1992), *Alliance Capitalism: The Social Organization of Japanese Business*. Berkeley: University of California Press.

Glazer, Nathan (1976), "Social and Cultural Factors in Japanese Economic Growth," in *Asia's New Giant: How the Japanese Economy Works*, Hugh Patrick and Henry Rosovsky, eds. Washington: The Brookings Institute, 816-98.

Graham, John L. and Yoshihiro Sano (1989), *Smart Bargaining: Doing Business with the Japanese*, revised edition, New York: Harper & Row.

Granovetter, Mark (1973), "The Strength of Weak Ties," *American Journal of Sociology*, 78 (May), 1360-80.

Gronhaug, Kjell and John L. Graham (1987), "International Marketing Research Revisited," *Advances in International Marketing*, 2, 121-37.

Hall, Edward T. (1976), *Beyond Culture*. Garden City, NY: Anchor Press/Doubleday.
_____ and Mildred Reed Hall (1987), *Hidden Differences: Doing Business With the Japanese*. Garden City, NY: Anchor/Doubleday.

Hofstede, Geert (1980), *Culture's Consequences*. Beverly Hills: Sage Publications.
_____ (1991), *Cultures and Organizations–Software of the Mind*. London: McGraw-Hill.

Iacobucci, Dawn and Niguel Hopkins (1992), "Modeling Dyadic Interactions and Networks in Marketing," *Journal of Marketing Research*, 29 (February), 5-17.

Ibarra, Herminia and Steven B. Andrews (1993), "Power, Social Influence and Sense Making: Effects of Network Centrality and Proximity on Employee Perceptions," *Administrative Science Quarterly*, 38 (June), 277-303.

Japan Travel Bureau (1994), *All about Japanese overseas travelers*. Tokyo: Japan Travel Bureau.

Kale, Sudhir (1986), Dealer perceptions of manufacturer's power and influence strategies in a developing country. *Journal of Marketing Research*, 23 (4), 387-393.

Kahle, Lynn R. (1986), "The Nine Nations of North America and the Value Basis of Geographic Segmentation," *Journal of Marketing*, 50 (April), 37-47.

Kluckhohn, Richard, ed. (1962), *Culture and Behavior: Collected Essays of Clyde Kluckhohn*, New York: Free Press of Glencoe/MacMillan.

Komiya, Ryutaro, Masahiro Okuno, and Kotaro Suzumura (1988), *Industrial Policy of Japan*. Tokyo: Academic Press.

Labianca, Guiseppe, Daniel J. Brass, and Barbara Gray (1988), "Social Networks and Perceptions of Intergroup Conflict: The Role of Negative Relationships and Third Parties," *Academy of Management Journal*, 41 (February), 55-67.

Mahajan, Vijay, Eitan Muller and Frank M. Bass (1990), "New Product Diffusion Models in Marketing: A Review and Direction for Research," *Journal of Marketing* 54 (January), 1-26.

March, James G. and Herbert A. Simon (1958), *Organizations*. New York: John Wiley & Sons, Inc.

March, Robert M. (1990), *Honorable Customer: Marketing and Selling to the Japanese in the 1990's*. London: Pitman.

March, Roger (1997). An exploratory study of buyer-seller relationships in international tourism: The case of the Japanese wholesaler and Australian suppliers. *Journal of Travel & Tourism Marketing*, 6 (1), 55-68.

McGuire, William J. (1985), "Attitudes and Attitude Change," in *The Handbook of Social Psychology*, third edition, Gardner Lindzey and Elliot Aronson, eds. New York: Random House.

Money, R. B., M. C. Gilly, and J. L. Graham (1998), Exploration of National Culture and Word-of-Mouth Referral Behaviors in the Purchase of Industrial Services in the U.S. and Japan. *Journal of Marketing*, 62 (October), pp. 76-87.

Morgan, James C. and J. Jeffrey Morgan (1991), *Cracking the Japanese Market*. New York: The Free Press.

Nairu, Tatsuhiko and David Flath (1993), "The Complexity of Wholesale Distribution Channels in Japan," in *The Japanese Distribution System, Opportunities and Obstacles, Structures and Practices*, Michael R. Czinkota and Masaaki Kotabe, eds. Chicago: Probus, 83-98.

Nakane, Chie (1970), *Japanese Society*. Berkeley: University of California Press.

Nakata, Cheryl and K. Sivakumar (1996), "National Culture and New Product Development: An Integrative Review," *Journal of Marketing*, 60 (January), 61-72.

Ouchi, William G. (1980), "Markets, Bureaucracies, and Clans," *Administrative Science Quarterly*, 25, 124-41.

_____ (1981), *Theory Z: How American Business Can Meet the Japanese Challenge*. Boston: Addison-Wesley.

Pascale, Richard (1978), "Communication and Decision Making Across Cultures: Japanese and American Comparisons," *Administrative Science Quarterly*, 23 (March), 91-110.

_____ and Anthony G. Athos (1981), *The Art of Japanese Management*. New York: Simon and Shuster.

Reingen, Peter H. and Jerome B. Kernan (1986), "Networks in Marketing: Methods and Illustration," *Journal of Marketing Research*, 13 (November), 370-8.

_____, Brian L. Foster, Jacqueline Johnson Brown, and Stephen B. Seidman (1984), "Brand Congruence in Interpersonal Relations: A Social Network Analysis, *Journal of Consumer Research*, 11 (December), 771-83.

Ronchetto, John R. Jr., Michael D. Hutt, and Peter H. Reingen (1989), "Embedded Influence Patterns in Organizational Buying Systems," *Journal of Marketing*, 53 (October), 51-62.

Roth, Martin S. (1995), "The Effects of Culture and Socioeconomics on the Performance of Global Brand Image Strategies," *Journal of Marketing Research*, 32 (May), 163-75.

Ruan, Danching, Linton C. Freeman, Xinyuan Dai, Yunkang Pan, and Wenhong Zhang (1997), "On the Changing Structure of Social Networks in Urban China," *Social Networks*, 19, 75-89.

Sakaiya, Taichi (1993), *What is Japan? Transformations and Contradictions*, New York: Kadansha International.

Sullivan, J. (1995). The major players in Asia's travel industry. *Travel and Tourism Analysis*, No. 1, 54-83.

Sullivan, Jeremiah and Richard B. Peterson (1988), "Factors Associated with Trust in Japanese-American Joint Ventures," *International Management Review*, 22 (2), 30-40.

Takada, Hirokazu, and Dipak Jain (1991), "Cross-National Analysis of Diffusion of Consumer Durable Goods in Pacific Rim Countries," *Journal of Marketing*, 55 (April), 48-54.

Tse, David K., June Francis, and Fan Walls (1994), "Cultural Differences in Conducting Intra-and Inter-Cultural Negotiations: A Sino-Canadian Comparison," *Journal of International Business Studies*, 25 (3), 537-56.

Tyson, Laura D'Andrea (1992), *Who's Bashing Whom? Trade Conflict in High-Technology Industries*. Washington: Institute for International Economics.

Van Zandt, Howard F. (1981) "Learning to do Business with 'Japan, Inc.,'" in *How Japan Works*. Cambridge, MA: Harvard Business School Press, 151-60.

Ward, James C. and Peter H. Reingen (1990), "Sociocognitive Analysis of Group Decision Making among Consumers," *Journal of Consumer Research*, 17 (December), 245-62.

Williamson, Oliver E. (1975), *Markets and Hierarchies*. New York: The Free Press.

Age and Cohort Effects:
An Examination
of Older Japanese Travelers

Xinran You
Joseph T. O'Leary

SUMMARY. The older travel market will make up a larger proportion of the travel market in the near future with profound impact on market size and potential. This research addressed the issue whether travelers' behavior changes over time through longitudinal and cohort comparisons of older Japanese outbound travelers in terms of travel propensity, destination activity participation and travel philosophy. Both the age effect and generation cohort effect were tested and the underlining patterns of the destination activity participation patterns relative to other age groups and previous generation cohorts were identified. The findings indicated that the older travel market is becoming more active compared to 10 years before. Travel characteristics of this market also change over time. *[Article copies available for a fee from The Haworth Document Delivery Service: 1-800-342-9678. E-mail address: <getinfo@haworthpressinc. com> Website: <http://www.haworthpressinc.com>]*

Xinran You is a PhD student, Department of Forestry and Natural Resources, Purdue University, West Lafayette, IN 47906 (E-mail: *xinran@fnr.purdue.edu*). Joseph T. O'Leary is Professor, Department of Forestry and Natural Resources, Purdue University.

The data utilized in this study were made available by the Canadian Tourism Commission. The data for Japan (1986) Pleasure Travel Market Survey was originally prepared by Market Facts of Canada Limited. The data for Japan (1995) Pleasure Travel Market Survey was originally prepared by Coopers and Lybrand Consulting. Neither the preparer of the original data nor the Canadian Tourism Commission bear and responsibility for the analysis or interpretations presented here.

[Haworth co-indexing entry note]: "Age and Cohort Effects: An Examination of Older Japanese Travelers." You, Xinran, and Joseph T. O'Leary. Co-published simultaneously in *Journal of Travel & Tourism Marketing* (The Haworth Hospitality Press, an imprint of The Haworth Press, Inc.) Vol. 9, No. 1/2, 2000, pp. 21-42; and: *Japanese Tourists: Socio-Economic, Marketing and Psychological Analysis* (ed: K. S. (Kaye) Chon, Tsutomu Inagaki, and Taiji Ohashi) The Haworth Hospitality Press, an imprint of The Haworth Press, Inc., 2000, pp. 21-42. Single or multiple copies of this article are available for a fee from The Haworth Document Delivery Service [1-800-342-9678, 9:00 a.m. - 5:00 p.m. (EST). E-mail address: getinfo@haworthpressinc.com].

KEYWORDS. Older traveler, Japanese tourists, market segmentation

INTRODUCTION

At the turn of the century, tourism researchers and destination marketers are concerned with one irreversible trend–the aging of the world population, especially in the industrialized countries. The decline in fertility levels, reinforced by continued declines in mortality levels, is producing fundamental changes in the population composition of most countries. It is estimated (U.S. Bureau of the Census 1996) that by the year 2020, the elderly (64 and over) will be the fastest growing population segment, increasing 88 percent by 2020 compared with a 28 percent increase for the rest of the population. Not only do people anticipate an increase in the proportion of older people in the total population, an absolute increase in numbers is also expected.

The maturing of the population, however, is assumed to exert a negative impact on travel, especially in terms of international travel (Sakai, Brown, and Mak 1997). This is because aging leads to the prospect of progressive loss of energy and mobility and a diminished propensity to pursue long distance travel. Researchers and destination marketers raise important questions such as: "Should destinations expect slower long term future growth rates in the longhaul travel market as a result of the phenomenal aging of population?" and "What developmental and product planning strategies should they be pursuing?"

One country that falls into the rapid aging category is Japan. Since Japan is a major international travel market for many longhaul travel destinations, the Japanese senior travel market has become a growing focus for researchers. In 1997 at the Travel and Tourism Research Association Annual Meeting (TTRA), Sakai et al. (1997) did a presentation on population aging and Japanese international travel. They addressed the issue of two countervailing demographic effects. On the one hand, the aging of the population has a negative effect on outbound travel propensity, while on the other the cohort effect has a positive effect on outbound travel propensity. Sakai et al. (1997), however, could not determine which effect would prevail due to a lack of data. The question they raised was: "Whether the future older generation will have a taste for travel and behave more like when they were young, or whether they will behave more like the current population of the same age. If the cohort effect swamps the age effect, Japanese overseas travel propensities will not fall." This is an important question that all destination marketing organizations that are targeting Japan are concerned about.

There are two issues here. From a market demand perspective, the concern would be the possible decline in growth rate of Japanese outbound travel due to aging. The question is: Is there a real decline in Japanese outbound travel demand as a result of aging population or would the cohort effect override the aging effect? While this has a profound impact, from the supply perspective, the possible change or evolution of travel desire, travel product preference and travel behavior might also raise the question whether and how destination marketers should adjust their travel products and packages accordingly to meet the changing requirement of the booming older travel market.

As Sakai and his colleagues discovered, there is no empirical research done to support or disprove the change or illustrate the evolution of change in travel behavior due to a generation cohort or an aging population effect. Do senior travelers today have the same travel behavior pattern as seniors in the preceding generation considering factors such as travel experiences and wider exposure to travel information in the current generation?

Therefore, it was the intention of this research to empirically address whether Japanese travelers' behavior changes over time through a longitudinal and cross-sectional comparison of older Japanese outbound travelers in terms of travel propensity, destination activity participation and travel philosophies. Both the age effect and generation cohort effect are tested and the underlying patterns of their travel behavior and vacation activity participation patterns relative to other age groups and their previous generation cohorts are identified.

RELATED LITERATURE

Japan: The Graying Population

Aging of the population is a global trend. The fastest growing part of the world's population is the elderly. Japan was a relatively youthful country earlier in the century. The average age of a Japanese was 26.7 in 1920, but Japan is aging faster than any other nation. Today that average age is almost 40.1 years. Almost 15 percent of the Japanese population is 64 and above. In the year 2000, Japan will become the country with the highest percentage of elderly in the population. In 2050, it is estimated, one out of three Japanese will be an elderly citizen. As is the case with many industrialized countries, the graying of the Japanese population is related to decreasing population growth rate as a result of a lower birthrate and longer life expectancy. Not only does the population growth rate decrease, but the actual population of Japan is expected to decline from 127,548,000 in the year 2010 to 123,620,000 in the year 2020. On the other hand, Japan as a population has the longest life expectancy in the world. In 1935, the average life expectancies of Japanese men and women were 46.92 and 49.63 years respectively. Today the life expectancies of Japanese men and women are 76.36 and 82.84.

In terms of travel, the increase of Japanese visitors in the past two decades has been spectacular. According to the World Tourism Organization (1995), Japan ranked third in international tourism expenditures in 1994 at $30,716 million, comprising 10.1 percent of the world total. While an obvious market for international destinations to focus their promotion and marketing efforts, the graying of the population has caused enormous concern in destination marketing organizations.

Advantaged Seniors: Family Life Cycle and Travel Propensity

Aging is believed to be negatively correlated with the propensity to travel long distances due to the changes in a person's physical energy and mobility (Sakai et al. 1997). However research has shown that there are some distinct advantages for seniors compared to other age groups in terms of travel and leisure activity involvement. This is because of the stage in the family life cycle that this group is in.

The idea behind the family life cycle concept is that a person passes through a predictable progress or series of stages which are defined by unique combinations of socioeconomic and/or demographic variables (Wells and Gubar 1996). The most popular version of family life cycle is a multidimensional construct which takes into account age, marital status, the presence of children and family income (Wells and Gubar 1996; Bojanic 1992). Compared with other age groups, senior people have entered into a special life cycle stage. Having progressed from "bachelor" stage to "empty nests" to "survivorship," they are free from family and work responsibilities. This means more free time for leisure activities and more disposable income. Household economics theory suggests that as a result of time and income constraints, an individual's market and household productivity, and their preferences for consumption and leisure, individuals allocate their available time among market work, household work and leisure pursuits (Bryant 1995). As individuals age, they become less and less involved with market work and household work. As a result of semi or full retirement and grown-up children, the time and economic resources that are allocated to leisure and travel increase.

Travel propensity for today's senior is assumed to be higher than previous age cohorts. Thanks to medical advances, improved diet, housing and public health conditions, and safer and more satisfying work, today's senior possesses better mental and physical health condition which contributes to better mobility. Moschis (1996, 1975) has indicated in his gerontographic study that the stereotypical picture of the elderly as infirm is exaggerated. It has been found that most elderly people remain active despite their ailments until their late seventies. In fact, research has shown that a significant number travel for pleasure on a regular basis. For many seniors, travel is the primary status symbol (Pederson 1994). Travel turns out to be a link between many elderly and the society. Studies reveal that today's seniors live longer and are more vigorous and influential than ever before. In fact, people believe that today's senior will age more slowly than previous generations physically and psychologically (Dychtwald 1997).

Experienced and Diversified Seniors

Other factors that may invite higher travel propensity include new life events, possible change of life value or style and more active and richer travel history that today's seniors have gained relative to the previous senior cohorts. Seniors today are becoming more active and adventurous both physically and intellectually, and travel and recreation are playing an increasing role in fulfilling older people's physical, educational, social and spiritual needs. Oppermann (1995) approached changing travel patterns from a multitemporal perspective of changing travel patterns. He suggested that generation or cohort differences are the important factor in changing travel patterns. Although a certain destination may be very popular for today's elderly market, the next generation may not visit that destination at all because they have other values and travel experiences resulting in a different travel destination choice set. Moschis (1996) argued that the consumer behavior of older adults is the outcome of several social, psychological, biophysical, life-time events, and other environmental factors. Different gerontographic characteristics of different generation cohorts would bring different consumption and behavior pattern.

Senior Travel Motivation and Behavior

Limited comparisons have been done across age groups in terms of travel motivation, destination choices and lodging preferences. Ryan (1995) reported findings from two studies of tourists over 55 and showed the important role of past experience in determining holiday choice and loyalty to a destination.

However, researchers often tend to treat the senior travel market as a homogeneous whole. Only limited studies can be found in further differentiating the senior travel market. Shoemaker (1989) segmented the senior Pennsylvania residents into 3 groups with cluster analysis. The first group was those who enjoyed shorter trips and prefer to return to a destination rather than visit a new one. A second group was called active resters. This group took travel as a means of meeting people, socializing and relaxing. The third group was the older set. They prefer taking all-inclusive package tours and going to a resort. But their travel reason was not very explicit. The findings suggested that members of the senior market can be segmented into smaller homogeneous groups based on their reasons for pleasure travel.

Gustin and Weaver (1993) found that underlying dimensions exist for the mature individual (defined as 55 and above) with regard to the selection criterion for lodging preference when traveling for pleasure purposes. Price and quality, reputation, comfort and security, and room features are the underlying dimensions that differ between the mature groups. The lower income group is more conscious to hotel prices, while the reputation of the facility or security systems are more important to females than males.

Salient variables that explain senior travel behavior and preferences remain to be identified. Zimmer et al. (1995) attempted to discern the differences between older adults who travel and those who do not. Using discriminant analysis, they found that age, education, and mobility problems emerged as the strongest distinguishing predictors in separating travelers from nontravelers.

Seniority and Activity Participation

In recreation and leisure research, there remains many opportunities to look at the role of leisure activities by the elderly. Rapoport and Rapoport (1975) in their study of life style in later years divided later life into three phases: preretirement (55-64), retirement (64-75) and old age (75 +). The first two phases still witness active leisure participation. Research on the determinants of activity in later years seems to indicate a significant trilogy: education, income and health. Where all three are high, the activity rates are high. If any one drops significantly, the pattern rapidly becomes relatively passive.

Gender-linked differences in leisure pastime are believed to exist and carry over into senior age. Gordon, Gaitz, and Scott (1976) found that senior male participation was greater in active, external pursuits, such as competitive sports and outdoor activities than their female counterparts. Of all the socioeconomic status variables, education is thought to be the most influential with respect to leisure participation among the elderly (Iso-Ahola 1980). Neulinger (1974) has argued that the higher the education level attained, the more exposure the person is likely to have had to leisure opportunities. Better educated people acquire a wider variety of leisure skills, especially in the arts, literature and music. Health and income are frequently cited variables by the elderly to explain their low activity participation. People may lack the energy and capability to engage in preferred leisure activities. Anderson and Langmeyer (1982) profiled the similarities and differences of the under-50 and over-50 travelers. Their findings revealed that a significantly higher percentage of those over 50 travel to visit historic sites. In contrast, those under 50 were more likely to travel for outdoor recreation and to visit manmade amusement facilities.

It appears that there are limited studies about the senior travel market, especially in senior traveler's vacation activity participation. However, what travelers actually do at a destination is directly linked to destination product planning and packaging. It remains to be discovered: (1) what vacation activities senior travelers tend to be engaged in, (2) whether senior traveler's vacation activities differ distinctly from other age groups, (3) whether differences exist within the senior segment due to different sociodemographic background, and (4) whether activity patterns of senior travelers change across consecutive generations and over successive generations.

Objectives of the Research

The objectives of this research were to: (1) test the generation cohort effect through comparative analysis on two successive senior age groups (55 to 64 years old) 10 years apart (1986 and 1995); (2) conduct a longitudinal analysis (over the span of ten years) and compare mature age group (45 to 55) in 1986 with senior age group (55 to 64 years old) in 1995, testing whether when the mature group progresses into senior age, their travel behavior changes; and (3) identify whether vacation activity participation patterns are shifting.

METHODOLOGY

Subjects and Data Collection

Two cross sectional data sets collected at two points 10 years apart dealing with Longhaul Pleasure Travel Market Surveys for Japan were merged and used for meta-analysis. The two data sets were collected in 1986 and 1995 respectively by the Canadian Tourism Commission (formerly Tourism Canada) and the former U.S. Travel and Tourism Administration, now Tourism Industries in the U.S. Dept. of Commerce. Using personal in-home interviews, approximately 1,500 and 1,200 respondents were contacted in the year 1986 and 1995 respectively.

All respondents were 18 years of age or older who took an overseas vacation outside the east Asia region in the past three years or intended to take such a vacation in the next two years. The two samples were identified using a national probability cluster sample consisting of geographical areas selected at random in which every household was approached and eligible respondents within households were randomly chosen to participate in personal interviews.

The surveys collected information on Japanese outbound travel including: (1) socio-economic and demographic characteristics such as age, gender, income, education, occupation and life cycle; (2) travel characteristics such as party size, length of stay and trip type; (3) activities engaged in the most recent trip, most recent trip in general and most recent trip to North America; (4) travel philosophy and benefits pursued; and (5) travel planning related information such as planning horizon and information sources.

Methodology

The 1986 data were originally in ASCII format and were transformed into SPSS executable format. The two questionnaires used for the 1986 and 1995 data collection were almost identical except for some minor changes over selected variables in terms of variable content and differences in scale or coding system. Some data preprocessing had been done such as dropping unneeded or incomparable variables that were different or synchronizing the coding system before file merging was carried out. The two datasets were then merged by means of adding cases.

People grow old biologically, psychologically and socially. There seems to be no consensus on the definition of an older person. Marketers, especially marketers of travel and leisure services tend to use age 50 or 55 as the lower boundary for defining the older consumer market (Moschis 1996; Dychtwald 1997). In line with this practice, this research used age 55 years and older to examine Japanese travelers. A total of 691 cases were selected. This included 462 cases from the 1986 survey and 229 cases from the 1995 survey.

New variables were created based on existing variables for facilitating statistical analysis. For instance, in order to measure traveler's destination activity involvement level, an activity involvement index was created by summing up the number of activities that a certain respondent had participated in during his most recent trip to a long haul destination. Factor analysis was employed to reduce a large group of activity variables into a smaller number of factors. These factors were then saved as variables for further analysis.

Two Multivariate Analysis of Variance (MANOVA) were conducted to examine the mean differences between the different groups under study in two sets of comparable variables: travel activities and travel philosophies, while taking into account the covariance between variables in each set. One-way ANOVA was used to test group differences in other trip-related variables, such as travel propensity and travel history. The three groups under examination for this step were the 1986 55-65 year old group (N = 185), the 1986 45-55 year old group (N = 196) and the 1995 55-65 year old group (N = 95). The 55-65 year old group was at the beginning senior life stage and was named "the young seniors" in this study. Figure 1 illustrates the structure of the comparisons.

In addition, two cluster analyses based on activity variables were con-

FIGURE 1. Layout of Comparative Studies

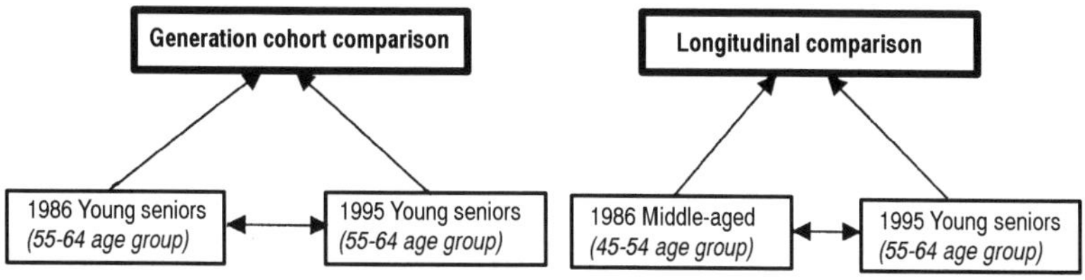

ducted on the 1986 senior travelers and 1995 senior travelers respectively in order to identify similarities or differences in their involvement patterns.

RESULTS AND DISCUSSION

Factor Analysis

Varimax rotation factor analysis was used to identify underlying dimensions or constructs in the 35 activity variables. Ten factors with eigenvalues greater than one were retained for further analysis (Tables 1 and 2). By summarizing variable information within each factor based on factor loadings, these ten factors are labeled as: (1) cultural heritage activity, (2) nature-oriented activity, (3) beach/water activity, (4) city based sightseeing/shopping, (5) visiting friends and relatives (VFR), (6) casino/gaming, (7) outdoor activity, (8) themed activity (theme parks, etc.), (9) coastal area sightseeing, and (10) skiing.

Generation Cohort Comparison

Two young senior groups, age 55 to 64 years old from both the 1986 and 1995 data, were selected for a cohort comparison. These were the same two segments, but 10 years apart. A new "cohort" variable from the 1986 and the 1995 data sets was created. MANOVA was used to test whether the 1995 seniors were the same as 1986 seniors in their vacation activity participation pattern (i.e., what senior travelers do during their overseas vacation), travel philosophies (i.e., what the senior travelers think of overseas travel). Then a one way ANOVA was used to examine other trip-related characteristics. The results are presented in Table 3.

Higher Activity Involvement

Are seniors today thinking and behaving the same way in overseas travel as seniors a decade before them? Results showed that overall the 1995 se-

TABLE 1. Rotated Component Matrix (Factor Loadings)

Destination Activities	Factor[a]									
	1	2	3	4	5	6	7	8	9	10
Visiting small towns and villages	0.548									
Visiting galleries/museums	0.610									
Places of historical interest	0.723									
Places of archaeological interest	0.695									
Commemorating important people	0.537									
Visiting national parks or forests		0.629								
Observing wildlife/bird watching		0.691								
Visiting mountainous areas		0.535								
Visiting protected lands		0.709								
Visiting scenic places		0.365								
Sunbathing or other beach activities			0.764							
Swimming			0.719							
Water sports			0.69							
Shopping				0.657						
Dining in restaurants				0.659						
Taking pictures or filming				0.586						
Sightseeing in cities				0.501						
Visiting friends or relatives					0.703					
Getting to know local people					0.572					
Casino/other gambling						0.643				
Visiting night clubs						0.524				
Hunting							0.643			
Horse riding							0.601			
Fishing							0.453			
Outdoor activities							0.516			
Visiting amusement park or theme park								0.553		
Attending spectacular sporting events								0.658		
Attending local festival								0.502		
Visiting coastal areas									0.567	
Visiting places of military sites									0.535	
Alpine skiing										0.736
Visiting health spas										0.455

[a] The 10 factors identified are labeled: (1) cultural heritage activity, (2) nature-oriented activity, (3) beach/water activity, (4) city based sightseeing/shopping, (5) visiting friends and relatives (VFR), (6) casino/gaming, (7) outdoor activity, (8) themed activity (theme parks, etc.), (9) coastal area sightseeing, and (10) skiing.

niors were much more active and participated in a wider variety of activities than their 1986 counterparts. Seniors in 1995 showed significantly ($\partial = .01$) higher activity involvement levels (average 11.12 activities versus 7.59 for 1986 seniors). The 1995 group had higher culture and heritage activity participation, more VFR activity, higher nature-based activity participation, and

TABLE 2. Eigenvalues and Variance Explained

Factors[a]	Eigen Value	Variance % Explained	Cumulative % of Variance Explained
1	3.921	8.811	8.811
2	2.891	7.811	16.622
3	2.525	7.612	24.234
4	2.322	6.822	31.056
5	1.824	5.841	36.898
6	1.610	4.946	41.843
7	1.442	4.795	46.638
8	1.327	4.585	51.224
9	1.202	4.250	55.474
10	1.097	4.058	59.532

a The 10 factors identified are labeled: (1) cultural heritage activity, (2) nature-oriented activity, (3) beach/water activity, (4) city based sightseeing/shopping, (5) visiting friends and relatives (VFR), (6) casino/gaming, (7) outdoor activity, (8) themed activity (theme parks, etc.), (9) coastal area sightseeing, and (10) skiing.

did more coastal area sightseeing. In terms of casino/gaming activities and outdoor risk-involving activities such as hunting, hiking or skiing, no significant differences were shown between the two groups.

Hub-and-Spoke Style

Results also indicated that senior travelers in 1995 preferred more of a hub-and-spoke travel style rather than rushing around from point to point. They tended to prefer to use a place as a base and stay a longer period, exploring more of what a destination can offer. This is reflected in their stronger preference to stay put once getting to a destination ($\overline{X}_{95} = 2.45$, $\overline{X}_{86} = 1.87$, P = 0.000).

Increased Sophistication

In many ways, the 1995 seniors appeared to be more sophisticated travelers than those from 1986. The 1995 seniors preferred less escorted or guided tours compared with their counterparts 10 years earlier ($\overline{X}_{95} = 3.01$, $\overline{X}_{86} = 3.4$, P = 0.000). They strongly liked flexibility on overseas travel ($\overline{X}_{95} = 3.39$), while their 1986 counterparts seemed to care less about it ($\overline{X}_{86} = 2.62$). One possible reason might be that this group of seniors tends to have more experience in overseas travel than the 1986 group. The average frequency of long-haul travel in the past 3 years was 3.88 trips for the 1995 senior travelers compared to 3.17 for the 1986 group. The 1995 young seniors appreciated travel as a life style much more than the 1986 young seniors. For them, money spent on overseas travel was well spent ($\overline{X}_{95} = 3.00$, $\overline{X}_{86} = 2.43$, P = 0.000).

No differences were found in the preference of "people who speak my

TABLE 3. MANOVA/ANOVA[a] Results of 55 to 64 Age Groups: 1986 and 1995

Dependent Variable	Mean		F Value	P Value
	1986 (N = 185)	1995 (N = 95)		
Destination Activities[b]				
Cultural heritage activity	0.079	0.514	7.62	.006***
Nature-oriented activity	0.074	0.721	18.181	.000***
Beach/water activity	− 0.65	− 0.081	29.256	.000***
City based sightseeing/shopping	− 0.67	0.354	42.373	.000***
VFR	− 0.3	0.074	5.361	.022**
Casino/gaming	− 0.03	− 0.059	0.049	0.825
Outdoor activity	− 0.12	− 0.007	0.843	0.36
Themed activity (theme parks, etc.)	− 0.04	− 0.302	11.54	.001***
Coastal area sightseeing	0.508	− 0.159	20.459	.000***
Skiing	− 0.26	− 0.208	0.167	0.683
Wilk's Lambda (Main effect) = .497, F = 17.329, P = .000				
Travel Philosophy[c]				
I like to have all my travel arrangements made before departure for overseas travel	3.43	3.64	5.769	.017**
I enjoy making my own travel arrangements	3.35	2.45	72.479	.000***
Once I get to the destination, I like to stay put	1.87	2.45	31.809	.000***
I like to go to a different place on each new trip	3.38	3.19	4.717	0.031**
I do not really like to travel	2.22	1.34	66.117	.000***
For me, money spent on overseas travel is well spent	2.43	3	26.514	.000***
I prefer escorted tours when vacationing overseas	3.4	3.01	12.338	.001***
I like flexibility on overseas holidays	2.62	3.39	51.823	.000***
It is important that people speak my language	2.62	2.84	3.156	0.077
Wilk's Lambda (Main effect) = .429, F = 38.279, P = .000				
Other Trip-Related Measurements				
Likelihood of another trip in next 5 years	3.32	3.33	0.021	0.886
Number of trips in past three years	3.17	3.88	7.648	.006***
Activity involvement level	7.59	11.12	35.043	.000***

[a]MANOVA analysis was done on destination activity variable set and travel philosophy variable set. ANOVA was done on other trip-related measurements.
[b] Destination activities were activity factors.
[c] Travel philosophy variables were rated on a 4 point scale, where 1 = Strongly disagree, 2 = Somewhat disagree, 3 = Somewhat agree and 4 = Strongly agree.
[d] **: 0.01 < P < 0.05, ***: 0.01 > P

own language." Both 1986 and 1995 seniors prefer that people they interact with at the destination speak their language. There was also no indication of significant differences between the two groups in the likelihood of another trip in the coming 5 years. Both groups showed the same strong interest. ($\overline{X}_{95}$ = 3.33, $\overline{x}_{86}$ = 3.32, P = 0.886).

Longitudinal Comparison

The later middle-aged subsegment (45 to 54 age group) in 1986 and young senior subsegment (55 to 64 age group) in 1995 were chosen for a longitudinal comparison. The two age groups represented the same cohort of people but at a different life stage. This was done to test if there was any changes in vacation activity participation, travel philosophies and other trip-related variables as people age. The MANOVA and ANOVA test results are presented in Table 4.

Older Yet More Active

The analysis revealed that as the same group of people marched from late middle age to early senior status, their travel vacation destination and travel philosophies changed. As people became older, they actually showed a higher level of activity involvement ($\overline{X}_{95} = 11.1$, $\overline{X}_{86} = 8.6$, P = 0.000). They are more actively engaged in culture and heritage, nature based sight seeing, beach/water activity, city based sightseeing/shopping, coastal area sightseeing, and themed activities such as visiting theme parks, etc. In this context, age does not show a negative relationship with vacation activity participation. However, no differences ($\alpha = 0.01$) were found in terms of involvement in visiting friends and relatives, wildlife related activities, or outdoor activities, such as horse riding, fishing, hunting, bird watching, etc.

Sense of Assured Security

Do seniors think about overseas travel differently now than when they were younger? As this group of people moved from middle age to the early senior life stage, their travel philosophy changes in many ways. They tended to prefer to make travel arrangement before departure more than before ($\overline{X}_{95} = 3.65$, $\overline{X}_{86} = 3.31$, P = 0.000). This tendency is reinforced in that they did not enjoy making their own travel arrangement as much as they did 10 years ago ($\overline{X}_{95} = 2.45$, $\overline{X}_{86} = 3.22$, P = 0.000). This suggests that as people age, the sense of security and convenience becomes more important.

Hub-Based Travel: Preferred Style

Compared with 10 years ago, the young senior prefers to stay in one place once they get to the destination rather than traveling to different places ($\overline{X}_{95} = 2.45$, $\overline{X}_{86} = 2.00$, P = 0.000). This is a change over the period. Possible explanations could be change of physical energy or a preference to travel to more places after they settled in a certain destination. This does not imply they were less active; rather they only chose to explore more and do more things at one place rather than traveling around. Along with the changed travel style, seniors actually showed a keener interest in travel in general and value more overseas travel than what was reported 10 years earlier ($\overline{X}_{95} =$

3.00, $\overline{X}_{86}$ = 2.26, P = 0.000). This phenomenon supports the advantaged senior image that researchers have discussed due to changing social obligations and more time and financial resources. This also agrees with Pederson's (1994) observation that travel is a primary status symbol and is a way that older people associate themselves with society.

Another interesting observation is that there is no statistical difference found in inclination to travel in the next five years. This raises a question about the assumption that travel propensity declines over time as people age. The result seems to agree with Sakai et al.'s (1997) speculation that cohort effect overrules the age effect.

Comparison of Clusters in 1986 with Clusters in 1995

Two cluster analyses based on destination activity participation were conducted separately on the 1986 and 1995 older-age groups, respectively. A two-stage procedure cluster analysis approach was adopted (Ketchen and Shook 1996). An agglomerative hierarchical cluster analysis was used first to define the number of clusters. The method for cluster formation used was Ward's method, which combined clusters with the smallest increase in the overall sum of the squared within-cluster distance. In the second stage, the solutions or the number of clusters defined from the hierarchical clustering were used as starting points for subsequent K-means clustering. Cluster memberships were saved for further comparisons between the cluster groups.

The 1986 older-age group was clustered using the vacation activity variables into three distinct clusters. Cluster 1 can be called *conventional mass travelers*. This group resembles very much the conventional mass traveler group in 1995. They prefer going to new places each trip and group tours serve them well. Their activities center around city and nature-based sightseeing.

Cluster 2 is called *social travelers*. They are involved heavily in people-oriented activities such as getting to know local people, visiting friends and relatives, playing golf or tennis, and eating out, besides the routine city sightseeing and shopping. This group prefers to stay in one place once they get to the destination. They seem to be more relaxed and go for depth rather than breadth in terms of activity participation. Instead of covering multiple places or doing multiple activities briefly, they tend to do fewer activity items but with more intensity.

Cluster 3 is the *inert travelers*. Their activities are mainly city sightseeing, shopping and eating out. This group participates in a narrow and limited range of activities.

Cluster analysis on the 1995 older-age group based on destination activities showed that the 1995 senior market can also be grouped into 3 clusters. Cluster 1 can be identified as *hyper-active travelers*. This group has distinct high

TABLE 4. MANOVA/ANOVA[a] Results of the 1986 "45 to 54 Age Group" and the 1995 "55 to 64 Age Group"

Dependent Variable	Mean		F Value	P Value
	1986 (N = 196)	1995 (N = 95)		
Destination activities[b]				
Cultural heritage activity	0.074	0.514	7.491	.007***
Nature-oriented activity	− 0.223	0.721	41.898	.000***
Beach/water activity	− 0.364	− 0.081	5.143	.025*
City based sightseeing/shopping	− 0.146	0.354	16.133	.000***
VFR	0.017	0.074	0.133	0.716
Casino/gaming	0.274	− 0.059	4.006	0.047*
Outdoor activity	− 0.088	− 0.0064	0.5	0.48
Themed activity (theme parks, etc.)	− 0.075	− 0.302	8.443	.004***
Coastal area sightseeing	0.347	− 0.16	12.554	.001***
Skiing	− 0.264	− 0.208	0.26	0.61

Wilk's Lambda (Main effect) = .562, F = 13.654, P = .000

Travel Philosophy[c]				
I like to have all my travel arrangements made before departure for overseas travel	3.31	3.64	13.486	.000***
I enjoy making my own travel arrangements	3.22	2.45	48.543	.000***
Once I get to the destination, I like to stay put	2	2.45	21.121	.000***
I like to go to a different place on each new trip	3.13	3.19	0.392	0.532
I do not really like to travel	2.11	1.34	51.885	.000***
For me, money spent on overseas travel is well spent	2.26	3	48.744	.000****
I prefer escorted tours when vacationing overseas	3	3.01	0.009	0.925
I like flexibility on overseas holidays	2.68	3.34	48.129	.000***
It is important that people speak my language	2.48	2.84	9.618	0.002***

Wilk's Lambda (Main effect) = .516, F = 27.625, P = .000

Other Trip-Related Measurements				
Likelihood of another trip in next 5 years	3.5	3.33	2.479	0.117
Number of trips in past three years	2.88	3.88	17.599	.000***
Activity involvement level	8.628	11.119	18.203	.000***

[a]MANOVA analysis was done on destination activity variable set and travel philosophy variable set. ANOVA was done on other trip-related measurements.

[b] Destination activities were activity factors.

[c] Travel philosophy variables were rated on a 4 point scale, where 1 = Strongly disagree, 2 = Somewhat disagree, 3 = Somewhat agree and 4 = Strongly agree.

activity involvement. They are enthusiastic travelers who actively participate in culture-oriented, people-oriented, nature-based as well as city-based holiday activities. They tend to be more sophisticated and more independent travelers. They express strong preferences toward flexibility on overseas travel.

Cluster 2 can be called the *inert travelers*. This group tends to have very limited holiday activity involvement. Some city sightseeing plus dining seems to be all they do. They do not appear to really enjoy overseas travel very much.

Cluster 3 can be named the *conventional mass travelers*. This group tends to have moderate holiday activity involvement. They do mostly nature-based or city sightseeing. They are less involved in culture and heritage activities such as visiting places of historical interest or museums, etc. They prefer pre-arranged, escorted tours and they seem to be risk averse (see Figure 2).

Comparing the two groups of clusters across the two sample periods, there are similarities and differences. The 1995 senior market seems to be more experienced, place higher values on overseas travel and have an overall higher activity involvement level. This trend is emphasized by the 1995 hyperactive traveler group.

Both cluster analyses reveal several permanent activity themes in the older Japanese travelers market over the comparison period: visiting scenic places, shopping, dining in a restaurant and sightseeing in cities. The activity scope has been expanding from city sightseeing, and nature sightseeing to cultural and heritage activities. Another interesting observation is that senior Japanese travelers overall tend to favor more infrastructure facilitated activities such as city sightseeing and visiting national parks, but also tend to be risk averse. Activities that are risky or consume more physical energy are consistently unpopular across the years among the senior Japanese travelers. These include activities like visiting wild lands, horse riding, hunting, and skiing.

Both cluster analyses do not show significant differences in socio-demographic variables. This is not very surprising since these groups are already homogeneous in the sense that they are seniors who actually travel overseas (see Tables 5-8).

CONCLUSION AND IMPLICATION

The older travel market will make up a large proportion of the travel market in the near future with profound impact on market size and potential. The increasing size of the older population puts more economic power in the hands of this group of travelers. The older travelers' market should not be misinterpreted as a less involved or interested market. As Pederson (1994) pointed out, it would be a myth to assume that future seniors will have the

FIGURE 2. Cluster Analysis on 1986 and 1995 Older Travelers

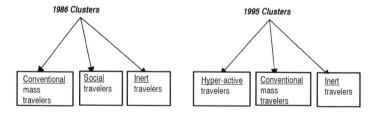

TABLE 5. Destination Activity Participation (1986) by Cluster

Activities	Cluster 1[a] (N = 67)	Cluster 2 (N = 31)	Cluster 3 (N = 76)	Chi-square
		(%)		
Golfing/playing tennis	4.5	12.9	6.6	0.171
Outdoor activity	4.5	6.5	5.3	2.129
Horse riding	1.5	3.2	0	1.162
Hunting	0	0	0	NA
Fishing	0	12.9	2.6	10.869***[b]
Attending spectator sporting event	1.5	3.2	0	2.129
Shopping	82.1	96.8	90.8	5.184
Short guided excursions/tours	55.2	61.3	43.4	3.538
Sightseeing in cities	91	100	94.7	3.196
Taking pictures or filming	26.9	12.9	19.7	47.020***
VFR	6	41.9	11.8	42.571***
Visiting amusement or theme parks	53.7	22.6	15.8	41.331***
Attending local festival	14.9	29	10.5	5.781
Visiting night clubs	22.4	35.5	3.9	18.335***
Visiting casinos/other gambling	6	19.4	5.3	6.544**
Visiting mountainous areas	16.4	9.7	2.6	8.116**
Visiting the coastal areas	7.5	38.7	5.3	25.389***
Visiting small towns and villages	10.4	9.7	3.9	2.442
Visit scenic places	95.5	71	38.2	52.686***
Visiting places of historical interest	70.1	58.1	10.5	56.000***
Visiting places of importance in military history	13.4	22.6	6.6	5.504
Visiting sites commemorating important people	47.8	35.5	3.9	36.736***
Places of archaeological interest	29.9	16.1	0	25.884***
Visiting health spas	10.4	3.2	0	9.023**
Dining in restaurant	64.7	90.3	76.3	7.000**
Visiting galleries/museums	71.6	64.5	17.1	47.458***
Sampling local foods	41.8	51.6	15.8	17.554***
Getting to know local people	9	64.5	22.4	35.563***
Observing wildlife bird watching	7.5	6.5	0	5.712
Visiting national parks or forests	55.2	58.1	11.8	36.168***
Visiting protected lands	4.5	0	0	4.875
Alpine skiing	0	0	0	NA
Sunbathing or other beach activities	1.5	19.4	14.5	9.771***
Swimming	1.5	32.3	7.9	23.294***
Water sports	0	6.5	1.3	5.339

a Cluster 1: conventional mass travelers. Cluster 2: social travelers. Cluster 3: inert travelers.
b **: 0.01 < P < 0.05, ***: 0.01 > P

same leisure behavior, travel desires and patterns, and interests as the present and recent senior market. The values and preferences that people have in earlier years of life generally carry through to middle and old age. Thus "it should not be automatically assumed that today's seniors want exactly what seniors did 10 years ago" (Browne 1984). Older travelers are likely to demand products and services suitable to their needs and life styles.

This research shows that what older Japanese travelers think about overseas travel and what they do at a destination are diverse and seem to have changed over time. Meanwhile, the widely held assumption that as people become older, their travel propensity declines does not seem to hold true. So

TABLE 6. Activity Factors and Trip-Related Measurement and Travel Philosophy (1986) by Cluster

	Cluster1[a] (N = 67)	Cluster2 (N = 31)	Cluster3 (N = 76)	F-Value
	(Mean)	(Mean)	(Mean)	
Activity Factors				
Cultural heritage activity	0.72	0.25	− 0.57	5.713***
Nature oriented activity	0.26	− 0.16	− 0.41	17.672***
Beach/water activity	− 0.88	− 0.37	− 0.55	8.622***
City based sightseeing/shopping	− 0.52	0.54	− 0.3	4.894***
VFR	0.72	− 0.16	− 0.64	19.554***
Casino/club-based activity	0.12	0.48	− 0.18	21.930**
Outdoor activity	− 0.26	− 0.15	0.058	3.774**
Themed activity	0.14	0.53	− 0.16	3.803***
Coastal area sightseeing	0.6	1.3	0.03	10.186***
Skiing	− 0.3	− 0.3	− 0.3	20.242***
Other Trip-Related Measurements				
Activity involvement index	9.3	12.6	5.5	110.053***
Likelihood of another trip in the next 5 years	3.18	3.52	3.32	2.273
Number of trips in past three years	3.9	3.77	3.08	3.392**
Travel Philosophy[c]				
I like to have all my travel arrangements made before departure	3.46	3.34	3.03	3.342**
I enjoy making my own travel arrangements	3.49	3.19	3.13	3.970**
Once I get to the destination, I like to stay put	1.86	1.83	2.03	1.009
I like to go to a different place on each new trip	3.4	3.03	3.21	2.708
I do not really like to travel	2.08	1.74	2.12	1.692
For me, money spent on overseas travel is well spent	2.6	2.53	2.36	2.432
I prefer escorted tours when vacationing overseas	3.39	2.97	3.27	2.921
I like flexibility on overseas holidays	2.42	2.73	2.44	1.760
It is important that the people speak my language	2.74	2.07	2.53	6.211**

[a] Cluster 1: conventional mass travelers. Cluster 2: social travelers. Cluster 3: inert travelers.
[b] **: 0.01 < P < 0.05, ***: 0.01 > P
[c] Travel philosophy variables were rated on a 4 point scale, where 1 = Strongly disagree, 2 = Somewhat disagree, 3 = Somewhat agree and 4 = Strongly agree.

in this sense, the analysis seems to support the dominance of the cohort effect rather than the age effect that Sakai et al. (1997) raised questions about. Results of the longitudinal comparison showed no decline in travel propensity as people moved from their late middle to early senior years. This finding seems to support that richer travel experiences and other social and economic factors favorable to the older travelers seem to have offset to a certain extent the negative impact that are associated with aging and immobility.

Furthermore, it should also be noted that the behaviors of older or senior markets change over time. Older travelers today have already demonstrated a more active participation pattern than their counterparts did a decade ago. The older travelers to come are likely to surpass their contemporary counterparts and may show an even more active and diversified travel behavior

TABLE 7. Destination Activity Participation (1995) by Cluster

Activities	Cluster1a (N = 54)	Cluster2 (N = 50)	Cluster3 (N = 125)	Chi-square
		(%)		
Golfing/playing tennis	9.3	14.8	11.2	0.561
Outdoor activity	14.8	3.7	12	2.197
Horse riding	0	7.4	1.6	5.382
Fishing	1.9	3.7	0.8	1.384
Attending spectator sporting event	0	0	0.8	0.641
Shopping	94.4	55.7	93.6	34.724***
Short guided excursions/tours	50	18.5	60.8	16.088***
Sightseeing in cities	94.4	51.9	97.6	56.679***
Taking pictures or filming	88.9	22.2	72.8	39.269***
VFR	42.6	14.8	8.8	28.897***
Visiting amusement or theme parks	31.5	3.7	14.4	11.716***
Attending local festival	27.8	11.1	8.8	11.454***
Visiting night clubs	22.2	0	23.2	7.744**
Visiting casinos/other gambling	9.3	0	15.2	5.39
Visiting mountainous areas	33.3	0	21.6	11.726***
Visiting the coastal areas	38.9	3.7	10.4	25.590***
Visiting small towns and villages	87	11.1	32	59.835***
Visit scenic places	98.1	25.9	86.4	67.374***
Visiting places of historical interest	85.2	18.5	32.8	50.462***
Visiting places of importance in military history	9.3	0	2.4	6.009
Visiting sites commemorating important people	53.7	3.7	8	55.244***
Places of archaeological interest	61.1	0	10.4	64.846***
Visiting health spas	7.4	0	7.2	2.096
Dining in restaurant	100	74.1	98.4	34.792***
Visiting galleries/museums	96.3	22.2	50.4	49.869***
Sampling local foods	96.3	14.8	63.2	53.676***
Getting to know local people	44.4	11.1	14.4	22.035***
Observing wildlife bird watching	24.1	11.1	18.4	2.029
Visiting national parks or forests	64.8	14.8	43.2	18.647***
Visiting protected lands	18.5	7.4	21.6	2.922
Alpine skiing	1.9	0	0.8	0.739
Sunbathing or other beach activities	18.5	18.5	16	0.221
Swimming	9.3	3.7	10.4	1.189
Water sports	11.1	3.7	5.6	2.277

aCluster 1: Hyperactive travelers. Cluster 2: Conventional mass travelers. Cluster 3: inert travelers.
b**: 0.01 < p < 0.05, ***: 0.01 > P

pattern. Since vacation activities are directly linked to travel product planning and packaging, a better knowledge of what older travelers do at a certain destination would provide opportunities to target this increasingly important market.

Results of this study identified important destination activity participation patterns of the older travelers' market. There is an urgency for destination organizations to develop and implement strategies for gaining a competitive advantage. It appears that there is a high demand for security and safety among Japanese older travelers while they travel overseas. Good travel infrastructure also appears to be very important to this group. Culture and heritage

TABLE 8. Activity Factors, Other Trip-Related Measurement and Travel Philosophy (1995) by Cluster

	Cluster1[a] (N = 54)	Cluster2 (N = 50)	Cluster3 (N = 125)	F-Value
		(Mean)		
Activity Factors				
Cultural heritage activity	1.76	0.1	− 0.4	99.643***
Nature oriented activity	0.94	0.63	− 0.073	5.541***
Beach/water activity	− 0.02	− 0.336	− 0.28	3.43
City based sightseeing/shopping	0.39	0.44	− 1.16	67.009***
VFR	0.6	− 0.3	0.11	17.948***
Casino/club-based activity	− 0.24	0.12	− 0.24	2.885
Outdoor activity	− 0.34	− 0.087	0.15	5.245***
Themed activity	− 0.168	− 0.38	− 0.34	1.6
Coastal area sightseeing	0.19	− 0.34	− 0.38	7.739***
Skiing	− 0.127	− 0.025	− 0.113	0.19
Other Trip-Related Measurement				
Activity involvement index	14.7	4.5	9.98	149.529***
Likelihood of another trip in the next 5 years	3.5	3.31	3.22	2.1234
Number of trips in past 3 years	4.64	2.96	3.9	7.789***
Travel Philosophy[c]				
I like to have all my travel arrangements made before departure	3.64	3.62	3.52	0.704
I enjoy making my own travel arrangements	2.7	2.3	2.5	0.704
Once I get to the destination, I like to stay put	2.46	2.33	2.62	3.968**
I like to go to a different place on each new trip	3.17	3.03	2.82	2.497
I do not really like to travel	1.28	1.41	1.64	2.588
For me, money spent on overseas travel is well spent	3.15	2.97	2.86	1.957
I prefer escorted tours when vacationing overseas	2.85	3.15	2.72	4.858
I like flexibility on overseas holidays	3.52	3.18	3.2	4.532**
It is important that the people speak my language	2.78	3	2.74	2.118

[a] Cluster 1: conventional mass travelers. Cluster 2: social travelers. Cluster 3: inert travelers.
[b] **: 0.01 < P < 0.05, ***: 0.01 > P
[c] Travel philosophy variables were rated on a 4 point scale, where 1 = Strongly disagree, 2 = Somewhat disagree, 3 = Somewhat agree and 4 = Strongly agree.

travel products have strong appeal that has grown among the older Japanese travelers. Shopping, as many previous studies indicated, has been an inseparable part of the whole overseas travel package. Although escorted tours still seem to be important and pre-departure arrangements are preferred to obtain that sense of security, increasing number of older travelers today seem to appreciate and demand more flexibility while they are at the destination.

The confounding problem with this analysis, of course, is the profound shifts in economic well being that have taken place in Japan. The 1995 survey used in the analysis was collected during a time in Japan when a significant downturn was already underway yet there was still substantial travel underway. Certainly, the travel behavior of all Japanese travelers along with seniors has been altered. Additional research will have to be done to determine new patterns of behavior associated with these national problems. In addition, this paper looks only at Japan. Do the same arguments made in this paper supporting a cohort effect hold for other Asian and non-Asian countries? The Pleasure Travel Market series can provide some insight to this question, but there are also other data that might also offer some new insights. It is hoped that researchers from around the globe will take up the challenge.

REFERENCES

Anderson, B. B., & Langmeyer, L. (1982). The under-50 and over-50 Travelers: A profile of similarities and differences. *Journal of Travel Research*, 20 (4): 20-24.

Bojanic, D. C. (1992). A look at a modernized family life cycle and overseas travel. *Journal of Travel & Tourism Marketing*, 1 (1): 61-79.

Bryant, W. K. (1995). *The Economic Organization of the Household*. Cambridge: Cambridge University Press.

Browne, C. (1984). The older traveler: Challenge and opportunities. *The Cornell H.R.A. Quarterly*, (August): 35-41.

Dychtwald, M. K. (1997). Marketplace 2000: Riding the wave of population change. *Journal of Consumer Marketing*, 14 (4): 71-275.

Gordon, C. C., Gaitz, C. M. & Scott, J. (1976). Leisure and lives: Personal expressivity across the lifespan. In R. H. Binstock & E. Shanas (Eds.). *Handbook of Aging and Social Sciences*. New York: Van Nostrand Reinhold.

Gustin, M. & Weaver, P. (1993). The mature market: Understanding dimensions and group differences of a potential market for the motel industry. *FIU Hospitality Review*, 1 (2): 49-59.

Iso-Ahola, S. E. (1980). *The Social Psychology of Leisure and Recreation*. Dubuque, IA: WM. C. Brown Co.

Ketchen, D. J., & Shook, C. L. (1996). The application of cluster analysis in strategic management research: An analysis and critique. *Strategic Management Journal*, 17: 441-458.

Moschis, G. P. (1996). *Gerontographics: Life Stage Segmentation For Marketing Strategy Development*. Westport, CT: Quorum Book.

MacNeil, R. D., & Teague, M. L. (1987). *Aging and Leisure*. Englewood Cliffs, New Jersey: Prentice-Hall, Inc.

Neulinger, J. (1974). *The Psychology of Leisure*. Springfield, IL: Thomas.

Oppermann, M. (1995). Family life cycle and cohort effects: A study of travel patterns of German residents. *Journal of Travel & Travel Marketing*, 4 (1): 23-43.

Pederson, B. (1994). Future seniors and the travel industry. *FIU Hospitality Review*, (Fall): 59-69.

Ryan C. (1995). Learning about tourists form conversations: The over-55s in Majorca. *Tourism Management*, 16 (3): 207-215.

Rapoport, R., & Rapoport, R. N. (1975). *Leisure and the Family Life Cycle*. Boston, MA: Routledge & Kegan Paul Ltd.

Sakai, M., Brown, J., & Mak, J. (1997). Population aging and Japanese international travel in the 21st century. Paper presented at the 1997 Travel and Tourism Research Association Annual Meeting, Norfolk, VA.

Shoemaker, S. (1989). Segmentation of the senior pleasure travel market. *Journal of Travel Research*, 27 (3): 14-21.

Silvers, C. (1997). Smashing old stereotypes of 50-plus America. *Journal of Consumer Marketing*, 14 (4): 303-309.

U.S. Bureau of the Census, (1996). *World Population at a Glance: 1996 and Beyond.* Author.

Wells, W. D., & Gubar, G. (1996). Life cycle concept in marketing research. *Journal of Consumer Research*, 3 (November): 355-363.

Zimmer, Z. et al. (1995). Whether to go and where to go: Identification of important influences on seniors' decision to travel. *Journal of Travel Research*, 33 (3): 3-9.

The Japanese Vacation Visitor to Alaska: A Preliminary Examination of Peak and Off Season Traveler Demographics, Information Source Utilization, Trip Planning, and Customer Satisfaction

Laura M. Milner
James M. Collins
Rumiko Tachibana
Rodney F. Hiser

SUMMARY. The current study examines data gathered on the Japanese visitor to Alaska during the summer of 1996 and winter of 1997. The survey focused on several topics: the demographic profile of the visitor, their motivations, the sources of information used, actual trip

Laura M. Milner is Professor of Marketing and James M. Collins is Associate Professor of Business Administration, Department of Business Administration, School of Management, University of Alaska Fairbanks. Rumiko Tachibana has relocated to Japan. Rodney F. Hiser is pursuing his PhD at the University of Alaska Fairbanks.

The authors gratefully acknowledge the assistance of Andreas Anger and Lorin Toepper as well as the assistance from the Alaska tourism industry without whom this study would not have been possible. The authors also wish to thank two anonymous reviewers for their helpful comments.

This study was supported by a grant from the U.S. Department of Education to the first author. The summer visitor data formed the basis for Rumiko Tachibana's Master's Project.

[Haworth co-indexing entry note]: "The Japanese Vacation Visitor to Alaska: A Preliminary Examination of Peak and Off Season Traveler Demographics, Information Source Utilization, Trip Planning, and Customer Satisfaction." Milner, Laura M. et al. Co-published simultaneously in *Journal of Travel & Tourism Marketing* (The Haworth Hospitality Press, an imprint of The Haworth Press, Inc.) Vol. 9, No. 1/2, 2000, pp. 43-56; and: *Japanese Tourists: Socio-Economic, Marketing and Psychological Analysis* (ed: K. S. (Kaye) Chon, Tsutomu Inagaki, and Taiji Ohashi) The Haworth Hospitality Press, an imprint of The Haworth Press, Inc., 2000, pp. 43-56. Single or multiple copies of this article are available for a fee from The Haworth Document Delivery Service [1-800-342-9678, 9:00 a.m. - 5:00 p.m. (EST). E-mail address: getinfo@haworthpressinc.com].

behaviors, and indices of customer satisfaction. Results indicate that the Japanese visitor to Alaska segment may be further subdivided based on season, winter and summer. Implications are discussed. *[Article copies available for a fee from The Haworth Document Delivery Service: 1-800-342-9678. E-mail address: <getinfo@haworthpressinc.com> Website: <http://www.haworthpressinc.com>]*

KEYWORDS. Japanese tourists, Alaska, off-season travel, eco-tourists

The Japanese are prolific travelers. Several recent trends in Japan fueled interest in traveling abroad. For instance, in the 1980s, Japan incurred an extreme trade surplus, which, although favorable to that nation, became a major international economic issue, particularly with the United States. The Japanese government recognized that international tourism could be used as a strategy to offset this surplus, and sponsored the "Ten Million Program," with the goal of having 10 million travelers abroad by 1991. This goal was attained in 1990 (*JTB Report,* 1996; Nozawa, 1992; Polunin, 1989). Even though Japan experienced an economic slowdown which lasted several years, and is currently struggling through an exchange-rate crisis, Japan's economy has been fairly strong and stable over a sustained period of time.

In terms of another important dimension, the Japanese mindset may be changing to include an increased emphasis on leisure. In stark contrast to other nations, Japanese workers do not utilize vacation time to a great extent, and they work longer hours. In response to international criticism of Japanese labor practices, the government began promoting the 5-day workweek (Morris, 1988; Polunin, 1989). There is speculation that extremely high prices of land and housing have forced some Japanese to forego the dream of owning their own home. The combination of these factors may increase discretionary time and money leading people to pursue leisure (Prime Minister's Office, 1995).

Certain subtrends are apparent in Japanese overseas travel as well. For instance, young people and women are the largest group of overseas travelers (*JTB Report,* 1994, 1995, 1996; Sternberg, 1993). Travel party size is decreasing, and "less than a third of Japanese travellers join group tours" (Sternberg, 1993, p. 52). Family travel has also increased. Sternberg (1993) notes that at the time, the Japan Travel Bureau was increasing the number of family packages to 16 for Australia alone and that Jetour Corporation anticipated that 25% of its summer business was going to be children.

LIFESTYLE SEGMENTS

Research by Cha, McCleary, and Uysal (1995) indicates six factors motivate Japanese tourists traveling overseas: relaxing; knowledge; adventure;

travel bragging; family; and sports. They argue that three profiles emerge from these factors: sports seekers, novelty seekers, and family/relaxation seekers. Other research indicates nature tourism as a major interest (*JTB Report* 1995, 1996; Moeran, 1983).

JTB Reports

The most intensive on-going study of Japanese overseas travel trends is carried out by the Japan Travel Bureau (JTB). Established in 1912, JTB is the oldest and largest travel agency in Japan.

Socio-demographic segments. According to JTB (*JTB Report* 1995, 1996), women are the most likely group to travel for pleasure with more than 80% of single women traveling for this reason and with the highest growth rate occurring among women in their 30's (8.8% in 1993, 20.4% in 1994, and 16.5% in 1995 compared to previous years). An important component of this female segment is women known as "office ladies." This group is defined by the JTB as single working women between the ages of 18 and 29 (Young OL) and between the ages of 30 and 44 (Adult OL). Other segments of Japanese visitors are: Children; Male Students; Female Students; Single, Unemployed Women; Housewives, Working Housewives; Single Men, Married Men, Middle Aged Group; and Elderly Group.

Trips and information sources. Regardless of age or gender, trips lasting between five and seven days are the most frequent. The major activity at overseas destinations is visiting "natural scenic attractions." Word-of-mouth, especially a recommendation or invitation from a family or friend, is an extremely strong motivator for the Japanese overseas traveler, with most also finding motivation in travel catalogs and travel guidebooks. However, those with a great deal of overseas travel rely less often on these sources and give more priority to travel magazines, television shows, and newspaper articles. Almost 52% of the vacation traveler used full packages. However, so-called "free-time" packaged tours (what Americans term combination tours . . . packages with independent components) were more favored by the "Office Lady" market than any other segment. Travelers with the most overseas experience were also most likely to be independents.

Japanese Visitors to Alaska

Overseas travelers comprise 7.5%, or 16,100 of the total number of vacation/pleasure visitors (214,666) to Alaska per year. Of these 16,100, Japanese visitors account for 11%, or 1770. Though their numbers are small, Japanese typically spend nearly triple the amount a "lower 48" visitor and one and a half times that of a German-speaking (German, Swiss, or Austrian) visitor while in Alaska: $1,555, $576, $1090 per person per trip, respectively. For the winter, they are the most important market. During the winter, overseas visitors account for 4% of total visitors, and of these, Japanese account for half, spending an average of $1022 in-state. These figures are based on research completed in 1993 and 1994 (State of Alaska, 1994 a-f), the last time the state gathered such data. However, John Beiler, Alaska Division of Tourism Asia Specialist surmises that each year the number of Japanese visitors has been increasing at a rate of 8-10% per year and depositing approximately $18 million dollars in the Alaska economy per year (personal communication, June 26, 1997; *Alaska Edition,* National Public Radio, March 26, 1998).

The current study serves several functions. First, this research was designed for the very pragmatic purpose of providing a more accurate profile of the Japanese visitor to Alaska. Specifically, the current study analyzes demographics, pre-trip and actual trip behaviors, as well as visitor satisfaction with the Alaska experience. Although overall motivations of the Japanese traveler, travel patterns, travel demographics, etc., have been studied as evidenced by such works as the JTB studies (JTB Report, 1994, 1995, 1996 as well as Cha, McCleary, and Uysal (1995), little is known about planning horizons, motivational sources, images, etc., to visit a particular place. Finally, this study provides an opportunity to investigate segmentation based on peak and off-season.

Ultimately this study allows for examination of variables that can be loosely identified as "push and pull factors." Much has been written about these factors (i.e., Bello and Etzel, 1985; Dann, 1977; Uysal and Hagan, 1993; Smith, 1983; Yuan and McDonald, 1990). Push factors usually originate in the tourist as motivations, and as described by Uysal and Hagan, the push factors pertinent to the current study include such topics as demographics and market knowledge. Pull factors are destination attributes, and of those specified by Uysal and Hagan, the most relevant for this study are marketed image including "formed negative/positive destination attributes" as well as quality of services and facilities. Thus, the current study allows for a preliminary examination of those push and pull factors specific to Alaska. However, because it is an initial investigation, no formal hypotheses are made concerning what factors might be found or how these factors might differ across summer and winter visitors.

METHODOLOGY

A survey was administered to Japanese residents visiting Alaska during the summer of 1996 and the winter of 1997. The survey, printed in Japanese, investigated the following major areas: demographics, information sources used to inspire their trip, information sources used to plan their trip, trip-planning behaviors, as well as trip satisfaction. The distribution points for the survey varied for summer visitor and winter visitors. During the summer, distribution focused on south-central Alaska, a major destination of most Japanese, but also extended as far north as Denali National Park, the home of Mt. McKinley. During the winter the distribution point focused in the interior of Alaska around Fairbanks. The major reason for the difference in survey distribution points is related to Japanese travel goals. Though both the winter and summer Japanese tourists are motivated by "natural scenic attractions," the trip itineraries change to emphasize the best that season has to offer. Therefore, trips taken in the summer tend to focus on glacier watching, observing wildlife, and experiencing openness/vastness. During the winter, the sole major motivation is to view the Northern Lights, or the Aurora Borealis. The best Aurora viewing in the state is around Fairbanks.

RESULTS

The 579 surveys were collected during the summer and 200 during the winter for a total of 779 respondents. These data strongly suggest that sharp differences exist between the groups of summer and winter vacationing Japanese tourists.

Demographics

While both the summer and winter traveler are typically well-educated females, who take packaged trips, as Table 1 shows, the average winter visitor also tends to be younger, more likely single, less well-off financially, and though frequently employed in a professional or technical field, they are often found in occupations like office/clerical or student. Further, the winter visitor is more likely to be an independent traveler than the summer visitor. The summer visitor is more likely to be married, and though employed as an administrator or professional-technical, housewives are also well represented.

Motivations

Motivations were assessed with two questions; the first asked respondents to indicate which information sources triggered or inspired their interest to travel to Alaska and the second asked what factors prompted their visit to Alaska. In both cases, respondents indicated the three most influential triggers. Table 2 shows the most influential sources triggering interest in traveling to Alaska during the summer and winter are friends, travel guides, bro-

TABLE 1. Visitor Demographics

	Summer	Winter
Gender	56.3% Female	64.5% Female
Average age	41.0 Years	35.5 Years
Average income	13.6 M¥	7.2 M¥
Four year college		
degree or higher	50.0%	49.5%
Marital Status		
Married	55.7%	36.4%
Single	44.3%	63.6%
Occupation	20.9% Administrators	19% Prof/Tech
[three largest	19.3% Prof/Tech	18.5% Office/Clerical
groups]	14.6% Homemakers	17.4% Students
Type of Trip		
Independent	22.4%	33.3%
Package	60.11%	45.8%
Combination	17.5%	20.8%

chures, and TV shows. Only in the case of brochures was the proportion of winter visitors indicating a particular trigger significantly different from the proportion of winter visitors that named the same trigger as important.

Table 3 indicates that for summer visitors, factors affecting the decision to visit were seeing particular sights (defined as wilderness, mountains, and tundra), wildlife (viewing various animals), the Alaska summer (Midnight Sun, warm climate), and having an adventure (visiting new areas, experiencing new things). For the winter visitor, the Alaska winter (defined by the Northern Lights, Cold, Snow/Ice), having an adventure, attending special events (defined as dog sledding, car traveling, cruises), and seeing particular sights were major motivators. Thus, there was overlap with the exception of special events for the winter visitor and wildlife for the summer visitor and, as might be expected, seeing an Alaska summer for the summer visitors and seeing an Alaska winter for the winter visitors.

Trip Planning

Several questions were used to assess travelers' sources of trip planning information and the degree to which travelers felt that information was relevant. Table 4 describes responses to a question asking respondents to indicate up to three general resources which were used to actually plan their trip. Summer and winter visitors both indicated that brochures, travel guides, and friends were three major sources of trip planning information. In addition, winter visitors' important factors also included travel agent and travel magazine categories. Without a doubt, the travel agent category might also have been an important factor for the summer visitor (particularly since so many of

TABLE 2. Information Sources Triggering Interest

	summer	winter	χ^2	p
Book	11.77	16.26	2.7	0.101
Magazine	9.56	11.33	0.5	0.468
Newspaper	11.60	6.90	3.6	0.058
Radio	0.70	2.00	2.5	0.114
TV News	8.40	11.40	1.7	0.198
TV Show	30.70	35.00	1.3	0.262
Movie	3.10	5.40	2.3	0.126
Internet	0.50	5.40	20.8	0.001
Travel Guide	36.90	31.00	2.2	0.135
Travel Magazine	17.06	16.75	0.0	0.918
Travel Documentary	11.43	9.85	0.4	0.535
Travel Show	4.10	7.40	3.5	0.062
Brochure	34.60	20.20	14.7	0.001
Advertisement	10.75	7.88	1.4	0.241
Friends	38.05	39.90	0.2	0.641
Workplace	3.41	4.43	0.4	0.505
Travel Agency[1]	0.85	10.34	42.6	0.001
Other	12.29	15.76	1.6	0.207

[1] In translating the survey into Japanese for the summer visitor, travel agency as an option was inadvertently omitted. The error was rectified for the winter visitor. The data for this choice by summer visitor was derived from their indications in the open-ended "other" choice that travel agent was an influencer.

TABLE 3. Factors Prompting Visit to Alaska

	summer	winter	χ^2	p
Native Culture	7.9	9.9	0.7	0.394
US Culture	2.5	1.6	0.6	0.444
Particular Sights	59.3	30.7	46.8	0.001
Gain Understanding	6.3	3.7	1.9	0.169
Special Events	9.7	31.2	51.2	0.001
Historic Attraction	2.3	2.1	0.0	0.838
Time Frame	18.9	5.7	18.8	0.001
Romance	2.5	21.4	74.3	0.001
Visit Friends	5.0	4.2	0.2	0.628
AK Summer	38.1	6.3	69.1	0.001
AK Winter	13.1	89.1	374.4	0.001
Outdoor	15.5	8.3	6.2	0.013
Affordable	1.6	3.1	1.6	0.199
Adventure	31.5	41.1	5.9	0.015
Wildlife	50.4	7.8	108.2	0.001
Business	2.0	2.6	0.3	0.605
Other	5.0	4.2	0.2	0.628

them utilize package tours) if it had not been inadvertently omitted from the summer questionnaire.

An intriguing question is related to how sufficient visitors view sources of information for planning purposes. Table 5 shows that most sources to be merely adequate with less than 10 percent for both groups feeling that the sources were very sufficient. Table 6 indicates why visitors may have made

TABLE 4. Resources Used to Plan Trip

	Summer	Winter	χ^2	p
Book	6.67	5.42	0.4	0.530
Magazine	4.96	5.91	0.3	0.598
Newspaper	6.67	5.91	0.1	0.706
Radio	0.68	0.99	0.2	0.670
TV News	5.64	4.43	0.4	0.509
TV Show	15.56	4.93	15.2	0.001
Movie	1.20	0.99	0.1	0.807
Internet	1.54	10.84	34.5	0.001
Travel Guide	67.52	62.07	2.0	0.157
Travel Magazine	24.10	23.15	0.1	0.784
Travel Documentary	9.91	6.40	2.3	0.132
Travel Show	7.35	9.36	0.8	0.360
Brochure	74.24	25.76	5.6	0.018
Advertisement	8.03	5.42	1.5	0.219
Friends	28.38	27.59	0.0	0.829
Workplace	3.42	3.94	0.1	0.729
Travel Agency[1]	2.05	26.60	118.4	0.001
Other	6.32	7.39	0.3	0.599

[1] In translating the survey into Japanese for the summer visitor, travel agency as an option was inadvertently omitted. The error was rectified for the winter visitor. The data for this choice by summer visitor was derived from their indications in the open-ended "other" choice that travel agent was an influencer.

TABLE 5. Japanese Tourists' Ratings of Information Sufficiency

	Experience Rating				
	1	2	3	4	5
	Not Very Sufficient		Somewhat Sufficient		Very Sufficient
Summer	7.32	17.07	50.00	19.86	5.75
Winter	2.99	13.93	44.78	30.85	7.46
$\chi^2 = 14.867$ p $\geq$ 0.005					

this evaluation. For winter and summer visitors, lack of availability as well as lack of specificity were major reasons given for inadequacy (see Table 7). Winter visitors may spend more time planning because they are more likely to take an independent or combination type of trip than the summer visitor (see Table 8). Table 9 shows resources particular to Alaska. As indicated for both the summer and winter visitor, Japan-based sources are the most important. Specifically, these include the Japanese travel books, *The Globe Trotter* and the *Blue World Guide* in addition to the Alaska Division of Tourism Office in Tokyo.

The Trip Itself

Regardless of whether visitors choose a package, independent, or combination type of trip, Table 10 indicates that the length for both the winter and

TABLE 6. Evaluation of Information

	Summer	Winter	χ^2	p
Not available	46.25	38.71	0.6	0.440
Not specific	43.75	51.61	0.6	0.421
Incorrect	13.75	12.90	0.0	0.900
Dated	11.25	9.68	0.1	0.798
Other	8.75	12.90	0.5	0.469

TABLE 7. Months Spent Planning Trip

	N	Summer Mean	St. Dev.	N	Winter Mean	St. Dev.	delta	t	
Planning	548	3.29	3.16	190	4.04	3.96	−0.75	−2.36	***

***p ≤ .01

TABLE 8. Type of Travel

	Combination	Independent	Package
Summer	17.51	22.38	60.11
Winter	20.83	33.33	45.83

$\chi^2 = 12.79$ p ≥ 0.002

TABLE 9. Sources of Information Used to Plan Trip

	Summer	Winter	χ^2	p
Globe Trotter	61.78	67.17	1.8	0.177
Blue World	28.26	26.26	0.3	0.590
AK Tokyo	20.47	22.73	0.4	0.504
AK visitor center	9.97	6.57	0.4	0.522
AK Vac Planner	1.27	0.51	0.8	0.370
Other AK brochure	17.75	15.15	0.7	0.404
Milepost	3.26	1.01	2.8	0.092
AK Budget Traveler	1.99	0.51	2.0	0.152
None above	9.78	13.64	2.2	0.134
Other	6.70	9.60	1.8	0.184

summer visitor was nearly 7 days with, in both seasons, the packaged tourist staying the shortest time, the combination tourist staying the intermediate length, and the independent tourist staying the longest.

Table 11 suggests most of the tour product was purchased in Japan prior to arrival in Alaska. A follow-up question examined additional purchases once in Alaska; 29.64 percent of summer visitors purchased additional sightseeing tours in Alaska while a significantly (p ≤ 0.05) higher percentage of winter visitors, 37.44, did so.

TABLE 10. Duration of Stay in Alaska by Type of Trip

	N	Summer Mean	St. Dev.	N	Winter Mean	St. Dev.	delta	t	
All visitors	487	6.78	3.69	170	6.66	2.67	0.12	0.45	
Combination	80	8.19	4.24	31	6.48	1.61	1.71	3.08	***
Independent	87	10.40	5.86	55	7.78	3.96	2.62	3.18	****
Package	297	5.45	1.10	77	5.99	1.43	−0.54	−3.09	***

**** p ≤ .001 *** p ≤ .01 ** p ≤ .025 * p ≤ .05

TABLE 11. Percentage of Japanese Tourists Purchasing Products and Services Prior to Their Trip To Alaska

	Summer	Winter	χ^2	p
Airfare to/fro AK	91.3	93.6	0.9	0.333
Airfare w/in AK	30.6	70.5	83.6	0.001
Short Distance Ground	22.8	22.5	0.0	0.950
Long Distance Ground	57.4	23.7	57.7	0.001
Accommodations	75.4	79.2	1.0	0.309
Food	73.6	26.0	6.2	0.013
Personal/Group Guide	48.9	31.2	16.1	0.001
Sight Seeing Tour	56.3	33.0	27.8	0.001

Trip Satisfaction

The Japanese visitor was asked three questions about the trip satisfaction. The first, featured in Table 12, examines their expectations and fulfillments with regard to images. Specifically, respondents were asked to indicate their three strongest images, before their trip and after they arrived. As becomes immediately obvious, the winter travelers' expectations were more accurate as evidenced by an absence of a large number of significant differences between the pre-and post-images. Both groups apparently experienced some surprises, e.g., a lack of igloos, and they also revised their perception of how cold the state is . . . they found it warmer than they expected. Similarly, all visitors were awed by the vastness, but yet caught off guard by the presence of urban life. Both groups expressed expectations of seeing a bigger Native presence than they actually experienced. For the winter people, the strongest images were the Aurora, Cold, and Dog Sledding. After their visit, Aurora is still first, followed by Vastness, followed by Dog Sled and Natural (tied at third). For the summer people, the pre-trip images are Aurora, Natural, and Glacier. The top three after having arrived are Natural, Glacier, and Vastness. So, in general, their expectations were met with regard to pre-conceived notions. The dramatic shift of Aurora for the summer visitor can be explained as follows: Japanese media have heavily featured information about Auroras;

TABLE 12. Images of Alaska, Before and After Trip

		Summer			Winter		
	Pre	Post	Difference	Pre	Post	Difference	
Igloos	0.02	0.00	−0.01 **	0.03	0.00	−0.03 ***	
Vast	0.24	0.46	0.23 ****	0.21	0.45	0.24 ****	
Natural	0.44	0.50	0.06 **	0.24	0.30	0.06	
Wilderness	0.08	0.12	0.04 ***	0.07	0.09	0.01	
Pipeline	0.02	0.04	0.01	0.07	0.05	−0.03	
Mountains	0.08	0.11	0.04 ****	0.07	0.11	0.04	
Car tour	0.00	0.03	0.02 ****	0.01	0.02	0.01	
Ocean tour	0.04	0.05	0.00	0.01	0.01	0.01	
Cold	0.19	0.07	−0.12 ****	0.49	0.18	−0.31 ****	
Snow	0.15	0.05	−0.10 ****	0.20	0.22	0.02	
Aurora	0.51	0.15	−0.36 ****	0.91	0.79	−0.11 ****	
Midnight sun	0.16	0.17	0.01	0.05	0.04	−0.01	
Rain	0.01	0.07	0.06 ****	0.00	0.00	0.00	
Cities	0.00	0.01	0.01 ***	0.00	0.04	0.04 ***	
Crowded	0.00	0.00	0.00	0.01	0.01	0.01	
Glacier	0.43	0.48	0.05	0.14	0.07	−0.08 ***	
Fish/hunt	0.09	0.07	−0.02	0.02	0.02	0.00	
Native	0.12	0.03	−0.08 ****	0.17	0.04	−0.13 ****	
Hike	0.02	0.03	0.01	0.02	0.02	0.00	
Camping	0.02	0.05	0.03 **	0.03	0.03	0.00	
Dogsled	0.11	0.02	−0.10 ****	0.28	0.30	0.02	
Wildlife	0.26	0.32	0.06 ***	0.06	0.06	0.00	
Parks	0.09	0.13	0.04 **	0.04	0.05	0.02	
Far away	0.08	0.05	−0.03 *	0.13	0.07	−0.06 *	
Other	0.02	0.05	0.03 ***	0.02	0.07	0.05 **	

**** $p \le .001$ **** $p \le .01$ ** $p \le .025$ * $p \le .05$

however seeing the Aurora Borealis, a night-time display, in the summer, during the "midnight sun" is problematic.

Respondents were asked to rate their overall Alaskan experience. Table 13 shows, that few were terribly dissatisfied. A follow-up question inquired as to whether they would recommend the trip to a friend. Overwhelming, they would. Both summer and winter Japanese visitors indicated that they would recommend the trip to others [91.42 and 94.79 percent, respectively].

Study Limitations

Two limitations to this study must be addressed. First, although over 35% of all Japanese estimated to have visited Alaska during the summer of 1996 through the winter of 1997 were sampled, this sample was not random in nature, so the possibility of non-response bias does exist. Second, because of the process of disaggregation into component groups necessarily results in comparisons of subsamples of relatively small size in the current study, one must recognize that sample size can effect the calculation of test statistics. However, small Ns are only an issue if the results are not significant. As such,

TABLE 13. Japanese Tourists' Ratings of Visit Experience

	Experience Rating				
	1	2	3	4	5
	Poor		Average		Excellent
Summer	1.61	9.82	39.29	35.00	14.29
Winter	0.51	5.61	27.04	44.39	22.45
$\chi^2 = 19.612$ $p \geq 0.001$					

a larger sample may be required to reveal significant differences, if indeed significant differences exist.

DISCUSSION

Major goals of the current study are to more accurately assess the profile of Japanese visitors to Alaska and to tentatively identify push and pull factors specific to Alaska. In this regard, the results reported here indicate that Alaska's experience with Japanese tourists mirrors wider trends in Japan's market for international tourism products. That is, the modal international traveler is a young female who is searching for experiences that are closely tied to beautiful natural phenomena and is likely to complete all travel within a week's time. Most are using package travel although there are trends toward travelers using combination trips as well as traveling independently.

However even though the overall profile is the same, niche markets can be established within this overall segment. The current study strongly suggests that the Japanese market for Alaskan tourism products may be cleanly broken into two nature-based segments grounded on season, winter and summer. Each seeks a unique nature-based experience, one based on the aurora, cold, and dog mushing, and the other based on nature, including glaciers. One is younger, single, and more likely to travel independently.

Japanese visitors provide unique economic opportunities for travel-related business located in northern latitudes. First, the Japanese represent a class of visitors who possess both financial resources and the willingness to invest in leisure activities located in these regions. Second, because the Japanese summer and winter cohorts appear to be quite different along several dimensions it seems to be the case that aggressively marketing to winter visitors will not appreciably cannibalize Japanese demand for summer activities. Because tourism facilities located in northern latitudes are typically underutilized during the winter months, this is a non-trivial issue. Third, the results uncovered here suggest that Japanese rely on sources of information that originate in Japan. This suggests that appropriate promotional strategies cannot ignore these distribution realities. In much the same manner as Americans use and prefer domestically produced travel planning aids, the Japanese extensively utilize travel planning products and services that are produced in Japan for planning their international travels. The one exception to this idea would be Internet-based marketing which would allow Alaskan and other circumpolar business to directly access the Japanese market in a manner that many Japanese might find comfortable. This is especially true if one is seeking out visitors with the characteristics of the Alaskan winter visitor. The current study found that winter visitors were significantly more likely to use the Internet than were the summer visitors. Apparently this is explained by the fact that major users of the Internet in Japan include the young and students (Cyberspace Japan, 1997). As shown in Table 1, these two groups are prominent in the winter profile. This suggests that a web-page describing an Alaskan attraction and properly executed in Japanese would elicit hits on an Internet search conducted in Japan.

Although the Japanese indicate that, in an overall fashion, they are happy with their experiences in the state, there is room for improvement. In particular, Japanese visitors expressed dissatisfaction with the sufficiency of information available to plan trips. Perhaps tourism related firms should attempt to position themselves vis à vis the Japanese travel planning industry in such a way as to insure that their products and services will be described in a timely and specific fashion. Finally, though the current study indicated that the Japanese were very willing to recommend Alaska to their friends, the fact that their response to the question concerning their "overall Alaska experience," was not as high as would be hoped, future research should explore specifically which components in their experience is lacking, be they accommodations, activities, food, transportation, or some combination.

REFERENCES

Bello, D. C. & Etzel, M. J. (1985). The rate of novelty in pleasure travel experiences. *Journal of Travel Research, 24,* 20-26.

Cha, S., McCleary, K. W., & Uysal, M. (1995). Travel motivations of Japanese overseas travelers: A factor-cluster segmentation approach. *Journal of Travel Research, Summer,* 33-39.

Cyberspace Japan (1997). WWW Usage Survey Results: 1995-1997 Overview. Available: http://www.csj.co.jp/English/index-2yr.html

Dann, G. (1977). Anomie, ego-enhancement and tourism. *Annals of Tourism Research, 4,* (4), 184-194.

JTB Report '94: All about Japanese overseas travelers (1994). Tokyo, Japan: JTB Overseas Travel Department.

JTB Report '95: All about Japanese overseas travelers (1995). Tokyo, Japan: JTB Overseas Travel Department.

JTB Report '96: All about Japanese overseas travelers (1996). Tokyo: Japan: JTB Overseas Travel Department

Moeran, B. 1983. The Language of Japanese tourism. *Annals of Tourism Research*, *10*, 93-108.

Morris, S. (1988). Outbound markets/market segment studies: Japanese leisure patterns. *Travel and Tourism Analyst*, *5*, 32-53.

Nozawa, H. (1992). A marketing analysis of Japanese outbound travel. *Tourism Management*, *13* (2), 226-234.

Polunin, I. (1989). Japanese travel boom. *Tourism Management*, *10* (1), 4-8.

Smith, L. J. S. (1983). *Recreation Geography*. London and New York: Longman.

Sternberg, R. (1993, October). Japanese go their own way. *Asian Business*, 52.

Prime Minister's Office (1995). *Heisei 7 nendo Kanko Hakusho*. Tokyo, Japan: Ministry of Finance Printing Bureau.

State of Alaska (1994a). *Alaska visitor statistics program: Alaska visitor arrivals, summer 1993*. Juneau and Ketchikan: McDowell Group.

State of Alaska (1994b). *Alaska visitor statistics program: Alaska visitor expenditures, summer 1993*. Juneau and Ketchikan: McDowell Group.

State of Alaska (1994c). *Alaska visitor statistics program: Alaska visitor patterns, opinions and planning, summer 1993*. Juneau and Ketchikan: McDowell Group.

State of Alaska (1994d). *Alaska visitor statistics program: Alaska visitor arrivals, fall/winter/spring, 93-94*. Juneau and Ketchikan: McDowell Group.

State of Alaska (1994e). *Alaska visitor statistics program: Alaska visitor expenditures, fall/winter/spring, 93-94*. Juneau and Ketchikan: McDowell Group.

State of Alaska (1994f). *Alaska visitor statistics program: Alaska visitor patterns, opinions and planning, fall/winter/spring 93-94*. Juneau and Ketchikan: McDowell Group.

Uysal, M. & Hagan, L. A. R. (1993). Motivation of pleasure travel and tourism. In M. A. Khan, M. D. Olsen, & T. Var (Eds.), *VNR's encyclopedia of hospitality and tourism*. New York: Van Nostrand Reinhold.

Yuan, S. & McDonald, C. D. (1990). Motivational determinants of international pleasure time. *Journal of Travel Research*, *29* (1), 42-44.

Hong Kong as a Travel Destination: An Analysis of Japanese Tourists' Satisfaction Levels, and the Likelihood of Them Recommending Hong Kong to Others

Vincent C. S. Heung
Hailin Qu

SUMMARY. The Japanese market is one of Hong Kong's major tourism markets, contributing significant numbers of inbound travelers and tourism receipts to the Hong Kong tourism industry. Nevertheless, this sector has dropped drastically since early 1997. In order to retain the potential Japanese market, and as a first step, this study examines the satisfaction levels of the Japanese tourists toward Hong Kong as a travel destination in terms of 31 travel attributes. Of these 31 travel attributes, 'Overall accessibility of Hong Kong' appears to be the top satisfaction attribute perceived by Japanese tourists. The 31 travel attributes

Vincent C. S. Heung is Assistant Professor of Marketing, Department of Hotel and Tourism Management, Hong Kong Polytechnic University. Hailin Qu is Professor, School of Hotel, Restaurant and Tourism Management, Oklahoma State University, Stillwater, OK 74078-6173.

Address correspondence to: Vincent C. S. Heung, Department of Hotel and Tourism Management, The Hong Kong Polytechnic University, Hung Hom, Kowloon Hong Kong (E-mail: hmvheung@polyu.edu.hk).

This research project was supported by a research grant from the Hong Kong Polytechnic University.

[Haworth co-indexing entry note]: "Hong Kong as a Travel Destination: An Analysis of Japanese Tourists' Satisfaction Levels, and the Likelihood of Them Recommending Hong Kong to Others." Heung, Vincent C. S., and Hailin Qu. Co-published simultaneously in *Journal of Travel & Tourism Marketing* (The Haworth Hospitality Press, an imprint of The Haworth Press, Inc.) Vol. 9, No. 1/2, 2000, pp. 57-80; and: *Japanese Tourists: Socio-Economic, Marketing and Psychological Analysis* (ed: K. S. (Kaye) Chon, Tsutomu Inagaki, and Taiji Ohashi) The Haworth Hospitality Press, an imprint of The Haworth Press, Inc., 2000, pp. 57-80. Single or multiple copies of this article are available for a fee from The Haworth Document Delivery Service [1-800-342-9678, 9:00 a.m. - 5:00 p.m. (EST). E-mail address: getinfo@haworth pressinc.com].

are then factor analyzed into eight dimensions: 'People'; 'Overall Convenience'; 'Price'; 'Accommodation and Food'; 'Commodities'; 'Attractions'; 'Culture'; and 'Climate and Image.' Multiple regression analysis was applied to examine the relative impact of each of the travel dimensions in affecting Japanese tourists' overall satisfaction with Hong Kong, as well as the their likelihood of them recommending Hong Kong to other people. Results reveal that 'Accommodation and Food' exert the most influential impact on both of the dependent variables. *[Article copies available for a fee from The Haworth Document Delivery Service: 1-800-342-9678. E-mail address: <getinfo@haworthpressinc.com> Website: <http://www.haworthpressinc.com>]*

KEYWORDS. Destination travel attributes, Hong Kong, Japanese tourists, satisfaction

INTRODUCTION

Hong Kong has long been a popular destination of Japanese travelers. For the past ten years (1987-1996), the number of Japanese visitor arrivals has increased about 1.3 times, from 1 million in 1987 to a record high of 2.3 million in 1996, with more than 70% of them traveling to Hong Kong for vacation purposes (Hong Kong Tourist Association, 1996). The 1996 figure represented 20.4% of total visitor arrivals, and Japan ranked as the top inbound market (see Table 1). Table 2 reports the Japanese tourists' expenditure in Hong Kong from 1987 to 1996. Tourism receipts from Japan have been reported as the major source of foreign exchange to the territory, accounting for more than 20% of total tourism receipts per annum on average between 1987 and 1996. In 1996, Japanese tourists spent nearly HK$19 billion in Hong Kong on various activities such as shopping, accommodation meals, entertainment, etc., equivalent to 22% of total tourism receipts (HK $82.4 billion) in that year.

Since 1997, Hong Kong's tourism industry has faced tremendous market turmoil, in particular in relation to the Japanese inbound sector. The Japanese market, which was once regarded as a high-generating market in terms of tourist arrivals and tourism receipts, has dropped significantly. A controversy about discriminatory pricing for Japanese tourists during the handover period discouraged inbound Japanese travel, leading to a 2.9% fall in tourism receipts to HK$39.8 billion in the first six months of 1997 (South China Morning Post, 1997). Worse still, unfavorable news about Hong Kong was widespread in Japanese documentaries, which reported that Hong Kong's hotels charged Japanese tourists three times more than they did other tourists. The drop in inbound Japanese travel not only reduced tourism receipts, but

TABLE 1. Visitor Arrivals from Japan, 1987-1996

Year	Number of Japanese Arrivals	Growth Rate (%)	Market Share (%)	Ranking
1987	1,033,525	42.1	23.0	Top 1
1988	1,240,470	20.0	22.2	Top 1
1989	1,176,189	− 5.2	21.9	Top 1
1990	1,331,667	13.2	22.4	Top 2
1991	1,259,837	− 5.4	20.9	Top 2
1992	1,324,399	5.1	19.0	Top 2
1993	1,280,905	− 3.3	14.3	Top 3
1994	1,440,632	12.5	15.4	Top 3
1995	1,691,283	17.4	16.6	Top 3
1996	2,382,890	40.9	20.4	Top 1

Source: A Statistical Review of Tourism 1987–1996, Hong Kong Tourist Association, Hong Kong.
* Data for 1992 and before excludes China visitors

TABLE 2. The Share of Japanese Tourist Expenditure as a Percentage of Total Tourism Receipts in Hong Kong, 1987-1996

Year	Total Japanese Tourist Expenditure (HK$M)	Total H.K. Visitor Receipts (HK$M)	Market Share (%)
1987	7,024.04	24,837.14	28.3
1988	9,149.21	32,496.16	28.2
1989	9,113.70	35,842.86	25.4
1990	9,227.19	37,977.86	24.3
1991	9,184.97	38,300.56	24.0
1992	9,034.46	46,698.76	19.3
1993	10,074.43	58,303.43	17.3
1994	12,165.18	62,511.87	19.5
1995	14,110.60	72,939.61	19.3
1996	18,501.85	82,462.38	22.4

Source: A Statistical Review of Tourism 1987-1996, Hong Kong Tourist Association, Hong Kong.
* HK$7.75 = US$1.0

has also undermined the reputation of Hong Kong as an international tourist destination. Falling tourist arrivals have been aggravated by the regional currency crisis, which has made Hong Kong an expensive destination in comparison with other Southeast Asian regions. Brevetti (1995) warned that Hong Kong had become less 'vacation-friendly' than previously, as high inflation had driven up prices. Consequently, the rising cost of staying in Hong Kong and the dwindling number of shopping bargains are continuously affecting the territory's tourism, hence reducing its competitiveness as a 'Shopping Paradise' and 'The Pearl of the Orient.'

In order to attract Japanese tourists, it is important to understand how they perceive Hong Kong as a travel destination. This study aims to examine Japanese tourists' satisfaction levels towards Hong Kong as a travel destination in terms of shopping, food, accommodation, entertainment, people, etc. Understanding the preferences and travel-related behavior of tourists is vital to tourism marketers in terms of market segmentation and the design of effective promotional campaigns. Nowadays, tourists are becoming more and more sophisticated. Their expectations regarding the quality and variety of tourism services have increased tremendously (Wade, 1995). To win customers requires an understanding of their preferences, and the development of services and facilities to satisfy those preferences. The specific objectives of this study are:

1. To identify Japanese tourists' levels of perceived satisfaction with Hong Kong as a travel destination in terms of a list of travel attributes;
2. To identify the underlying dimensions of travel attributes, as perceived by Japanese tourists, in relation to Hong Kong as a travel destination;
3. To examine the relative impact of the underlying dimensions of travel attributes in influencing Japanese tourists' overall levels of satisfaction with Hong Kong as travel destination; and,
4. To examine the relative impact of the underlying dimensions of travel attributes influencing Japanese tourists' likelihood of recommending Hong Kong to other people.

It is believed that a comprehensive understanding of the leisure travel destination decision process is likely to make a substantial contribution to the practice of tourism marketing. By identifying major attributes that affect destination selection and their relationships with tourist characteristics, tourism marketers will be better able to influence consumer behavior, to consumer satisfaction and repeat patronage.

LITERATURE REVIEW

Travel Attributes

Um (1987) defined travel attributes as the set of attributes which, when aggregated together, describe a place as a travel destination. They include all elements that are related to a destination and to traveling to the place, such as the destination's physical and cultural characteristics, the mental and actual distance required to get to the destination, and so on. Lancaster (1966) mentioned that customers do not choose goods themselves, but rather the attributes possessed by the goods, and that they use the attributes as input factors that produce utility. Mok and Armstrong (1996) noted that tourists generally have limited knowledge about a destination that they have not previously visited. Hence, their destination choice is often dependent upon symbolic information acquired either from the media or from social groups.

The current tourism literature has mostly reported findings about tourist perceptions and satisfaction levels towards traveling in Western societies. Relatively few studies have addressed the Asian aspect. Mayo and Jarvis (1981) stated that travel attributes may be perceived differently by members of different cultural groups. Mill and Morrison (1985) mentioned that tourists from different countries and cultures generally have different perceptions as to their favorite attractions.

Goodrich (1977) reported that his sample of American Express international travelers had considered four important factors in their travel planning. The four attributes were: entertainment; purchase opportunities; climate for comfort; and cost. Holloway (1986) stated that the success of a tourist destination (as a consumer product) depended upon the interrelationship of three basic factors: its attractions; its amenities or facilities; and its accessibility for tourists. Supported by the Pennsylvania Bureau of Travel Development, Shih (1986) identified some important travel attributes, including visitor safety; reasonable prices; good accommodation; and relaxing vacations. Van Raaij (1986) sawed a travel destination as a product that is partly 'given' and partly 'man-made.' In the 'given' part, there are a number of natural features of a tourist destination, such as the climate, scenery, beaches, mountains, historic-cultural buildings, and so forth. In general, these 'given' features may determine the tourist segments, e.g., active vs. passive vacationers; and vacationers with cultural, sports, or other preferences. In the 'man-made' part, there exist features such as hotel and transportation facilities, package tours and facilities for sports and recreation, which can be adapted to customer preferences, subject to budget restrictions. These 'man-made' services and facilities can be designed by tourism marketers to satisfy the preferences of the consumer segments in the 'given' part. It is important to evaluate consumer behavior with regard to existing tourist products so that 'man-made' characteristics can be better tailored to consumers' needs and 'given' characteristics can be better positioned in the market place (Van Raaij, 1986).

Regarding Hong Kong as a travel destination, Siu et al. (1987) observed that the effective marketing of Hong Kong tourism requires an understanding of how tourists from different geographic and cultural backgrounds perceive Hong Kong's attributes. Yau and Chan (1990) surveyed 600 tourists with an instrument covering 31 major travel attributes emphasized by tourists in general. Seven travel attributes were extracted by means of factor analysis. They were: infrastructure; entertainment and attractions; services in hotels and restaurants; quality of food and the proximity of restaurants; price; climate; and friends and relatives. Mok's study (1995a; 1995b) looked into the Asian perspective by examining Hong Kong and Taiwanese outbound travelers' perceptions of Australia as a leisure destination. They reported that safety appeared to be the top priority as perceived by both Hong Kong and Taiwanese travelers. The other travel attributes, in order of perceived importance, were: scenic beauty; cultural interests; friendliness of local people; price of trip; services in hotels and restaurants; quality and variety of foods; shopping facilities and services; climate; entertainment; recreational and sports facilities; destination distances from place of residence; and, friends and relatives at destination. A report by the Hong Kong Tourist Association (1995) addressed eight common needs of tourists. They included: ease of visa application and relaxed travel regulations; easy and safe travel; competitive prices; sufficient information about facilities, attractions, services and events; sufficient hotel accommodations; ease of access; commodities with great variety at reasonable prices; and attractions and relaxing activities.

An understanding of the perceived importance of various travel attributes to tourists is an important step in facilitating market segmentation and promotion. Successful tourism marketing requires an understanding of the factors that affect a destination's image and attractiveness (Ahmed and Krohn, 1990; Haahti, 1986). From a cultural perspective, examining the differences in perceptions helps in creating different marketing themes for those different market segments (Mok and Armstrong, 1995b).

Customer Satisfaction

Studies of consumer behavior emphasize customer satisfaction as the core of the post-purchase period (Westbrook and Oliver, 1991). A traditional definition of customer satisfaction follows the disconfirmation paradigm of consumer satisfaction/dissatisfaction (CS/D), which suggests that CS/D is the result of interaction between the consumer's post-purchase evaluation and pre-purchase expectations (Berkman and Gilson, 1986; Czepiel and Ronsenberg, 1977; Engel et al., 1990). Anton (1996) had a more contemporary approach, defining customer satisfaction as a state of mind in which an individual's needs, wants, and expectations throughout the product or service life have been met or exceeded, resulting in repurchase and loyalty. In the tourism literature, Pizam et al. (1978) defined satisfaction as the result of the interaction between a tourist's experience at the destination area and the expectations he or she had about that destination. The tourist is satisfied when the weighted sum total of experiences compared to the expectations results in feelings of gratification (positive disconfirmation). The tourist is dissatisfied when his or her actual experiences compared with expectations result in feeling of displeasure (negative disconfirmation). However, recent research studies have viewed satisfaction from the perspective of performance evaluations, making the inclusion of the disconfirmation process unnecessary (Churchill and Suprenant, 1982; Cronin and Taylor, 1992). In this study, we measured Japanese tourists' satisfaction levels with Hong Kong by assessing their perceptions of travel attributes.

The concept of satisfaction is defined by marketers as post-purchase behavior that is of strategic importance to businesses because of its influence on repeat purchases and word-of-mouth recommendations (Berkman and Gilson, 1986; Westbrook and Oliver, 1991). As customer satisfaction can result in favorable word-of-mouth publicity, an understanding of this concept is essential for tourism businesses (Fornell, 1992; Halstead and Page, 1992). Therefore, in order to retain customers, tourism marketers need to understand fully those travel attributes are most likely to influence customers' choice intentions. Berry and Parasuraman (1991) pointed out that as customer satisfaction is influenced by the availability of customer services, the provision of quality customer service is an increasingly important concern of businesses. Chon et al. (1995) mentioned that failure to pay attention to influential attributes in choice intention may result in a customer's negative evaluation, and may thus lead to unfavorable word-of-mouth.

Japanese Travelers

Japanese tourists are unique in many ways. They love to travel, they travel in groups, they finance their trips in unique ways, and they are young in age (Nishiyama, 1989). As reported by the Japan Travel Bureau (JTB) in 1994, leisure and free-time activities were at the top of purposes for vacation travel for the past ten years. More and more people are tending to travel with a spouse, family member and relatives. As Japanese society ages, more elderly travelers are going overseas, while the largest percentage of departures in 1994 was in the category of women in their 20s. There has been remarkable growth in the number of travelers aged under 20 for the past 10 years. There has been an increasing number of repeat travelers and a stronger trend towards individual travelers. The most important activities at a destination have been unchanged for the past five years, centering on shopping, local sightseeing and city sightseeing. The preferences in types of destination show 'nature' and 'sunshine, blue seas and white beaches' in the first and second position for the past five years. The three major factors hindering overseas travel are cost, language and security (JTB, 1994).

METHOD

The Instrument

The questionnaire, translated into Japanese, consisted of four sections. The first section contained questions asking for traveling information of respondents, such as purpose of trip, source of information, the number of times the respondent had visited Hong Kong, length of stay, type of hotel at which the respondent stayed, and commodities bought. The second section consisted of 31 statements that captured the major travel features of Hong Kong in terms of accommodation, food, shopping, entertainment, transportation, sightseeing, infrastructures, prices, people, culture, etc. These 31 statements (destination attributes) were identified through professional advice from academic and tourism bodies in Hong Kong and a comprehensive review of the findings from major destination studies (Goodrich, 1977; Holloway, 1986; Shih, 1986; Van Raaij, 1986; Siu et al., 1987; Yau & Chan, 1990; Mok and Armstrong, 1995a 1995b). Respondents were asked to rate their perceived satisfaction levels towards each of the statements on a 5-point Likert scale, ranging from 1 (very dissatisfied) to 5 (very satisfied). The third section featured two questions that were aimed at rating the Japanese tourists' overall satisfaction levels towards Hong Kong as a travel destination (Likert scale: 1-very dissatisfied to 5-very satisfied), as well as their likelihood of recommending Hong Kong to other people (Likert scale: 1-very unlikely to 5-very likely). The last section contained four questions designed to extract respondents' demographic characteristics, such as including gender, age, occupation and annual income.

Two pilot tests were conducted, and several items were reworded so as to improve the readability and clarity of the questionnaire instrument.

The Sample

In this study, the target populations included those Japanese tourists who were to leave Hong Kong in the survey period. In this context, "tourists" are defined as those who cross a border for leisure or business and stay at least 24 hours, but less than one year (Mill and Morrison, 1985). Using a convenience sample approach, data were gathered in the departure area of the Hong Kong International Airport during 25th-31st December 1997 and 2nd-8th February 1998, through a closed-ended, self-administered questionnaire.

Data Analysis

In this study, simple frequencies were performed on the tourists' demographic and traveling profiles; their overall satisfaction levels towards Hong Kong; their likelihood of returning; and the likelihood of them recommending Hong Kong to others. Mean rating was used to rank the respondents' satisfaction levels towards the 33 destination attributes.

Principal components analysis with varimax rotation was employed to reduce the 31 travel attributes into a few, correlated and meaningful dimensions. The component factor model was used in the study. The purpose of using the component factor model is to predict and determine the minimum number of factors needed to account for the maximum portion of the variance represented in the original set of variables (Hair et al., 1998). Only items with factor loadings of 0.50 or above and eigenvalues greater than or equivalent to 1 were extracted. The reliability of the factors was assessed using Cronbach's coefficient alpha (Churchill, 1979).

Multiple regression analysis was used to examine the relative importance of the travel dimensions (predicting variables) in contributing to tourists' overall satisfaction levels (dependent variable), and their likelihood of recommending Hong Kong to other people. The two dependent variables (overall satisfaction levels and likelihood of giving a recommendation) were regressed against the factor means of the independent variables (the travel dimensions), respectively. The reason for using factor mean, or summated scale, for each factor was that it included the variables loading highly on the factor and excluded those having little impact on the factor (Hair et al., 1995). Thus, each surrogate factor could be easily replicated on subsequent samples because the summated scales were just averaged for each factor and were comparable between samples. Multicollinearity was examined to see whether the seven travel dimensions were highly correlated to each other, undermining the explanatory power of each independent variable on the variance of the dependent variable.

RESULTS AND DISCUSSIONS

Demographic and Traveling Characteristics of the Respondents

A total of 630 questionnaires were done in the two survey periods, in December 1997 and February 1998. Of 630 questionnaires, 522 usable questionnaires were generated, representing a response rate of 82.8%. Table 3 shows the demographic and traveling characteristics of the respondents. Nearly 70% of the respondents were males, and the majority of respondents

(70%) were aged between 18 and 34 years old. The four most common occupations of the respondents were: civil servant (19.4%); student (18%); professional (15.5%); and white collar worker (13.8%). In terms of income, 22.5% of the respondents had an annual income of less than US$10,000; 18.8% had an annual income of between US$10,001 and US $30,000; 28% were between US$30,001 and US$50,000; and 31.7% earned more than US $50,000 annually. With regard to traveling characteristics, almost 55% of the respondents were first-time visitors; and 72% were on vacation, whereas only 6% were on business. More than 95% of the respondents stayed in hotels during the trip in question, while the rest stayed with friends or relatives and hostels. Nearly 50% of the respondents sought information about Hong Kong through travel brochures or magazines; while 26% and 10% of the respondents were recommended by travel agencies or friends and relatives, respectively.

Mean Ratings of the Thirty-one Travel Attributes

Table 4 shows the mean ratings of Japanese tourists' satisfaction levels in relation to the 31 travel attributes in Hong Kong. In order of highest to lowest levels of satisfaction, accessibility of Hong Kong was found to be the top travel attribute as perceived by Japanese tourists, followed by convenience of shopping arcades, variety of food, convenience of transportation, ease of immigration and customs procedures, etc. The 31 travel attributes can be broadly classified into three segments according to their satisfaction scores. Travel attributes of higher perceived satisfaction levels included such aspects as overall convenience, food variety and quality, commodity variety, hotel accommodations and services, and open street markets. Travel attributes of medium satisfaction levels as perceived by Japanese tourists included mainly attractions, culture, product quality, absence of language barrier and safety. Travel attributes with low satisfaction levels were associated with aspects such as prices, human interaction, and cleanliness.

Respondents' Overall Satisfaction and the Likelihood of Their Recommending Hong Kong to Others

Frequencies on respondents' overall satisfaction levels with Hong Kong, and their likelihood of recommending Hong Kong to others are shown in Table 5. More than 70% of respondents were satisfied with Hong Kong as a travel destination, and 78% of respondents indicated that they would recommend Hong Kong to others, respectively.

Travel Dimensions

Principal components analysis with varimax rotation was used to identify the underlying dimensions on the 31 travel items. Twenty-nine out of 31

TABLE 3. Demographic and Traveling Profiles of Japanese Tourists

Sex	N = 518	%	Time to Hong Kong	N = 513	%
Male	354	68.3	First-Time Visitors	281	54.8
Female	164	31.7	Repeat Visitors	232	45.2
Age	**N = 513**	**%**	**Purpose of Visit**	**N = 522**	**%**
18-24 years old	156	30.4	Business/Meetings	31	5.9
25-34 years old	206	40.2	Visit Friends/Relatives	33	6.3
35-44 years old	81	15.8	Vacation	376	72.0
45-54 years old	50	9.7	En Route	61	11.7
55-64 years old	18	3.5	Others	21	4.0
65 years old or above	2	0.4			
Accommodation	**N = 403**	**%**	**Source of Information**	**N = 510**	**%**
Friends and Relatives	7	1.7	Travel Agencies	133	26.1
Hostel	6	1.5	Airlines	32	6.3
3-Star Hotel	87	21.6	Travel Brochures/Magazines	242	47.5
4-Star Hotel	234	58.1	TV/Radio Commercials	11	2.2
5-Star Hotel	69	17.1	Friends/Relatives	52	10.2
			Business Associates	19	3.7
			National Tourist Organizations	14	2.7
			Internet	5	1.0
			Others	2	0.4
Occupation	**N = 516**	**%**	**Annual Income***	**N = 489**	**%**
Management/Administration	32	6.2	≤ US$10,000	110	22.5
Professional	80	15.5	US$10,001-$20,000	27	5.5
Self Employed	16	3.1	US$20,001-$30,000	65	13.3
White Collar Worker	71	13.8	US$30,001–$40,000	82	16.8
Blue Collar Worker	14	2.7	US$40,001-$50,000	55	11.2
Sales	32	6.2	US$50,001-$60,000	40	8.2
Civil Servant	100	19.4	US$60,001-$70,000	37	7.6
Student	93	18.0	US$70,001-$80,000	15	3.1
Retired/Not in Work Force	23	4.5	US$80,001-$90,000	13	2.7
Others	55	10.7	≥ US$90,001	45	9.2
			* HK$7.75 = US$1.0		

TABLE 4. Japanese Tourists' Satisfaction Levels in Relation to the Travel Attributes in Hong Kong

Ranking	Destination Attributes in Hong Kong	Valid N	Mean[1]	Std Dev[2]
1	Hong Kong is highly accessible.	520	3.99	0.89
2	Shopping arcades are conveniently located in Hong Kong.	518	3.86	0.87
3	There is great variety of food in Hong Kong.	520	3.85	0.96
4	Transportation is convenient within the city.	518	3.80	0.94
5	Immigration and customs procedures are simple.	520	3.76	0.93
6	Hotel accommodations are comfortable in Hong Kong.	517	3.73	0.99
7	There is great variety of commodities in department stores.	518	3.68	0.95
8	Hong Kong has interesting open street markets.	519	3.66	0.92
9	Quality of food is satisfactory.	520	3.63	0.99
10	Hotel services are satisfactory.	518	3.62	0.96
11	Hong Kong has attractive natural and scenic spots.	522	3.58	1.05
12	Climate and weather is acceptable in Hong Kong.	522	3.53	0.92
13	Quality of products is satisfactory.	520	3.53	0.90
14	Hong Kong is a mixture of Chinese and Western culture.	519	3.50	0.87
15	There are interesting cultural events in Hong Kong.	519	3.39	0.89
16	Hong Kong is a gateway to China and other Asian countries.	515	3.39	0.94
17	Hong Kong has attractive urban and city sightseeing.	521	3.38	0.85
18	Hong Kong is a cosmopolitan city.	522	3.38	0.89
19	Hong Kong gives a positive image after handover in 1997.	515	3.36	0.80
20	There is no language barrier in Hong Kong.	516	3.33	0.97
21	Hong Kong is a safe place to visit.	521	3.29	0.97
22	Prices of air tickets are reasonable.	522	3.28	0.91
23	Hong Kong has an interesting night life.	519	3.28	0.93
24	Hotel/restaurant/retail labor force are helpful and efficient.	518	3.24	0.99
25	Hotel facilities are satisfactory.	506	3.21	0.89
26	Prices of food are reasonable.	518	3.18	1.03
27	Hong Kong people are friendly and courteous.	521	3.16	1.00
28	Immigration/customs/police labor force are helpful and efficient.	520	3.15	0.97
29	Prices of commodities are reasonable.	521	3.10	1.01
30	Prices of hotels are reasonable.	518	3.08	0.99
31	Hong Kong is a clean and tidy place.	520	2.89	1.03

[1] Mean Scale: 1–very dissatisfied to 5–very satisfied
[2] Std Dev: Standard Deviation

items from the factor analysis resulted in eight factor groupings, explaining 63.8% of the travel variance. It was found that most of the factor loadings were greater than 0.60, indicating a good correlation between the travel items and the factor grouping they belonged to. All the eight dimensions had a Cronbach's alpha of more than 0.60, which is considered a good indicator of internal consistency (Nunnally, 1967). Each dimension was named according

TABLE 5. Japanese Tourists' Overall Satisfaction Towards Hong Kong and the Likelihood of Their Making Recommendations

Overall Satisfaction Levels (N = 511)			Likelihood of Making Recommendations (N = 520)		
	N	%		N	%
Very Satisfied	154	30.1	Very Likely	150	28.8
Satisfied	208	40.7	Likely	207	39.8
Neutral	112	21.9	Neutral	128	24.6
Dissatisfied	28	5.5	Unlikely	26	5.0
Very Dissatisfied	9	1.8	Very Unlikely	9	1.7
Mean[1]: 3.9 (0.95)			Mean[2]: 3.9 (0.94)		

[1] Mean Scale: 1–very dissatisfied, 5–very satisfied
[2] Mean Scale: 1–very unlikely, 5–very likely
Standard deviations are in parentheses

to the common characteristics of variables it included. Table 6 shows the result of the factor analysis in terms of: (1) factor name destination items; (2) factor loadings; (3) communalities; (4) eigenvalues; (5) percentage of variance; and (6) factor mean.

Factor 1, 'People,' explained 26% of the variance with an eigenvalue of 8.13. This factor included four items, which are associated with the human interaction between local people and tourists, as well as the cleanliness of the destination. This factor had the mean value of 3.11, which was the lowest one among the eight factors, implying that Japanese tourists were least satisfied with the attitude of local people and the cleanliness of Hong Kong.

Factor 2 was labeled 'Overall Convenience,' and it explained 8.3% of the variance with an eigenvalue of 2.56. This factor had the highest factor mean of 3.85, and comprised three attributes associated with the overall convenience of Hong Kong in terms of immigration and customs procedures, shopping malls and transportation.

Factor 3, 'Price,' was the next-to-last factor that was perceived as satisfactory by the Japanese tourists, with a factor mean of 3.16. This factor explained 6.6% of the variance and had an eigenvalue of 2.05. This factor contained four attributes associated with price, such as hotel, commodities, food and air ticket.

Factor 4 was labeled 'Accommodation and Food.' With an eigenvalue of 1.94, this factor explained 6.2% of the variance. This factor had a mean value of 3.61, covering aspects such as hotel accommodations, quality of services and facilities, and variety and quality of food.

Factor 5, 'Commodities,' was associated with four attributes; variety of commodities, quality of commodities, open street markets and shopping ar-

TABLE 6. Factor Analysis Results with Varimax Rotation of Japanese Tourists' Satisfaction Levels with Travel Attributes

Travel Dimension[1]	Factor Loading	Communalities	EV[2]	Pct of Variance[3]	Factor Mean[4]
Factor 1–People (α = 0.83)[5]			8.13	26.2%	3.11 (0.81)
Helpful and efficient labor force in public sector	0.7946	0.7270			
Helpful and efficient labor force in private sector	0.7582	0.6977			
Friendly and courteous local people	0.7316	0.6405			
Clean and tidy place	0.7102	0.6198			
Factor 2–Overall Convenience (α = 0.79)			2.56	8.3%	3.85 (0.77)
Convenient immigration and customs procedures	0.8258	0.7446			
Convenient shopping arcades	0.7783	0.6984			
Convenient transportation within the city	0.6856	0.5948			
Factor 3–Price (α = 0.83)			2.05	6.6%	3.16 (0.80)
Reasonable prices in hotels	0.7994	0.7059			
Reasonable prices of commodities	0.7831	0.7177			
Reasonable prices of food	0.7236	0.6498			
Reasonable prices of air tickets	0.7097	0.6220			
Factor 4–Accommodation and Food (α = 0.81)			1.94	6.2%	3.61 (0.72)
Comfortable hotel accommodations	0.8199	0.7549			
Satisfactory hotel services	0.7773	0.7555			
Satisfactory hotel facilities	0.7283	0.6063			
Great variety of food	0.5275	0.7101			
Satisfactory quality of food	0.5269	0.6640			
Factor 5–Commodities (α = 0.82)			1.62	5.2%	3.68 (0.73)
Great variety of commodities	0.8048	0.7441			
Satisfactory quality of commodities	0.7929	0.7481			
Interesting open street markets	0.6794	0.5893			
Convenient shopping arcades	0.5817	0.5758			
Factor 6–Attractions (α = 0.70)			1.31	4.2%	3.40 (0.68)
Attractive urban and city sightseeing	0.7571	0.6547			
Interesting night life	0.6990	0.5516			
Cosmopolitan city	0.5924	0.6067			
Attractive natural & scenic spots	0.5661	0.4799			
Factor 7–Culture (α = 0.75)			1.10	3.5%	3.45 (0.79)
Mixture of Chinese and western culture	0.7500	0.7119			
Interesting cultural events	0.6866	0.6138			
Factor 8–Climate and Image (α = 0.63)			1.06	3.4%	3.39 (0.68)
Acceptable climate and weather	0.7329	0.6186			
Positive image after 1997 handover	0.5904	0.5586			
Safe place to visit	0.5233	0.6032			

[1] 29 Destination Attributes Captured in Eight Factors
[2] EV : Eigenvalue
[3] 63.8% of Cumulative Variance Explained
[4] Mean Scale : 5–very satisfied, 1–very dissatisfied
Standard Deviations are in parentheses
[5] Cronbach's Alpha

cades. This factor explained 5.2% of the variance and had an eigenvalue of 1.62. This factor had a mean value of 3.68 and was ranked second as a factor that was perceived as satisfactory by Japanese tourists, after 'Overall Convenience.'

Factor 6 included four destination items: sightseeing, night life, cosmopolitan city and scenic spots. Labeled 'Attractions,' this factor explained 4.2% of the variance with an eigenvalue of 1.31 and a factor mean of 3.40.

With an eigenvalue of 1.1 and 3.5% of the variance explained, factor 7 captured two destination attributes: mixture of Chinese and western culture, and cultural events of Hong Kong. This factor was named 'Culture' and had a factor mean of 3.45.

The last factor was named 'Climate and Image', and included three items: climate, safety and positive image after the 1997 handover. With a factor mean of 3.39, 'Climate and Image' explained 3.4% of the variance and had an eigenvalue of 1.06.

Determinants of Japanese Travelers' Overall Satisfaction with Hong Kong

Multiple regression analysis was employed to examine the impact and relative importance of eight travel dimensions (independent variables) derived from the factor analysis in contributing to Japanese tourists' overall satisfaction with Hong Kong (dependent variable). As shown in Table 7, in predicting of the 'Goodness-of-Fit' of the regression model, the multiple correlation coefficient (R), coefficient of determination (R^2) and F-ratio were examined. Firstly, the R of the eight travel dimensions on respondents' overall satisfaction was 0.514, meaning that there was a moderate correlation between independent and dependent variables. Secondly, the R^2 was 0.264, suggesting that approximately 27% of the variation of the Japanese tourists' overall satisfaction was explained by the eight travel dimensions. Lastly, an F-ratio of 42.427 (significant at 0.000) meant that the results of the regression model could hardly have occurred by chance. Except for the relatively low percentage of R^2, the data fit the model well in predicting the variance of Japanese tourists' overall satisfaction levels in relation to the eight travel dimensions.

In order to explain the relative importance of the eight travel dimensions in contributing to the variance in the Japanese tourists' overall satisfaction with Hong Kong, standardized coefficients, or betas, were examined. Results revealed that four travel factors remained significant in the equation with a different value of the beta coefficients, thus contributing different weights to the variance in tourists' overall satisfaction. In order of importance, the main factors affecting Japanese tourists' overall satisfaction were: Factor 4 (Accommodation and Food, beta = 0.265); followed by Factor 1 (People, beta = 0.191); Factor 3 (Price, beta = 0.161) and Factor 7 (Culture, beta = 0.108).

Therefore, it could be interpreted that a one-unit increase in satisfaction with the 'Accommodation and Food' factor would lead to a 0.265 unit (or 26.5%) increase in the tourists' overall satisfaction with Hong Kong, other variables being held constant. To assess multicollinearity among independent variables, three measures were adopted: the tolerance value, the variance inflation factor (VIF), and condition index. Results showed that there were no significant indications of multicollinearity. The tolerance value was bigger than 0.10, the VIF was less than 10, and the condition indices were less than 30 (Belsley et al., 1980). The four other travel dimensions were excluded in the regression model and did not explain the variance in Japanese tourists' overall satisfaction levels with Hong Kong.

Determinants of Japanese Travelers' Likelihood of Recommending Hong Kong to Other People

Table 8 shows the results of the regression analysis of the eight travel dimensions (independent variables) in relation to the Japanese' tourists' likelihood of recommending Hong Kong to other people (dependent variable). In prediction, the R of the eight travel dimensions on respondents' overall satisfaction was 0.500; the R^2 was 0.264; and the F-ratio was 39.353 (significant at 0.000). Similarly, with the exception of the relatively low percentage of R^2, the regression model could be said to have achieved a satisfactory level of 'Goodness-of-Fit' in predicting the variance of Japanese tourists' likelihood of recommending Hong Kong to other people in relation to the eight travel dimensions.

In order to explain the relative importance of the eight travel dimensions in contributing to the variance in the tourists' likelihood of recommending Hong Kong to other people, standardized coefficients, or betas, were examined. Results revealed that four travel dimensions remained significant in the equation with a different value of the beta coefficients, thus contributing different weights to the variance in tourists' overall satisfaction. The four travel dimensions were Factor 4 (Accommodation and Food, beta = 0.209); Factor 3 (Price, beta = 0.198); Factor 7 (Culture, beta = 0.176); and Factor 6 (Attractions, beta = 0.142).

CONCLUSION AND MARKETING IMPLICATIONS

The primary purpose of this study was to examine Japanese tourists' satisfaction with Hong Kong as a travel destination. It has measured the satisfaction levels of 31 travel attributes; factor-analyzed them into eight travel dimensions; examined the relative impact of each of these travel di-

TABLE 7. Regression Analysis Results of Japanese Tourists' Overall Satisfaction Levels with Hong Kong in Relation to the Eight Travel Dimensions

Dependent Variable:	Japanese tourists' overall satisfaction levels with Hong Kong as a travel destination		
Independent Variables:	Eight orthogonal factors : People (F1), Overall Convenience (F2), Price (F3), Accommodation and Food (F4), Commodities (F5), Attractions (F6), Culture (F7), Climate and Image (F8)		

Prediction: Goodness–of–Fit

Multiple R	.514		
R Square	.264		
Adjusted R Square	.258		
Standard Error	.799		
Analysis of Variance			
	Degree of Freedom	Sum of Squares	Mean Square
Regression	4	108.290	27.073
Residual	472	301.182	.638
F = 42.427	Sig. F = .000		
Durbin-Watson	1.749		

Explanation: Variables in the Equation

Independent Variable	Unstandardized Coefficients (B)	Standardized Coefficients (Beta)	T-value	Sig.
Accommodation and Food–Factor 4	.341	.265	6.085	.000
People–Factor 1	.219	.191	4.166	.000
Price–Factor3	.189	.161	3.618	.000
Culture–Factor7	.130	.108	2.523	.012
Constant	.973		4.102	.000

Collinearity Diagnostics:	Tolerance	Variable Inflation Factor (VIF)	Condition Index
Accommodation and Food–Factor 4	.820	1.219	10.317
People–Factor 1	.744	1.343	11.758
Price–Factor 3	.784	1.276	13.107
Culture–Factor 7	.854	1.171	16.642
Constant			1.000

mensions in influencing Japanese tourists' overall satisfaction levels; and examined the relative impact of each of these travel dimensions in contributing to Japanese tourists' likelihood of recommending Hong Kong to other people. 'Accessibility of Hong Kong' appears to be the travel attribute that Japanese tourists are most satisfied with. The results support Holloway's study (1986) that accessibility of a destination is important in attracting tourists. In this study, those top attributes can be categorized into several aspects, namely, accessibility and convenience of Hong Kong (in terms of shopping arcades and open street markets, transportation, and immigration and customs procedures); variety and quality of food; variety of commodities; and hotel accommodations and services.

TABLE 8. Regression Analysis Results of Japanese Tourists' Likelihood of Recommending Hong Kong to Other People, in Relation to the Eight Travel Dimensions

Dependent Variable:	Japanese tourists' likelihood of recommending Hong Kong to other people		
Independent Variables:	Eight orthogonal factors: People (F1), Overall Convenience (F2), Price (F3), Accommodation and Food (F4), Commodities (FS), Attractions (F6), Culture (F7), Climate and Image (F8)		

Prediction : Goodness-of-Fit

Multiple R	.500		
R Square	.250		
Adjusted R Square	.241		
Standard Error	.795		
Analysis of Variance			

	Degree of Freedom	Sum of Squares	Mean Square
Regression	4	99.552	24.888
Residual	478	302.299	.632
F = 39.353	Sig. F = .000		
Durbin-Watson	1.774		

Explanation: Variables in the Equation

Independent Variable	Unstandardized Coefficients (B)	Standardized Coefficients (Beta)	T-value	Sig.
Accommodation and Food–Factor 4	.267	.209	4.903	.000
Price–Factor 3	.229	.198	4.668	.000
Culture–Factor 7	.207	.176	3.841	.000
Attractions–Factor 6	.193	.142	3.136	.002
Constant	.852		3.395	.000

Collinearity Diagnostics:	Tolerance	Variable Inflation Factor (VIF)	Condition Index	
Accommodation and Food–Factor 4	.864	1.157	12.563	
Price–Factor 3	.875	1.143	10.765	
Culture–Factor 7	.751	1.332	17.698	
Attractions–Factor 6	.770	1.299	14.164	
Constant			1.000	

Using factor analysis, eight travel dimensions, incorporating 29 attributes, were identified: 'People'; 'Overall Convenience'; 'Price'; 'Accommodation and Food'; 'Commodities'; 'Attractions'; 'Culture' and 'Climate and Image.' These travel dimensions have been reported as prime factors in destination choice selection in various studies (Goodrich, 1977; Mok, 1995a 1995b; Shih, 1986; Yau and Chan, 1990). An examination of the factor means of each of the dimensions revealed that 'Overall Convenience' scored the highest satisfaction level among Japanese tourists; followed by the dimensions of 'Commodities'; 'Accommodation and Food'; 'Culture'; 'Attractions'; 'Climate and Image'; 'Price'; and 'People.' Factor analysis results support the notion that Hong Kong has long been renowned as a destination in terms of its accessibility, offering a 'Food Paradise' and a 'Shopping Paradise.' Tourism marketers should address these issues in their advertising and promotional campaigns to attract Japanese travelers. Furthermore, government and tourism marketers should ensure consistency between entry-exit facilities such as the new Chek Lap Kok airport (advanced facilities, capacity, and extensive operating hours), sea terminals, and road and rail links. Simplifying immigration and customs procedures, as well as visa applications, would probably be appreciated by international travelers when they make decisions about their destination.

With regard to the regression results, it was found that three travel dimensions were common in influencing Japanese tourists' overall satisfaction level and the likelihood of their recommending Hong Kong to other people. The three travel dimensions were: 'Accommodation and Food'; 'Price' and 'Culture.' Despite the high price of accommodation, it is interesting to note that 'Accommodation and Food' was the most influential factor in contributing to Japanese tourists' overall satisfaction with Hong Kong, as well as to the likelihood of recommending Hong Kong to other people. This factor, in fact, was ranked third, after the 'Overall Convenience' and 'Commodities' factors. The latter two factors, however, were found to be statistically insignificant in affecting Japanese tourists' levels of satisfaction. According to statistics from the Hong Kong Tourist Association, hotel bills and meals outside hotels accounted for nearly 30% and 10% of tourists' spending, respectively (Hong Kong Tourist Association, 1996). Results of this study indicate that 390 (75%) tourists stayed at hotels for this trip. This signals to hoteliers that they should maintain the quality of the services in their hotels in order to satisfy their customers. Accommodation is an indispensable constituent of the journey, and travelers, regardless of whether they are business or vacation-travellers, need comfortable accommodations for refreshment and recovery. Hong Kong's image as a 'Food Paradise' can be promoted through various types of international food fairs held in Hong Kong, in order to attract international travelers.

The 'Price' factor included the overall price of the trip (prices in hotels, commodities, food and air tickets). Tourism marketers should be alert to the increasing cost of trips to Hong Kong, especially in light of the recent Asian economic crisis and the devaluation of the currencies of many Southeast Asia countries, which threatens Hong Kong's competitiveness as a travel destination. To re-establish Hong Kong as Asia's number one destination, Cathay Pacific launched the 'Two-for-One' air fare package for international tourists who visited Hong Kong between January 1 and February 15, 1998. This campaign also involved 59 hotels, and hundreds of restaurants, shops and tourist attractions such as Ocean Park, which offered discounts and free gifts

(South China Morning Post, 1997). Further special tourism-related packages like this should be promoted with cooperation between the government, the private sector and the Hong Kong Tourist Association, in order to increase Hong Kong's competitive power.

The 'Culture' factor included two destination attributes: 'Mixture of East and West' and 'Interesting culture events.' This signals that tourism marketers should be concerned with maintaining the cultural heritage of Hong Kong. Hong Kong, as a former colony of Great Britain, is likely to attract international tourists who seek to explore the post-handover cultural dynamic. The government, in association with tourism marketers, should take all reasonable steps to protect and enhance existing cultural attractions and events. For example, the Hong Kong Tourist Association could prepare new promotional materials and self-guided walking tours dealing with the Chinese city and its Chinese heritage and the colonial city and its colonial heritage (Hong Kong Tourist Association, 1995). The government should also encourage property owners to retain, refurbish and find new tourism uses for suitable remaining colonial and traditional Chinese buildings (Hong Kong Tourist Association, 1995).

The 'People' factor was the second most important factor in determining the satisfaction levels of Japanese tourists, yet this factor scored lowest in terms of Japanese tourists' satisfaction level. Thus, a tourist who is satisfied with his or her human-interacting activity is more likely to be satisfied than a tourist who perceived local people being unfriendly. Proper training aimed at improving the courtesy, helpfulness and efficiency of the workforce should be undertaken in both the public and private sectors. The labor workforce in these two sectors should be aware of the importance of service quality, and should provide prompt and efficient responses to tourists' requests. The Hong Kong Tourist Association's 'Smile Campaign' has for many years attempted to educate the private workforce to smile at tourists, addressing the importance of courtesy and honesty. It is suggested the promotional message should not only include the private workforce, such as retail service providers, hotel receptions and taxi drivers, but should also include the public sector workforce, such as immigration and customs staff. In fact, proper training is essential to delivering a quality tourism product. In view of the seriousness of the pollution problem worldwide, the increased importance of environmental conservation in recent years has led many countries to educate their citizens to be more responsible in preserving the quality of the environment. Take Singapore as an example. Its reputation for cleanliness and tidiness has attracted significant numbers of tourists for many years. The success of Singapore has depended not only on legislation that imposes serious penalties on law-breakers, but also on civil education programs that educate citizens, especially youngsters, about the importance of environmental conservation.

Hong Kong should be no exception. It is time for the Hong Kong government and its citizens to learn to preserve their living place.

The 'Attractions' factor was found to a significant exert impact on Japanese tourists' likelihood of recommending Hong Kong to other people. A destination's attractions are prime in affecting the likelihood of its being selected (Holloway, 1986; Mok, 1995a 1995b; Yau and Chan, 1990). The 'Attractions' factor consisted of four variables: 'Attractive urban and city sightseeing'; 'Interesting night life'; 'Cosmopolitan city'; and 'Attractive natural and scenic spots.' Tourism marketers should take note of this, and should promote Hong Kong as an urban, cosmopolitan city with numerous tourist attractions and a busy night life scene. As reported by the Hong Kong Tourist Association (1995), Hong Kong still has many underutilized urban, urban fringe, countryside, coastal and island assets. Many existing attractions draw a limited number of tourists, because they may not be aware of or find it difficult to get to these attractions. It is therefore suggested that government and tourism planners should encourage increasing usage of a wide range of attractions by enhancing signage and transportation system. And both the public and private sectors should co-operate to maintain the existing urban tourism attractions such as traditional forms of shopping and the colonial and Chinese heritage. They should also search for new tourism products to strengthen the competitive advantage of Hong Kong in the face of increasingly fierce international competition. For instance, thanks to the development the new airport at Chek Lap Kok and its supporting infrastructure, the western part of Lantau Island and other outlying islands could be promoted as 'The Leisure Islands' for travelers.

In short, customer satisfaction is a key factor for any repeat business. As Japan is one of the major markets for Hong Kong tourism, it is essential to continue marketing Hong Kong to the Japanese travelers. Effective travel management relies to a large degree on understanding of travelers' satisfaction and destination choice behavior.

LIMITATIONS AND DIRECTIONS FOR FUTURE STUDIES

Limitations

Due to the practical difficulties of employing random sampling techniques in data collection, the convenient sampling technique was used in the study. The results of Japanese tourists' demographic and traveling profile were compared with the Hong Kong Tourist Association 1997 annual survey report. It was found that the distribution of Japanese tourists' traveling and demographic data in the study were very similar or close to those reported by the Hong Kong Tourist Association. It indicated that the samples selected in the study were reasonably representative of the target population.

Future Research

There are at least two possible areas for future research: (1) A study on the satisfaction level of each segment group based on demographic or traveling variables such as age, occupation and purposes of visit are recommended; and (2) A longitudinal research is also recommended to explore any significant difference on the relative importance of the eight travel dimensions (factors) on overall satisfaction level or likelihood of recommending Hong Kong to others between two time points: 1998 and 2000.

REFERENCES

Ahmed, S. A. (1988). Understanding residents' reaction to tourism marketing strategies. *Journal of Travel Research*, 13-18.

Ahmed, S. A., Barber, M. and Astous, A. (1998). Segmentation of the Nordic winter sun seekers market. *Journal of Travel & Tourism Marketing*, *7* (1), 39-63.

Ahmed, Z. U. and Krohn, F.B. (1990). Reversing the United States' declining competitiveness in marketing international tourism: A perspective on future policy. *Journal of Travel Research*, *24*, 23-29.

Anton, J. (1996). *Customer Relationship Management: Making Hard Decisions with Soft Numbers*, Upper Saddle River, New Jersey: Prentice Hall, Inc., 73.

Belsley, D. A., Kuh, E. and Welsch, R. R. (1980). *Regression Diagnostics: Identifying Influential Data and Sources of Collinearity*. New York: Wiley.

Berkman, H. W. and Gilson, C. (1986). *Consumer Behavior: Concepts and Strategies* (3rd ed.). PSW-Kent: Boston.

Berry, L. L. and Parasuraman, A. (1991). *Marketing Services: Competing through Quality*. New York, NY: The Free Press.

Brevetti, F. (1995). Tourism hit by high prices. *Asian Business*, November, 42.

Chon, K. S., Christianson, D. J. and Lee, C. L. (1995). Modeling tourist satisfaction: Japanese tourists' evaluation of hotel stay experience in Taiwan. *Australian Journal of Hospitality Management*, *2* (1), 1-6.

Churchill, G., Jr. (1979). A paradigm for developing better measures of marketing constructs. *Journal of Marketing Research*, *16*, 64-73.

Churchill, G. A., Jr. and Suprenant, C. (1982). An investigation into the determinants of customer satisfaction. *Journal of Marketing Research*, *19*, 491-504.

Cronin, J. J., Jr. and Taylor, S. A. (1992). Measuring service quality: A reexamination and extension. *Journal of Marketing*, *56*, 55-68.

Czepiel, J. A. and Rosenberg, L. J. (1977). The study of consumer satisfaction: Addressing the 'so what' question. In K. H. Hunt (Ed.), *Conceptualization and Measurement of Consumer Satisfaction and Dissatisfaction*, Cambridge, MA: Marketing Science Institute, 92-119.

Engel, J. F., Blackwell, R. D. and Miniard, P. W. (1990). *Consumer behavior* (6th ed.), Hinsdale, IL: Dryden Press.

Fornell, C. (1992). A national customer satisfaction barometer: The Swedish experience. *Journal of Marketing*, 56, 6-21.

Goodall, B. and Ashworth, G. (1988). *Marketing in the Tourism Industry.* United Kingdom: Croom Helm.

Goodrich, J. N. (1977). Benefit bundle analysis: An empirical study of international travelers. *Journal of Travel Research*, 26 (2), 6-9.

Haahti, A. J. (1986). Finland's competitiveness position as a destination. *Annals of Tourism Research*, 13 (1), 11-35.

Hair, Jr. J. F., Anderson, R. E., Tatham, R. L. and Black, W. C. (1995). *Multivariate Data Analysis with Readings.* New York: Prentice Hall Inc.

Halstead, D. and Page, T. J., Jr. (1992). The effects of satisfaction and complaining behavior on consumers' repurchase behavior. *Journal of Satisfaction, Dissatisfaction and Complaining Behavior*, 5, 1-11.

Hong Kong Tourist Association. (1995). *Visitor and Tourism Study for Hong Kong: Strategy Report.* Hong Kong Tourist Association.

Hong Kong Tourist Association. (1997). *A Statistical Review of Tourism 1996.* Hong Kong Tourist Association.

Holloway, J. C. (1986). *The Business of Tourism.* London: Longman Publishing Ltd.

JTB. (1994). *JTB Report '94-All about Japanese Overseas Travelers.* Japan Travel Bureau.

Lancaster, K. J. (1966). A new approach to consumer theory. *Journal of Political Economy*, 74, 132-157.

Mayo, E. J. and Jarvis, L. P. (1981). *The Psychology of Leisure Travel: Effective Marketing and Selling of Travel Services.* Boston, MA: CBI Publishing Co.

McIntosh, R. W. and Goeldner, C. R. (1990). *Tourism: Principles, Practices, Philosophies.* New York: John Wiley & Sons, Inc.

Mill, R. C. and Morrison, A. M. (1985). *The Tourism System: An Introductory Text.* Englewood Cliffs, NJ: Prentice Hall, Inc.

Mok, C. and Armstrong, R. W. (1995a). Leisure travel destination choice criteria of Hong Kong residents. *Journal of Travel & Tourism Marketing*, 4 (1), 99-104.

Mok, C., Armstrong, R.W., and Go, F.M. (1995b). Taiwanese Travelers' Perception of Leisure Destination Attributes. *Australian Journal of Hospitality Management*, 2 (1), 17-22.

Mok, C. and Armstrong, R.W. (1996, Autumn). Sources of information used by Hong Kong and Taiwanese leisure travelers. *Australian Journal of Hospitality Management*, 3 (1), 31-35.

Nunnally, J. C. (1967). *Psychometric Theory.* New York: McGraw-Hall Inc.

Pizam, A., Neumann, Y., and Reichel, A. (1978). Dimension of tourism satisfaction with a destination area. *Annals of Tourism Research*, 5, 314-322.

South China Morning Post. (1997). *South China Morning Post*, August 25.

South China Morning Post. (1997). *South China Morning Post*, November 15.

Scott, R. D., Schewe, C. D., and Frederick, D. G. (1978). A multi-brand and multi-attribute model of tourist state choice. *Journal of Travel Research, Summer*, 17 (1), 23-29.

Shih, D. (1986). VALS as a tool of tourism market research: The Pennsylvania experience. *Journal of Travel Research*, *24* (4), 2-11.

Siu, A., Yu, D., and Lit, V. (1987). A marketing strategy for Hong Kong Tourist Association to promote Hong Kong as a tourist attraction in 1987. *Proceedings of The Conference on The Changing Environment of Management in Hong Kong*, Baptist College, Hong Kong, 133-139.

Stevens, B. F. (1992). Price Value Perceptions of Travelers. *Journal of Travel Research*, *31*, 44-48.

Um, S. (1987). *The role of perceived inhibitors and perceived facilities in the pleasure travel destination choice process*. Unpublished Ph.D thesis, Texas A & M University.

Van Raaij, W. F. (1986). Consumer research on tourism: Mental and behavioral constructs. *Annals of Tourism Research*, *13*, 1-9.

Wade, K. R. (1995). Segmentation: when, what, why, how and so what? *Proceedings of the 20th Annual TTRA Conference*, Acapulco, Mexico, 10-14.

Westbrook, R. A. and Oliver, R. L. (1981). The dimensionality of consumption emotion patterns and consumer satisfaction. *Journal of Consumer Research*, *18*, 84-91.

Woodside, A. G. and Sherrell, D. (1977). Traveler evoked, inept, and inert sets of vacation destinations. *Journal of Travel Research*, *16* (1), 14-18.

Woodside, A. G. and Lysonski, S. (1989). A general model of traveler destination choice. *Journal of Travel Research*, *27* (4), 8-14.

Yau, O. H. M., and Chan, C. F. (1990). Hong Kong as a travel destination in South-East Asia: A multidimensional approach. *Tourism Management*, *11* (2), 123-132.

Social and Cultural Factors Influencing Tourists' Souvenir-Purchasing Behavior: A Comparative Study on Japanese "Omiyage" and Korean "Sunmul"

Mi kyung Park

SUMMARY. One of the major parts of tourist shopping is the purchasing of souvenirs as presents for people. There are many motives for souvenir purchasing that seem to be influenced by the culture and customs of a society. This study attempts to bring light to the various social and cultural factors influencing the purchasing of souvenirs by tourists in Japan and Korea, to make predictions about tourists' souvenir-purchasing behavior in the future, and present keys to the sales promotion of souvenir goods. The results of the analysis show, as a common point, both Japanese and Korean tourists use souvenirs as a means of supporting a relationship with others, although some differences may exist in "what," and "how" souvenirs should be given. *[Article copies available for a fee from The Haworth Document Delivery Service: 1-800-342-9678. E-mail address: <getinfo@haworthpressinc.com> Website: <http://www.haworthpressinc. com>]*

KEYWORDS. Souvenir-gift, Omiyage, Sunmul, social/cultural factors

Mi kyung Park is Research Associate, College of Tourism, Rikkyo University.

Address correspondence to: Mi kyung Park, College of Tourism, The Rikkyo University 1-2-26, Kitano, Niza-shi Saitama-ken, Japan 352-8558. (E-mail: mikyunglj@ yahoo.com).

[Haworth co-indexing entry note]: "Social and Cultural Factors Influencing Tourists' Souvenir-Purchasing Behavior: A Comparative Study on Japanese "Omiyage" and Korean "Sunmul." Park, Mi kyung. Co-published simultaneously in *Journal of Travel & Tourism Marketing* (The Haworth Hospitality Press, an imprint of The Haworth Press, Inc.) Vol. 9, No. 1/2, 2000, pp. 81-91; and: *Japanese Tourists: Socio-Economic, Marketing and Psychological Analysis* (ed: K. S. (Kaye) Chon, Tsutomu Inagaki, and Taiji Ohashi) The Haworth Hospitality Press, an imprint of The Haworth Press, Inc., 2000, pp. 81-91. Single or multiple copies of this article are available for a fee from The Haworth Document Delivery Service [1-800-342-9678, 9:00 a.m. - 5:00 p.m. (EST). E-mail address: getinfo@haworthpressinc.com].

INTRODUCTION

One of the major parts of tourist shopping is the purchase of souvenirs as presents for people. Although these presents are not always asked for, most people buy some kind of souvenir. According to Gordon (1986) tourists often feel they cannot go home without 'something' for so and so precisely because the souvenir gift is an 'entry-or-re-entry fee,' required by the culture at large.

One reason why tourists buy souvenirs, is to express love and thanks to their family and friends, while they feel a moral obligation toward colleagues and bosses who know about their vacation. In both Japan and Korea, the custom of giving money to people going on vacation exists, in order to cover a part of their travel expenses. In the case of receiving money before departure, one feels a psychological obligation to reciprocate by buying souvenir gifts. Consequently, it is thought that this custom and ritual will give rise to purchasing souvenirs as presents for those who gave cash as a present.

The aim of this paper is to bring light to various social and cultural factors influencing the purchasing of souvenirs by tourists in Japan and Korea, to make predictions about tourists' souvenir purchasing behavior in the future, and present clues to the sales promotion of souvenir goods.

THE SOCIAL AND CULTURAL BACKGROUND OF JAPANESE AND KOREAN TOURISTS' SOUVENIR PURCHASES

Gifts in Japanese and Korean Everyday Life

Gift giving in the summer (in Japanese, Chugen, and in Korean, according to the old calendar August 15th, Chusuk sunmul), and the year-end gift giving (in Japanese Seibo, in Korean Semo) are seen to be annual events of gift giving that are held in both Japan and Korea. On such occasions, presents are given to bosses, relatives, seniors or people to whom one owes debts of gratitude.

To examine the various similarities and differences between Japanese and Korean annual gift giving, first, the majority of gifts given in the summer, or at the end of the year consist of food or practical items. According to the results of the Sanwa Bank Home Consultant survey (1998), Japanese summer gifts mainly consist of beer and juice drinks, while year-end gifts include ham and sausage. As for the gifts people most wanted, merchandise vouchers or gift vouchers topped the list for both the summer and winter gift giving seasons.

Similar to Japan, in the big cities in Korea, department stores sell gift sets, for both summer and winter gift giving, mainly consisting of seasonings or other food products. In the countryside, people often visit their boss and relatives in person, taking gifts such as liquor or fruit. Similar to the Japanese, Koreans ranked gift vouchers for clothes and shoes as their number one choice (Chosunilbo, 1997).

On the other hand, when considering the value and type of present to give, Japanese consumers not only pay attention to the recipient, but also to the accepted standard of the gift-giving market. According to Inoue (1977), as a conformist group, Japanese consumers determine their behavior based on their consciousness of public opinion. In this way, seasonal gift giving is a strongly regulated behavioral area. Opposed to this, Koreans care more about their personal relationship with those to whom they are giving the gift, rather than public opinion, their dignity or "face" as regards to the recipient. Thus, the Japanese observe the rules of returning gifts much more than Koreans.

Generally, in Japan, to reciprocate in gift giving is common practice. How one reciprocates by buying a gift is a virtue of their up-bringing. Kurita (1984) says that Japanese summer and year-end gift giving is to make up for any unknown trouble one may have caused or any unacknowledged assistance one may have received from another. One may also infer that the common everyday Japanese greeting of "Thank you/sorry for the other day" also comes from this ritual.

The History and Etymology of Japanese "Omiyage" and Korean "Sunmul"

Souvenir gifts that are given to the family and friends upon returning from a vacation are called "omiyage" in Japanese and "sunmul" in Korean. The difference between Japanese "omiyage" and Korean "sunmul" is that "omiyage" is only used for presents given when returning from travel, which is different from the ordinary presents or "okurimono." On the other hand "sunmul" includes not only the meaning of "omiyage," but also encompasses the general meaning of presents given at any time, such as Christmas presents, birthday presents, New Year's gifts, and gifts given when visiting.

For the purpose of understanding modern Japanese and Korean purchasing habits regarding souvenirs, the history and etymology of "omiyage" and "sunmul" should be compared.

Japanese "omiyage" and Korean "sunmul" have a number of similarities. Firstly, both words originally have the meaning of "an offering prepared on an altar." The most widely used theory for the origin of the word "omiyage," is the "Miyake" theory. The original meaning of "miyake" is a vessel containing a food offering to God. It is said that a food offering to God would consist of that region's freshest products. These offerings would then be taken away in due time, and would later be eaten together with others. The offerings prepared on an altar would be then taken home as gifts to those who were not present. In other words, offerings to God, eaten together by those present, and then taken to people who were not present, which become "omiyage" souvenirs (Kurita, 1984).

In Korea, the meaning of "sunmul" itself is a food offering prepared on an altar. When holding religious ceremonies for the ancestors of one's family and relatives, everyone eats and drinks prepared offerings together, (in Korean called "umbok"), since it is customary for everyone present to participate in the feast. In the case that a community has a religious ceremony, cows and pigs are offered up on the altar as animal sacrifice, and the food is shared among everyone present. Those present, never fail to take home a part of these blessings for their family. In this way, bit by bit, the food is shared out, and everyone is able to partake in the blessing (Lee, 1977).

As previously mentioned, both Japanese and Koreans have the custom of giving money to their relatives, neighbors and friends before they set off on a journey. In the Japanese language, this custom of "senbetsu" has a direct relationship with "omiyage" (souvenirs).

If you look at the history of "senbetsu" and "omiyage," from the middle of the Edo era, the custom of visiting shrines and temples became widespread for the ordinary masses in Japan. In many cases, as a representative of a group, this visit took the form of a group tour, and in this system, it was not unusual for each participant to be a representative of his or her community.

For representatives visiting these shrines and temples, "Warajizeni" (straw sandal money) was needed. Money was given to the travelers to cover traveling expenses. From another point of view, this money made the journey possible and the custom of giving money for straw sandals has been passed on from generation to generation, to become the modern form of "senbetsu." As such, the return gift of a souvenir becomes indispensable for the traveler. Thus, it becomes a publicly known homecoming report.

CONTENT ANALYSIS OF OPINIONS ON JAPANESE "OMIYAGE" AND KOREAN "SUNMUL" SOUVENIRS

Procedure

The objectives of the analysis are to examine and compare the motives between Japanese "omiyage" and Korean "sunmul," along with clarifying the various underlying social and cultural factors influencing tourists' souvenir purchasing in each country.

The Japanese content analysis was made through the "postcard report concerning souvenirs" recorded in "Gendai Fuzoku Tsushin" (The Modern Public Morals Report) '77-'86 in Tsurumi (1987), and the Korean content analysis was undertaken by a questionnaire survey on opinions and impressions concerning "Sunmul."

The postcard report contributions came from members of the Gendai Fuzoku Kenkyukai (Modern Public Morals Study Group). The 100 contributors ranged in age from those born between 1900 to 1969, a range of 70 years that comprised of 53 men and 47 women. The analysis is based on 88 postcards sent between 1982 and 1986. The opinions were summarized and based on the written statements. They were examined from the standpoint of the role, and image of souvenirs, specifically focusing on the human relationship aspect. Opinions and impressions concerning "Sunmul," were collected by a survey conducted in Korea between March and May of 1997, and the analysis is comprised of the impressions of 44 replies.

The Content Analysis of Self-Description on "Omiyage" and "Sunmul" Souvenirs

Based on the opinions of Japanese "omiyage" and Korean "Sunmul," the role of souvenirs and the purchasing motives are analyzed. Japanese opinions are categorized as:

1. *A means of assisting social intercourse and lubricating oil for social relationships.*

   I once received a bottle of wine from a renowned writer who had returned from Australia. As we hadn't had a very close friendship, I was rather embarrassed. I remember re-evaluating the meaning of a "souvenir". . . . Westerners have showy gestures. Gestures are a means of assisting words. Japanese people have showy souvenirs. Exchanging gifts is a means of assisting social intercourse. Those with a complete understanding of the rules of gift giving, and strictly follow these rules will be very skillful at social intercourse in Japan.

   Souvenirs! In the end, anything will do. "Here you are, a souvenir," hand it over with a grin, and your friend will be delighted to receive it whatever it may be. Putting aside people fixated with souvenirs, the most important issue for us is that souvenirs are lubricating oil for social relationships.

2. *As a means of communication.*

   I like buying souvenirs, but this has less to do with the fact that I am interested in the item itself, but probably more to do with the fact that I am interested in the communication that arises from the gift-giving. . . .

When I go on an overseas vacation, one of the activities I enjoy is buying souvenirs for female friends. However, I am not sure whether or not the women pick up on the message I have entrusted with the souvenir.

3. *While on vacation, souvenirs allow us to feel a bond of the heart and share the feelings and circumstances with those who were not able to go on vacation together with us.*

There are many types of souvenirs, but by large, food items are the most common. An old proverb states that there are little things that are as delicious as meibutsu (a local specialty), but when you get a souvenir from an acquaintance, you are always very happy. Essentially, traveling on vacation should be enjoyed individually and be totally self centered. But if they think about me during their vacation, it makes me very happy. In other words, quality, taste, or lack of taste has nothing to do with souvenirs. It is the mutual consideration that makes us happy. . . .

4. *A mirror that reflects the gift giver's social understanding and etiquette.*

. . . It seems to be something that is hard for foreigners to understand, but Japanese people can tell about one's cultural up-bringing, by looking at the souvenirs received. The souvenir becomes a mirror that reflects their degree of social understanding and etiquette. As a bond of the relationship between people, we feel a lot of anxiety over what present to give.

5. *Evidence that one has been to a region or a country, at the same time it is proof that ones knows something that is unknown to others. It derives from one's desire to be paid due recognition and difference from other people.*

Buying souvenirs while traveling is both fun and troublesome. The reasons I buy souvenirs are (1) I think I want to share enjoyment and meibutu (local specialties) with other people, (2) I don't want to betray other people's expectations that I'll surely buy them some souvenirs on my travel, (3) I want to make up for past wrongs in one go, (4) I wish everyone to know I've been abroad. Whichever of these four reasons is taken, the type and value of the souvenir bought can be determined.

6. *Due to a guilty conscience of going off and having fun all by oneself.*

I think to travel is to release oneself from normal everyday life, and to relax as much as one is inclined to. But, in the middle of this is the unique exception of buying souvenirs. Somehow, there is a feeling of obligation. Unexpectedly, this may cut into your vacation behavior. . . . I wonder if it comes from a guilty conscience of escaping from troublesome everyday life. . . . At the final stage of travel, people seek souvenirs.

. . . Souvenirs are a form of compensation for going out and enjoying yourself, just like the small box of sushi a businessman brings home after a late night out drinking.

7. *As a return present to the person who gave senbetsu.*

When I went on vacation, I received money (senbetsu) from several people. I was relieved when some people asked clearly for souvenirs, but there were many other people who just expected something. . . . Choosing souvenirs in a foreign country for someone whose tastes you don't know well, is troublesome because conventional gifts such as ballpoint pens, ties, lighters, etc., are seldom warmly received, and they don't leave any lasting impression.

The following are Korean opinions and their analysis on souvenirs, based on the open-ended questionnaire.

1. *"Sunmul" is an expression of affection and a way of showing one's true feelings.*

I personally don't feel that it goes against common courtesy to go on vacation and not buy souvenirs. However, because it is commonly accepted that "vacation means souvenirs," I feel I have no other choice but to buy something. Korean people especially have the tendency to focus on a souvenirs' material value. Souvenirs are tokens that express one's feelings. More than the price of the souvenir, I think it's best to bear in mind that person's true intentions.

Recently many people who give and receive souvenirs do so as a formality without any emotion. I think it's best not to give this type of souvenir. Souvenirs for close friends given with love are fine, but handing over souvenirs to company colleagues as a courtesy is meaningless.

2. *Korean society culture and customs, traditional etiquette, social convention.*

Whatever the society, each has its own culture and customs, and individuals have their place in that society. As a member of a group or family, it is impossible to ignore the group consciousness or their way of thinking and to live alone as one thinks right. Souvenir purchasing on a trip sometimes springs from the heart but many times one cannot help buying souvenirs because of the social pressures of being a member of a group, or what people think. I could not ignore the people around me, even when I went on my honeymoon. One is obliged to buy souvenirs suitable to one's status in society.

3. *Souvenirs are to meet people's expectations.*

Somehow, everybody, either your friends, acquaintances, or company colleagues, expect a souvenir when you go on vacation. They take it for granted that you will buy something. . . . The tourists themselves want to give something more expensive as a self-manifestation, so they tend to prefer first class articles. If one gives small mementos, they may be seen as lacking sincerity.

4. *An expression of affection and thanks.*

When returning from a vacation, buying souvenirs is an act of courtesy to people who are close to you, or to whom you owe a debt of gratitude. As human relationships become more alienated and more complicated in modern society, the fact that we can show consideration for and share with people, is a desirable feature associated with vacation souvenirs. . . .

5. *A standard of the persons evaluation of me.*

The consideration shown by Korean and Japanese tourists toward others, has one good point. This is the exemplified by the purchase of souvenirs. As far as I know, in Korea the way of thinking seems to be that the price of the souvenir sometimes signifies its equivalence to the person you give it to. In this way, if you give a gift, which is cheap, the people might ask themselves "what does this person think of me?" and get a misleading impression of your evaluation of him/her. . . .

6. *The conditions for good souvenirs are specialty goods that show the country or region you visited, practical commodities, or economical, reasonably priced things.*

Every tourist destination has rows of souvenir shops. But it is fairly difficult to find the souvenirs suitable to buy others. I think such souvenirs that suit your friend's tastes, or are practical, make good souvenirs. For example, key-chains are one of the most universal types of souvenirs, even though the person you are purchasing for may have several in their possession.

> . . . According to the Korean National Tourism Organization, the results of a survey of citizens who traveled overseas in 1997 showed that products most often bought by tourists were; cosmetics, spirits, clothes, and toys. As for the reasons for shopping overseas, 45.4% of respondents said "prices were cheaper" and 35.6% replied that they thought that "vacation souvenirs should be foreign goods."

As mentioned above, the motives and reasons Japanese and Koreans have for purchasing souvenirs have many common traits. These include: the customs and publicly accepted practices of the society's culture, an expression of thanks and friendship, the wish not to disappoint people who are expecting souvenirs, and obligations to those people who gave money before the vacation.

On the other hand, the differences are based on the fact that Japanese tourists compared to Koreans, see souvenirs more as a means of assisting social communication, and as a way of making those people who were not able to go on the vacation together with you feel the same level of satisfaction. In this way, one of the main motives for Japanese souvenir-purchasing, is to focus on a feeling of solidarity with the people left behind at home and not have to feel sin or a guilty conscience.

Opposed to Japanese feelings regarding souvenirs as a method of consideration or communication, Koreans see souvenirs as a mutual sharing of affection and a method of showing one's sincerity.

Furthermore, Japanese see souvenir giving as a chance to feel superior in endeavoring to find something nice and in having proof that they have been somewhere, or know something other people do not. Through souvenir-giving they want to differentiate themselves from others.

This may also be observed in the terms and phrases used in the opinions about souvenirs mentioned above. Japanese tourists use terms such as matter of common knowledge, communication, bonds of affection, superiority, and guilty conscience. On the other hand, Koreans use terms such as truth, sincerity, the sharing of feelings, and abiding to one's social status and formality.

Both Koreans and Japanese regard souvenir giving as a way of maintaining a relationship with another person, but there are apparent differences concerning "what," and "what kind of" souvenir to give between the two nationalities. From the analysis it may be seen that Japanese, regardless of the content, concentrate on the idea of "giving/receiving something" as a function of maintaining a relationship. Koreans, on the other hand, focus on "what to give" and have the impression that souvenirs play a function of self-expression.

CONCLUSION

In order to make sightseeing rich and enjoyable, and to create "enjoyable shopping," it is crucial to mention what sort of merchandise will be demanded as souvenirs in this modern age, and to enhance the economic effect of tourism.

This study, in attempting to make clear the various factors influencing tourists' purchasing of souvenirs, examines Japanese and Korean purchasing habits regarding souvenirs, specifically focusing on the human relationship aspect. Since both Japan and Korea have the same Asian cultural background, the motives and reasons for buying souvenirs have a number of similarities for both nations, despite the fact that some differences also exist.

Lee (1977) claimed that around the individual there exist three concentrated circles; the spheres of empathy, obligation, and community. Western people are in the community sphere, while the Japanese are closely tied to the sphere of obligations. In comparison to this, Koreans feel obligated by the sphere of human empathy.

Judging from the purchase of souvenirs, if the souvenir is given as a mere formality, Koreans feel a strong sense of incongruity and are particular about giving gifts with love and affection. Thus, it follows that Koreans will not only give a souvenir, but also take more care in choosing "what" to give than the Japanese. Presumably, the choice of souvenirs for Koreans usually starts with, not the idea of giving something valuable, but of something which will please the recipient. In contrast to Korean "affection," the Japanese have "obligation." They buy souvenirs in order to fulfill this obligation. Thus, for the Japanese, it may be said that the choice of souvenir is made based on the idea of not letting down the recipient.

Both Koreans and Japanese attach importance to choosing souvenirs that represent the country or region visited, for souvenirs to be reasonably priced, or gifts which suit their partner's tastes. However, the Japanese often buy food as souvenirs for their friends. This, as previously mentioned, may be connected to the history of souvenirs, or possibly since food, once eaten, does not remain and has little connection to the interests of the person receiving the souvenir. In contrast to this, Koreans prefer to buy tangible souvenirs that last afterwards. They believe that such souvenirs will remind the recipient of you, and can leave a lasting memory. Furthermore, the importance attached to non-bulky souvenirs by the Japanese has a connection to the fact that Japanese housing conditions are already cramped, and care is taken not to trouble the recipient to find a place to put it. However, for Koreans, more than the content of the souvenir, its looks are held important as it is thought that cheap looking souvenirs will not be satisfactory.

In predicting future souvenir purchasing behaviors of tourists examined in this study, it is thought that the "proof," "evidence" or "boastful talk" of traveling somewhere will not play an important role. However, when giving presents to people, good souvenirs are strongly related to what and to whom to give. Additional significance will be placed on souvenirs with the emphasis of "a strong impact is not necessary but, as a sign of friendliness," and "maybe he won't be delighted, but he definitely won't hate it." With this motive in mind, souvenirs will be given as a means of maintaining human relationships. Additionally, such local specialty items that you hardly get unless you actually visit the region, will further become the focus of attention.

Through analyzing the souvenir purchasing habits of tourists, this study gives us an insight into understanding Japanese and Korean society and culture. Also, it has been clarified that the purchasing behavior of tourists has something to do with the social and cultural factors of the country, and indicates trends in what kind of souvenir purchasing behavior will be observed in the future. In order to further this study, it will be important to expand the study group, and to include the analysis of motives related to the souvenir-purchasing behavior of nationalities other than the Japanese and Koreans.

REFERENCES

Chosunilbo (1997). *Chosunilbo* (Chosun Daily Newspaper), August 9.

Gordon, B. (1986). The Souvenir: Messenger of the Extraordinary. *Journal of Popular Culture*, 20 (3), pp. 135-146.

Inoue, T. (1977). *"Sekentei" no Kozo–Shakaisinrisi eno Kokoromi*. (The Construction of "Appearances"–Social Psychology History Trials). Tokyo: NHK books.

Kurita, Y. (1984). Zoto/Okurimono Ko (Thoughts on Gifts and Gift Giving). In N. Ishige et al. (Eds.), *Kurashi no Bunkajinruigaku* (Cultural Anthropology of Life). Kyoto: PHPkenkyujo.

Lee, G. T. (1977) *Hangukin ui Uisikguzo: Hangukin un Nuguinga* (The Construction of Korean Attitudes: Who Are the Korean). Seoul: Munrisa.

Sanwa Bank Home Consultant. (1998). *Kinsenkara mita Otsukiai Chosa* (A Survey of Socializing from the Viewpoint of Money). Sanwa Bank Home Consultant.

Tsurumi, S. (1987). *"Gendai Fuzoku Tsushin '77-86."* (The Modern Public Morals Report '77-86). Tokyo: Gakuyoshobo.

Japanese Tourists' Experience of the Natural Environments in North QLD Region– Great Barrier Reef Experience

Edward Kim
Diane Lee

SUMMARY. The North Queensland (QLD) region has been one of the fastest growing tourist destination for the international travel markets and has been recognized as a significant tourism icon in Australia. Surrounded by World Heritage areas such as the Great Barrier Reef (GBR) and Wet Tropical Rainforest, the North QLD region offers a range of unique and distinctive natural tourist attractions. Although the North QLD region is being recognized as one of the fast growing tourist destinations for Japanese tourists, few studies have been conducted in terms of understanding Japanese tourists' experiences towards the natural environment.

With a focus on the GBR trip in the North QLD region this study determined the importance of the GBR in Japanese holiday choice and elicited opinions on some reef-related issues. This study also attempted to compare Japanese visitor activities and behavior with a previous sample of English speaking respondents who took part in a similar survey during 1996.

The results indicated that not only do Japanese Tourists see Australia

Edward Kim is Lecturer, Tourism Program, James Cook University of North Queensland Cairns Campus, Australia (E-mail: Edward.Kim@jcu.edu.au). Diane Lee is Lecturer, Tourism Program, Murdoch University, Perth, Australia. (E-mail: Dlee@central.murdoch.edu.au).

[Haworth co-indexing entry note]: "Japanese Tourists' Experience of the Natural Environments in North QLD Region–Great Barrier Reef Experience." Kim, Edward, and Diane Lee. Co-published simultaneously in *Journal of Travel & Tourism Marketing* (The Haworth Hospitality Press, an imprint of The Haworth Press, Inc.) Vol. 9, No. 1/2, 2000, pp. 93-113; and: *Japanese Tourists: Socio-Economic, Marketing and Psychological Analysis* (ed: K. S. (Kaye) Chon, Tsutomu Inagaki, and Taiji Ohashi) The Haworth Hospitality Press, an imprint of The Haworth Press, Inc., 1999, pp. 93-113. Single or multiple copies of this article are available for a fee from The Haworth Document Delivery Service [1-800-342-9678, 9:00 a.m. - 5:00 p.m. (EST). E-mail address: getinfo@haworthpressinc.com].

as a great opportunity to experience a unique and different culture, but they also regard Australia as a stimulating destination where they can get involved in some adventurous activities.

Focussing on the GBR as a major drawcard for Japanese visitors, it was found that the 'Experiencing Nature' in a very natural, unstructured way, was the most important motivational factor for a GBR trip. There is potential to improve the enjoyment levels of Japanese visitors to the GBR by providing more information on day activities of the reef tours, by providing more education and through improvement of service and facilities on the boats. *[Article copies available for a fee from The Haworth Document Delivery Service: 1-800-342-9678. E-mail address: <getinfo@haworthpressinc.com> Website:<http://www.haworthpressinc.com>]*

KEYWORDS. Australia, Great Barrier Reef, Japanese visitors, motivation, satisfaction

INTRODUCTION

The highest rates of growth in visitor arrivals into Australia in recent years have been from emerging Asian markets (Kim, 1997). Understanding the diversity and characteristics among visitors from these markets is vital for planning to meet the requirements of the fastest growing source of visitors. Nature-based environmental activities are shown to be the most desirable experiences for holiday travellers to Australia (Childs, 1991; Blamey, 1995). In particular, coastal and marine related activities such as visiting the coastline, beaches, islands, and seeing the Great Barrier Reef (GBR) are the most favored type of activities (Kim, 1996).

Importance of Understanding Japanese Visitors' Behavior Patterns in the North QLD Region

The North Queensland (QLD) region has been one of the fastest growing tourist destinations for international travel markets and has been recognized as a significant tourism icon in Australia. According to Cairns Port Authority (ABS, 1997), the number of international tourist arrivals to this region have increased dramatically up to 263.6% in the past 10 years. Surrounded by World Heritage areas such as the Great Barrier Reef and Wet Tropical Rainforest, North QLD region offers a range of unique and distinctive natural tourist attractions.

The Great Barrier Reef Marine Park obtained World Heritage listing in 1981 (UNESCO, 1998). The Great Barrier Reef World Heritage area extends more than 2000 kilometers along the east coast of Australia, there are over 750 islands included within its boundaries and the Great Barrier Reef Marine Park cover an area of some 350 000 km^2. It contains the world's largest collection of coral reefs, being made up of approximately 3400 individual reefs. Due to the natural values for which the GBR has been recognized, tourism to the area is becoming increasingly popular (Shafer, Inglis, Johnson & Marshall, 1998). The tourism industry within the GBR primarily consists of general day trip boat operators, overnight boat trips, specialist dive trips, and game fishing trips (Burns, 1997). Popular tourist activities are snorkeling, diving and glass bottom boat viewing of the coral in the Great Barrier Reef.

In 1992, 604,900 Japanese visitors arrived in Australia (BTR, 1998) and by 1997, Japanese arrivals to Australia totalled 766,000 (IVS, 1998). These visitors represented 25 and 19 per cent of all international visitors to Australia, respectively (IVS, 1996; IVS, 1998). This decrease in the proportion of international visitors originating from Japan can be seen to be a reflection of the current 'Asian Economic Crisis' although it is interesting to note that Australia as an outbound destination has fared better than other destinations. During 1997 and 1998 Japanese outbound travel to Australia decreased by 8.1% whilst total Japanese outbound travel decreased by 10.4% (ATC, 1998). According to the Bureau of Tourism Research (BTR)(1998), Japanese tourists account for 32 per cent of international commercial visitors to the GBR. Japan has became the largest tourist market for the North QLD region over last decade occupying nearly half of total international market shares (ABS 1997).

There is a growing belief among tour operators that despite recent economic difficulties, Japan will continue to be a major source and destination for tourism and so they are very concerned with developing appropriate products and promotional campaigns. Although the North QLD region is being recognized as one of the fast growing tourist destinations for Japanese tourists, few studies have been conducted yet in terms of understanding Japanese tourists' experiences towards the natural environment.

With a focus on the GBR trip in the North QLD region the study determined the importance of the GBR in Japanese holiday choice and elicited opinions on some reef-related issues. This study also attempted to compare Japanese visitor activities and behavior with a previous sample of English speaking respondents who took part in a similar survey during 1996. This research was part of the Co-operative Research Center's Reef Research (CRC Reef) program undertaken in conjunction with the Pai Chai University and James Cook University Korean-Australian Study Center and was aimed at understanding and managing the GBR.

Sustainable tourism requires quality experiences for visitors as well as effective management of negative visitor impacts. A knowledge of tourists' perceptions and experiences of the GBR can therefore be a powerful tool for managing tourist use and developing promotional strategies. The results to be presented in this paper will provide both insights in cross cultural differences in different tourist markets and examples of how information about tourists can be used to guide management decisions for quality evaluation, destination image development and promotional activities.

Methodology

A questionnaire was developed to determine reasons for undertaking a holiday in Australia, travel preferences, experience and importance of the GBR. Attitudes to specific issues of reef quality, level of development and phenomena which may affect Japanese enjoyment were pretested. Bilingual research assistants participated in the pretesting, data collection, interview verification, and data-coding. Japanese tourists were interviewed during March and September 1997, representing the off-peak summer tourist season and the peak winter tourist season. Data collection was primarily undertaken on a big boat carrying over 100 people. Participants were given the questionnaire during the return trip and asked to hand it back to the research assistant on completion. Interviewing took place at several locations along the length of the GBR in North QLD. This technique resulted in a Japanese sample of 272 respondents. Data was collected in a similar manner, during 1996, from 1423 English speaking visitors.

Moscardo and Pearce (1986) noted that many surveys become overly concerned with the demographics of tourists, and avoid the true items of interest–such as multiple measures of tourist motivation, interest, and satisfaction. It was argued by Pearce and Moscardo that the analysis of tourists' satisfaction should evaluate two important elements simultaneously: the demographic and psychological profiles of tourists in a particular environment and tourists' cognitions and reactions to the tourist setting. This approach was regarded as a useful tool to ascertain reasons for visitation and to highlight tourists' needs and preferences, and suggests ways in which the organization can meet these requirements. For the purpose of this study, the measurement of satisfaction was introduced from research undertaken by Moscardo and Pearce (1986) and Pearce (1988). The study was designed to measure both components of tourists' satisfaction: the demographic and psychological profiles of Japanese tourists both to Australia and to the GBR region, and tourists' cognition to their travel experiences in the GBR region.

The Concept of the Travel Career Ladder as a Tourist Behavior Framework

Understanding the expectations and needs of international tourists requires special study to examine the cultural conditions that will enable the develop-

FIGURE 1. Pearce's Travel Motivation Model–The Travel Career Ladder

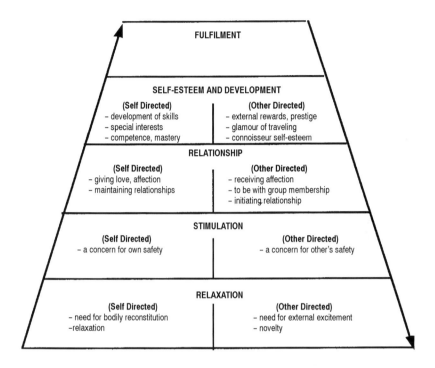

ment of the emergent market to the full (Ahmed, 1989). For the purpose of this study, the "Travel Career Ladder (TCL)" concept, outlined in various studies, was used to examine the Japanese tourists' expectations of Australia as a holiday destination.

Pearce (1988) argued that there are five different hierarchical travel career steps affecting tourist behavior. Like a career at work, people may start at different levels and they are likely to change levels during their life-cycle (Figure 1). The direction of change within the TCL is variable, some individuals may "ascend" the ladder predominantly on the left hand side of the system, while others may go through all steps on both the left and right hand side of the model. One motive at a time tends to be dominant but people may have several motives influencing their tourism activities.

People at the lower level of the TCL, emphasize basic services (food, space, toilets) and enjoy a sense of escape. They want to increase their stimulation and arousal, but not in dangerous or threatening situations. They are concerned with safety and security. On the other hand, people at the higher levels are concerned with developing their skills, knowledge, abilities and special interests.

By using the TCL concept, a new theoretical approach has been applied in several empirical case studies; visitor preference and satisfaction at an historic theme park (Moscardo and Pearce, 1986), new developments for a modern theme park (Dreamworld) (Pearce, 1991), and visitor motivation in Climbing Ayers Rock (Fielding, Pearce, and Hughes, 1992). Pearce argues that tourists have different travel careers which influence their tourist behavior; tourists at a certain stage of their travel career seek to satisfy specific needs so that different satisfaction levels depend on their travel career level. Such treatments of the TCL concept have proven to be practical and useful in predicting the pattern of visitor motivation–how people will change the type of holiday they choose over their life-span. Further, this model is likely to be more widely used as both a descriptive and a predictive tool to understand motivation, the assessment of tourist satisfaction, and cross-cultural understanding of international visitors.

A questionnaire was constructed to determine the psychographic profiles of the respondents by focusing on their motives and expectations for travelling to Australia and to the GBR. The travel motivation questions asked were based on Pearce's TCL model, as a response to a variety of simultaneously occurring motives or needs. Questions were derived from each stage of the ladder and were revised for the Japanese because of their different cultural background. These questions were to determine relevant motivations in the culture. Seventeen motivation statements derived from the TCL were converted into questions for travel motivation of Japanese visitors towards Australian trips and twelve statements were converted into questions for GBR trips. The scores on the questions for the groups were compared by examining the importance ratings on the five point Likert scales, where 1 = very important to 4 = not at all important.

RESULTS

A survey question asked respondents to note the type of group they were travelling with. The results detailed in Table 1 indicate that over half of the respondents (54.4% of Japanese and 58% of English speaking travellers) visited the region travel with their partner, either a husband, wife, boyfriend or girlfriend. Following this, the next largest travel parties for both groups are parties of friends. Business associates contribute a larger percentage to the Japanese group (9%) than the English speaking group (4%), for which business associates ranked as the least common travel companion. However, 9% of English speaking respondents noted their travel party as consisting of organized groups whilst only 4% of Japanese visitors travelled with orga-

TABLE 1. Description of Travel Party–Multiple Response

Travel Party	% of Japanese Respondents	% English Speaking Respondents
Wife, husband, girlfriend or boyfriend	54	58
Friends	9	24
Business associates/colleagues	9	4
I'm alone	5	10
Organised group/club	4	9
Father/mother	5	4
Other relatives	2	5
Child(ren) over 12	2	4
Child(ren) under 12	2	6

nized groups or clubs. English speaking respondents ranked travelling with children (10%) slightly higher than the Japanese visitors (4%).

Table 2 highlights the most frequent modes of transport utilized to travel both to and within the region. Nearly all Japanese travellers (91%) arrive in the region by aeroplane, with 3% arriving by coach/bus. English speaking visitors travel to the region in a similar pattern but a greater percentage arrive by coach (17%) and fewer arrive by air (74%). For both Japanese and English speaking visitors, the coach/bus mode is the most popular method for travelling within the region, being utilized by approximately 53% per cent of visitors. Planes are also used within the region by 9% and 8% per cent of all international visitors. The use of self drive and rental vehicles reflects a slightly higher use by English speaking visitors over Japanese visitors, particularly when travelling to the region. On arrival, more Japanese noted that they drove themselves within the region than other international visitors, it is possible that this is a reflection of the fact that Japanese drivers feel comfortable with the Australian road system of driving on the left hand side.

Table 3 highlights the fact that of the 272 Japanese visitors who travelled to the North QLD region during the period of data collection, 230 (85%) were first time visitors. Almost 5 per cent were visiting for the second time with 7% having visited more than twice. Of the English speaking visitors surveyed, 88% were visiting the GBR for the first time with 9% being on their second visit but only 3% indicating that they had visited the region more than twice. These repeat visitation figures indicate that the Japanese are more likely to be regular repeat visitors than the other international visitors to the GBR.

Table 4 presents the breakdown of GBR trip bookings. Of the 272 Japanese who visited the reef 101 (33.1%) did not make their own booking as the visit was part of a package tour to the region, this compares notably with English speaking visitors of whom only 18.7% indicated that their reef booking arose from package tours. Approximately 35.7 per cent of Japanese

TABLE 2. Main Forms of Transport Used

	To the Region		Within the Region	
	Japanese %	English Speaking %	Japanese %	English Speaking %
Self Drive	1	5	13	11
Rental	1	2	4	11
Coach	4	17	53	54
Plane	91	74	9	8
Other	2	2	3	16

TABLE 3. Visitation Experience–North QLD Region

Visitation Experience	Japanese %	English Speaking %
First time	85	88
Second time	5	9
More than second time	7	3

TABLE 4. Reef Trip Booking

Booking	Japanese %	English Speaking %
Directly with the reef operator	4.9	11.3
Through accommodation/information centre	15.4	46.2
Through a local tour company	35.7	19.6
Didn't book. This visit is part of a package tour to the region	33.1	18.7

respondents booked their trip through a local tour company whilst English speaking visitors tended to book tours through their accommodation facility.

To determine the average length of stay by Japanese tourists in the North QLD region, respondents were asked how many days they had spent in the region and how much longer they planned to stay.

Tables 5 and 6 show the breakdowns of actual time spent in the region. The results highlight that the majority of Japanese travellers surveyed (95.5%) had been in the region for less than a week with 30% spending more than one week in Australia.

These demographic details provide a basis for analysis of the following sections of results. The initial section will address the motivations for travelling to Australia and the GBR for Japanese visitors and the second section will make comparisons between the experiences of the Reef for the Japanese visitors and English speaking visitors.

TABLE 5. Plan to Spend in Australia (Japanese)

Plan to spend in Australia	Frequency	%
< 1 week	200	65.6
1 wk > 2wks	64	21.0
2 wks > 3 wks	13	4.3
3 wks > 4 wks	4	1.3
> 4 wks	12	3.9

TABLE 6. Length of Stay in the North QLD Region (Japanese)

Time	Spent in the region %
0	6.2
1 day	18.4
2 days	23.6
3 days	16.1
4 days	12.8
5 days	4.3
6 days	3.6
7 days	3.3
> a week	6.2

Travel Motivation of Japanese Visitors Towards Australian Trips

Table 7 presents the results of a Varimax rotated factor analysis of 17 statements used to identify the travel motivation factors sought by the respondents. The outcome of the analysis suggests that there are 5 factors underlying the set of travel motivation statements. To determine these factors, a combination of the eigenvalue rule (i.e. > 1) indicating the strength of the variable in the overall analysis and the percentage of the variance attributed to the variable has been applied.

The dimensions of benefits sought were the composite of variables whose factor loadings were higher than 0.4. These items were measured on four-point Likert-type scales, where 1 = very important to 4 = not at all important.

The first factor of Japanese tourists' motivations for Australian Trips was defined as "Exciting Experience" since the motivation statements deal with the having fun, being entertained, finding thrills and excitement including seeing a foreign destination. The second factor of travel motivation was defined as "Cultural Experience." This factor is a combination of "Self-directed Relationship" and "Self-directed/Self-development" motives defined in the original application of the Travel Career Ladder. Here the emphasis is on learning about and experiencing different cultures. The third motivation factor was defined as "Self-Esteem and Development" which corresponded closely to those defined in the original application of the Travel Career Ladder instrument by Pearce (1988). The fourth factor of travel motivation

TABLE 7. Travel Motivation Factors for Japanese Visitors to Australia (Principal Component Factor Analysis–Varimax Rotation)

Factors	Factor Loading				
	Factor 1	Factor 2	Factor 3	Factor 4	Factor 5
1. Exciting Experience (1.8)					
• Being daring and adventuresome (1.8)	**.7264**	.3420	.0766	.0576	.1342
• Being physically active (2.1)	**.7120**	.1509	.1973	.1317	.0046
• Finding thrills and excitement (2.3)	**.7100**	.0111	.1208	−.0895	.2041
• Getting a change from a busy job (1.6)	**.6596**	.0139	.0520	.1041	.1813
• Having fun, being entertained (1.8)	**.6004**	.0864	.3971	.1726	−.1325
• Seeing a foreign destination (1.5)	**.4492**	.3271	.3316	.1607	−.1400
2. Cultural Experience (1.8)					
• Seeing a culture different from my own (1.6)	.0935	**.8493**	.0435	.0637	−.0021
• Unique/different cultural groups (1.7)	.1070	**.8264**	.0334	.0377	.0152
• Learning new things (2.0)	.1645	**.7456**	.0433	−.0842	.1028
3. Self-Esteem (2.6)					
• Talking about the trip after I return home (2.4)	.2129	.0243	**.7719**	.0855	.0843
• Going to places my friends haven't been (2.8)	.2053	.0414	**.7422**	−.1090	.0987
• Opportunity to get away from it all (2.6)	.1061	.0870	**.4983**	.3363	.4914
4. Family Relationship (2.0)					
• Being together as a family (2.0)	.1099	.0929	.1684	**.8636**	−.0035
• Activities for the whole family (2.1)	.1084	−.0863	−.0925	**.8509**	.0539
5. Relaxation (2.7)					
• Experiencing a simpler lifestyle (2.5)	.0406	.1763	−.0073	.1352	**.7576**
• Getting away from the demands of home (2.9)	.2278	−.1371	.1776	−.1630	**.6045**
Eigenvalue	4.55	1.97	1.60	1.26	1.01
Reliability Coefficient (Cronbach's Alpha)	0.78	0.72	0.77	0.68	−0.09
Total Variance Explained	61.1%				

defined as "Family Relationship" relates directly to the "Relationship' level of the Travel Career Ladder. Finally the fifth motivation factor, defined as "Relaxation" incorporating the needs for getting away from demands of home to a simpler lifestyle, refers directly to the first level of the TCL (Pearce, 1988).

Cronbach's alpha coefficient scores were used in order to determine whether the factors are statistically valid in order to use in further analysis. The fifth factor, "Relaxation" was excluded in the further analysis due to the low reliability coefficient score of under 0.5.

Important Motivational Factors of an Australian Trip

In order to distinguish the importance of different motivational factors on the travel career ladder in Australian trips for Japanese tourists, mean ratings were calculated for each factor and their individual factor scores. Table 7 shows the calculated means, along with the full list of motives, grouped according to factors.

In reviewing the mean ratings for each factor, the "Exciting Experience" factor on the TCL was perceived to be most important to Japanese travellers, with the individual motives rating 'seeing a foreign destination' (1.5) and 'getting a change from a busy life' (1.6) and 'having fun, being entertained' (1.8) and 'being daring and adventuresome' (1.8).

However, analysis of the individual mean ratings of each factor group shows that there are other important components in motivating Japanese visitors to take an Australian trip. The components making up the factors of 'Cultural Experience' and 'Family Relationship' are particularly important. Important individual motives identified were 'seeing a culture different to my own' (1.6), 'unique/different cultural groups' (1.7), 'learning new things' (2.0) and 'being together as a family' (2.0).

Travel Motivation by Age-Groups

Japanese society has been changing in many ways during the last couple of decades. The younger generation has been exposed more to the outside world than the older generation. The younger generation is becoming more sophisticated with an international outlook. The research attempted to determine differences between the younger generation and the older generation.

To test for significant differences in motivation for Australian trips, respondents were divided into two different age-groups. This division for grouping ages resulted in 55% (156) subjects being placed in the 'younger group,' which was those less than 30 years and 45% of the sample (127 subjects) placed in the 'older group,' being those 30 years and older. Table 8 illustrates the age breakdown of the respondents.

Mean motivation scores for the two groups for each level of the travel career ladder was calculated and a statistical comparison was made. A t-test was then conducted to determine whether the two groups were significantly different in their travel career levels for Australian trips. The analysis revealed that both groups appear to have very similar motives, however a significant difference does exist between the groups in the level of 'Exciting Experience' and 'Self-Esteem.' The younger group rated "Exciting Experi-

TABLE 8. Age Category (Japanese)

Age Category	Frequency	Percent (%)	
< 21	20	7.1	Younger Group
21-29	136	48.1	156 (55.1%)
30-39	65	23.0	
40-49	32	11.3	Older Group
50-59	21	7.4	127(44.9%)
60-69	6	2.1	
> 69	3	1.1	
Total	283	100	

ence" motivation of 'being daring,' 'finding excitement,' 'having fun' and 'seeing foreign destination' higher than the older group. The younger group also rated the 'Self-Esteem' motivation of 'going places friends haven't been' higher than the older group. Table 9 shows the results for the travel career level based on age.

Travel Motivation of Japanese Visitors towards GBR Trips

The Varimax rotation factor analysis technique was used on the 12 travel motivation statements to determine Japanese Tourists' motivations towards GBR trips (see Table 10). An analysis of the eigenvalues suggested that there are three underlying factors, with a cumulative variance of 58 per cent. Reliability tests on each of the three factors yielded Cronbach's alpha coefficients above 0.50, which indicated that the three-factor solution can be accepted.

The first travel motivation factor was defined as 'Experiencing Nature' since the motivation statements deal with 'being close to nature,' 'seeing coral in its natural environment,' 'appreciating the beauty of the Great Barrier Reef,' 'experiencing something new and different.' The second travel motivation factor was labelled as 'Experiencing Excitement.' This factor referred directly to 'Stimulation' needs on the Travel Career Ladder and included such items as excitement and being active. The third factor, defined as 'Relaxation' also corresponds directly with the Travel Career Ladder level of

TABLE 9. Travel Motivation by Age-Groups (Japanese)

TCL	Travel Motives	Mean Scores		t Value	df	Prob.
		Younger (N = 156)	Older (N = 127)			
Stimulation	• Being daring and adventuresome	1.71	2.03	− 3.61	262.46	.000
	• Being physically active	2.02	2.21	− 1.99	258.40	.048
	• Finding thrills and excitement	2.23	2.45	− 2.10	250.46	.037
	• Getting a change from a busy job	1.62	1.68	− 0.73	262.86	.472
	• Having fun, being entertained	1.64	2.03	− 4.07	231.67	.000
	• Seeing a foreign destination	1.32	1.73	− 4.46	181.18	.000
Cultural Experience	• Seeing a culture different from my own	1.66	1.71	− 0.65	254.13	.518
	• Unique/different cultural groups	1.76	1.83	− 0.81	258.05	.416
	• Learning new things	1.94	2.10	− 1.64	251.33	.102
Self-Esteem	• Talking about the trip after I return home	2.34	2.55	− 2.03	253.48	.043
	• Going to places my friends haven't been	2.63	3.02	− 2.83	205.98	.005
	• Opportunity to get away from it all	2.52	2.69	− 1.38	249.87	.168
Family Relationship	• Being together as a family	2.06	2.06	− 0.01	154.21	.993
	• Activities for the whole family	2.14	2.03	1.10	255.62	.274

TABLE 10. Travel Motivation Factors for Japanese Visitors to the GBR (Principal Component Factor Analysis–Varimax Rotation)

Factors	Factor Loading		
	Factor 1	Factor 2	Factor 3
1. Experiencing Nature (1.7)			
• Seeing coral in its natural environment (1.4)	**.7377**	.3333	−.0339
• Seeing marine life in detail (2.0)	**.6781**	.0067	.1997
• Being close to nature (1.5)	**.6714**	.4222	.1098
• A learning/educational experience (2.2)	**.5915**	.0980	.3831
• Seeing the beauty of the Great Barrier Reef (1.6)	**.5099**	.3655	.2960
2. Experiencing Excitement (2.0)			
• Being physically active (1.9)	.2623	**.7324**	−.0150
• Swimming amongst the marine life (2.1)	.0324	**.7064**	.2402
• Provides excitement (2.1)	.2321	**.6305**	.0434
3. Relaxation (2.0)			
• An opportunity to rest and relax (1.8)	.0225	.1324	**.6708**
• Provides a chance to escape (2.2)	.1752	.2136	**.6123**
• An opportunity to be with friends, partners or family (2.0)	.1368	.4787	**.4965**
Eigenvalue	4.88	1.09	1.00
Reliability Coefficient (Cronbach's Alpha)	0.79	0.71	0.51
Total Variance Explained		58%	

'Relaxation.' This factor included the items of 'a chance to escape' and opportunity to be with friends/family.'

Important Motivational Factors of a GBR Trip

In distinguishing the importance of different motivational factors in GBR trips, for Japanese travellers, an analysis of the mean ratings for each factor indicates that 'Experiencing Nature' is the most important benefit gained from a visit to the Great Barrier Reef, however the learning/educational experience' (2.2) when related to 'Experiencing Nature' is the least important benefit for Japanese visitors. The components of experiencing nature in a very natural, unstructured way, such as; 'seeing coral in its natural environment' (1.4); 'being close to nature' (1.5); 'seeing the beauty of the GBR' (1.6) and; experiencing 'something new and different' (1.7) were all regarded as important benefits of a Great Barrier Reef trip. Table 11 details the full listing and mean scores of Great Barrier Reef benefits, grouped according to factors.

Motivation for Travelling to the GBR by Previous Reef Travel Experiences

Table 11 provides a breakdown of other coral reefs visited by Japanese travellers. Interestingly, most respondents who had been to coral reefs had

TABLE 11. Previous Visits to Other Coral Reefs (Japanese)

Place	Frequency	%
Japan	85	51.5
Hawaii	26	15.8
Southeast Asia	14	8.5
South Pacific	7	4.2
Mediterranean	5	3.0
Other coral reefs in world	5	3.0
NZ	1	0.6
Other coral reefs in Australia	1	0.6

done so in Japan, 20% of coral reef visits had been undertaken in Hawaii and the South Pacific and only 0.6% had previous coral reef experience in Australia.

It was hypothesized that travel motivation to the GBR would vary between those who had visited coral reefs before and those who were visiting a reef for the first time. To test for significant differences in motivation for travelling to the GBR, respondents were asked to state whether they had visited any coral reefs before this trip so that they could be divided into two groups based on their coral reef travel experiences. Table 12 presents the results of the preliminary analysis. The division resulted in 13% of the sample (25 subjects) being placed in a 'non-experienced group' and 87% of the respondents being placed into an 'experienced group.'

Mann-Whitney Non-Parametric test indicated that there were no significant differences travel motivation between the two groups

Motivation for Travelling to the GBR by Age-Groups

As outlined earlier, to test for significant differences in motivation for Australian trips, respondents were divided into two different age-groups (refer to Table 8). Table 13 illustrates that the two age groups are statistically different in their travel career levels, in relation to motivations for visiting the GBR. Analysis indicates that (at $p < .05$) there are significant differences in travel motivation factors for the different age groups. The motivational factor of 'Experiencing Nature' is significantly more important to the respondents who are less than 30 years old, particularly those components of 'seeing coral in its natural environment,' being close to nature' and experiencing 'something new and different.' The motivating factor of 'Experiencing Excitement' was also more important to the younger respondents with the components of 'being physically active' and 'swimming amongst the marine life' being significantly more important to those under 30 years. The element of 'escape' was a significantly more important contributor in motivation for the younger

TABLE 12. Previous Coral Reef Experience

Coral Reef Experience	Frequency	Percent (%)	
No	25	12.6	Non-Experienced Group
Yes	173	87.4	Experienced Group
Total	305	100	

TABLE 13. Travel Motivation by Age-Groups

TCL	Travel Motives	Mean Score		t Value	df	Prob.
		Younger (N = 156)	Older (N = 127)			
Experiencing Nature	• Seeing coral in its natural	1.39	1.59	− 2.82	259	.005
	• Seeing marine life in detail	2.04	2.16	− 1.34	241.38	.183
	• Being close to nature	1.45	1.70	− 2.27	173.37	.024
	• Learning/educational experience	2.15	2.27	− 1.30	243.27	.196
	• Seeing the beauty of the GBR	1.55	1.69	− 1.81	256.22	.072
	• Something new and different	1.70	1.88	− 2.16	255.18	.031
Stimulation	• Being physically active	1.85	2.16	− 3.29	240.32	.001
	• Swimming amongst the marine life	2.00	2.29	− 2.70	226.81	.008
	• Provides excitement	2.21	2.35	− 1.23	249.20	.218
Relaxation	• An opportunity to rest and relax	1.78	2.00	− 2.36	233.22	.019
	• Provides a chance to escape	2.07	2.26	− 2.05	249.96	.041
	• An opportunity to be with friends	2.07	1.98	0.93	250.44	.353

respondents, where they were motivated on a trip to the GBR because it 'provides a chance to escape.'

Visitor Activities

The following sections address the activities of Japanese visitors to the GBR and compares these activities with summary activities of the English speaking sample of GBR visitors obtained in 1996.

Tables 14 and 15, list reef activities and non-reef activities respectively, the top percentage of activities ticked by respondents as activities that they either have done or intend to do on this trip. A total percentage for each activity summing both the 'have done' and 'intend to do' responses has also been calculated and compared with the earlier sample of English speaking respondents. Of the reef activities listed the majority of respondents ticked that they 'have done', and 'intend to do' the following activities; 'snorkeling' (65.2%), 'swimming' (53.8%) and 'glass bottom boat/semi-sub coral viewing' (29.1%). In viewing the non-reef activity responses, the majority of respondents reported that they have done and intend to do 'shopping–local

TABLE 14. Types of Activities–Reef

Reef Activities	Japanese			English Speaking
	Have done (%)	Intend to do (%)	Have done and intend to do	Have done and intend to do %
Snorkeling	53.4	11.8	65.2	81
Swimming	42.3	11.5	53.8	80
Glass bottom boat–coral viewing	17.0	12.1	29.1	51
Scuba diving	21.0	5.6	26.6	31
Viewing marine animals	16.1	5.6	21.7	62
Visiting islands	8.5	10.2	18.7	44
Fishing	5.6	8.5	14.1	12
Sailing	3.0	5.6	8.6	21
Cruises of one or more nights	1.0	5.6	6.6	16

TABLE 15. Types of Activities–Non Reef (Top 10 Activities)

Other Activities	Japanese			English Speaking
	Have done (%)	Intend to do (%)	Have done and Intend to do	Have done and intend to do %
Shopping (local arts and crafts	42.3	26.6	68.9	70
Markets	34.1	14.8	48.9	57
Relax	32.5	11.8	44.3	70
Visiting zoos, etc	28.9	11.5	40.4	39
Visiting scenic landmarks	23.3	11.8	35.1	50
Casinos, gambling	17.0	12.5	29.5	25
Day trip tours of the rainforest	18.0	10.5	28.5	45
Rainforest walks less than one hour	21.3	6.9	28.2	76
Visit beaches	18.7	7.2	25.9	65
White water rafting	12.1	13.4	25.5	20

arts and crafts' (68.9%), and 'relaxing' (44.3%), 'visit zoos' (40.4%) and 'visit scenic landmarks'(35.1%). The table indicates that the English speaking responses followed a similar pattern, although with higher percentages of respondents indicating their desire to be involved with the activity. Notable differences appear for Reef activities such as 'viewing marine life' which ranks 3rd in the list of activities for the English speaking sample but 6th for the Japanese.

Table 15 again indicated higher participation rates in activities by English speaking respondents with the notable exceptions of 'casinos, gambling' and 'white water rafting.' For these activities Japanese participation was higher than that of the English speaking sample. Another impressive difference with the ranking of these non-reef activities can be noted by the fact that 'rainforest walks of < 1 hour' rated as the primary non-reef activity for English speaking visitors with a 76% participation rate indicated but ranked 8th as the most common activity with a participation rate indicated by only 28% of the Japanese sample.

Best Features of Great Barrier Reef Visit

Respondents were asked to indicate what was the best feature of their GBR trip. Table 16 shows the breakdown of responses given. Over 70 per cent of respondents reported reef activities such as snorkeling and swimming as their best feature, followed by 'enjoyment of seeing unique natural environments' (21.3%). The English speaking provided a broader range of 'best features' for the Great Barrier Reef visit however both groups rated activities on the reef as the best feature of the trip whilst viewing wildlife was seen as a best feature by a larger percentage on English speaking respondents, the Japanese noted the simple enjoyment of seeing the total environment as the second best feature for all respondents.

Suggested Improvements for GBR Visit

Table 17 presents the breakdown of suggestions given by Japanese visitors and the English speaking visitors for improvement for GBR trips. An analysis of the results indicate that the major concern identified by Japanese respondents was the need for more information on day activities on reef tours (60.3%) and more education (13.0%). Following these suggestions, approximately 11 per cent of Japanese respondents suggested improved boat and reef facilities for personal safety. Thirty-four percent (34%) of the English speaking group noted that their GBR trip required no improvements and 13.5% saw the only improvement as being more time on the reef. Suggested improvements by this group focussed on improvements to the boat facilities and services with 18% of respondents providing this suggestion. Tighter controls on the impact of tourism were suggested for improving the Reef trip by 12% of the English speaking visitors whilst this suggestion was not apparent from the Japanese sample.

It is interesting to note that whilst Japanese visitors did not enjoy the 'boat facilities and services' as part of their best experience (4%) and English speaking visitors did note the 'boat facilities and services' as contributing to their best experience (13%), it was the English speaking visitors who suggested most improvements relating to the boat and facilities.

Respondents were asked to rate how much they enjoyed their GBR experience on a ten-point Likert scale, where 0 = not at all to 10 = very much. Figure 2 illustrates that over half (50%) the sample had an enjoyment rating of 8 or above indicating that they were highly satisfied. Forty-four per cent of respondents had a rating between 7 and 5 reporting an enjoyable trip, with the

TABLE 16. Best Feature of Great Barrier Reef Visit

Best Feature	Japanese %	English Speaking %
Activities on reef (e.g., Snorkeling, swimming, etc.)	71	42
Seeing the reef	21	8
Learning about reef ecology	4	–
Seeing wildlife	4	24
Boat facilities and services	4	13
Other features	–	13

TABLE 17. Suggested Improvements for Great Barrier Reef Visit

Suggested Improvements	Japanese %	English Speaking %
More information on day activities on reef tour	60	–
More education	13	8
Personal safety on the ship and reef	11	–
Boat facilities and safety	7	18
Better standards of services/staff	5	–
More time at the reef	–	14
Control impacts (litter, touching visitor numbers, etc.)	–	12
Other	–	14

FIGURE 2. Japanese Visitors Enjoyment Levels

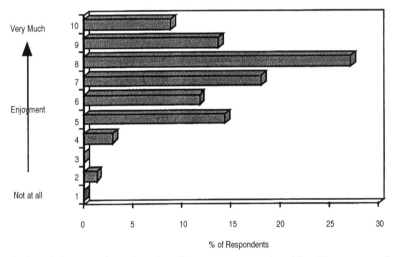

% of Respondents

remainder of the sample rating the trip as not very enjoyable. The mean rating was calculated at 7.2, the median 7 and the mode 8. Overall these results indicate that although a large proportion of Japanese visitors on Great Barrier Reef trips are fairly satisfied, there is great scope for improvement.

Results from the English speaking sample graphically portrayed in Figure 3 indicated that five people did not enjoy their trip at all (a response of less than 1%). However almost 40% of the sample rated the trip with a 10 indicating the top level of enjoyment, the mean level of enjoyment for this group was 8.8, indicating a very high level of satisfaction with the enjoyment of the trip and a much higher level than the mean score of 7.2 for the Japanese survey.

DISCUSSION

The primary purpose of the present study was to examine Japanese tourists travel motivations towards Australian trips. The secondary aim was to make brief comparisons between Japanese visitors and English speaking visitors to the GBR.

The need for Experiencing Excitement and Cultural Experiences were suggested to be of great importance to Japanese travellers. Japanese place major emphasis on being stimulated whilst experiencing different cultures and seeing foreign destinations. The results indicated that 'being together as a family' was also perceived to be an important motivational factor for Japanese tourists travelling to Australia. Not only do they see Australia as a great opportunity to experience a unique and different culture to their own they also regard Australia as a stimulating destination where they can get involved in some adventurous activities.

FIGURE 3. English Speaking Visitors Enjoyment Levels

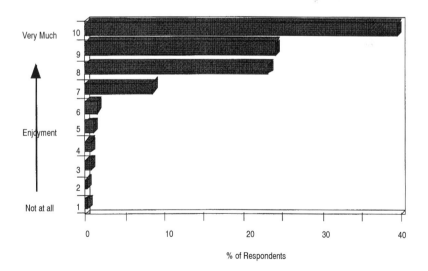

% of Respondents

Focussing on the GBR as a major drawcard for Japanese visitors, it was found that the 'Experiencing Nature' in a very natural, unstructured way, such as 'seeing coral in its natural environment,' 'being close to nature' and 'seeing the beauty of the GBR' was the most important motivational factor of a GBR trip.

The secondary aim of this paper was to compare Japanese with other visitors to the GBR region. This comparison indicated that there were some communalities amongst the two groups and some notable differences. The differences focussed on levels of activity rather than simply style of activity. The Japanese were more likely to have booked tours as part of a package. In determining how satisfied visitors were with GBR trips, it was found that a greater number of English speaking respondents were highly satisfied with their trips than the Japanese but in both groups of visitors there were few who indicated that they did not enjoy the trip.

Pearce (1988) argues that tourists at a certain stage in their travel career seek different travel experiences and select particular forms of travel and types of destinations. By using the five steps in the Travel Career Ladder to explain tourism motivation, this study investigated whether different motivations actually influence Japanese tourists' choice of holiday products. As previous research has indicated that experiencing natural environments is the most important motivating factor for international tourists when deciding to travel to Australia, this study focused on the importance of the GBR and specific reef-related issues. Results of this study suggested that there is potential to improve the enjoyment levels of Japanese visitors to the GBR and some suggestions are that more information is provided on the day activities of the reef tours, that more education is provided and that service and facilities on the boats improve. It is implied that Japanese tourists can be highly motivated to learn about the marine life through experience and viewing the coral in its natural environment.

Sustainable tourism requires quality experiences for visitors as well as effective management of negative visitor impacts. A knowledge of tourists' behavior patterns of the GBR can therefore be a powerful tool for managing tourist use and developing promotional strategies. This study provided both insights in cross cultural differences in different tourist markets and examples of how information about tourists can be used to guide management decisions for quality evaluation, destination image development, and promotional activities.

REFERENCES

Ahmed, S. A. (1989). Psychological profiles of Srilankans versus tourists, *Annals of Tourism Research*, 16 (3), 345-359.
Australian Bureau of Statistics (1997). *Overseas Arrivals and Departures*. Canberra.
Australian Tourist Commission (1998). *Tourism Pulse*, June 1998. Canberra, ACT.

Blamey, R. (1995). *The Nature of Ecotourism.* Canberra, ACT: Bureau of Tourism Research.

Bureau of Tourism Research (1996). *International Visitor Survey.* Canberra, ACT.

Bureau of Tourism Research (1997). *International Visitor Survey,* December Quarter. Canberra, ACT.

Bureau of Tourism Research (1998). *Australian Tourism Data Card.* Canberra, ACT.

Burns D. L. (1998). A profile of marine tourism marketing and future options. *Reef Tourism 2005–Technical Report.* Cairns: Cooperative Research Center for Ecologically Sustainable Development of the Great Barrier Reef.

Childs, R. (1991). *Japanese perceptions of the natural environment.* Canberra, ACT, Bureau of Tourism Research.

Fielding, K., Pearce L. P., and Hughes, K. (1992). Climbing Ayers Rock: Relating visitor motivation, time perception and enjoyment. *The Journal of Tourism Studies,* Vol. 3, No. 2, 49-57.

Kim, E. Y. J. (1996). Overview of Coastal and Marine Tourism in Korea. *The Journal of Tourism Studies,* Vol. 7, No. 2, 46-53.

Kim, E. Y. J. (1997). Korean Outbound Tourism: Pre-Visit Expectations of Australia. *Journal of Travel & Tourism Marketing,* Vol. 6, No. 1, 11-20.

Moscardo, G.M. & Pearce, P.L. (1986). Historic theme parks: an Australian experience in authenticity. *Annals of Tourism Research,* 13, 467-479.

Pearce P. L. (1988). *The Ulysses Factor.* Springer-Verlag: New York.

Pearce P. L. (1991). Dreamworld. A Report on Public Reactions to Dreamworld and Proposed Development at Dreamworld. Townsville: Department of Tourism, James Cook University.

Shafer, C. S., Inglis, G. J., Johnson, V. Y. & Marshall, N. A. (1988). Visitor Experience and Perceived Conditions on Day Trips to the Great Barrier Reef. *CRC Reef Research Center Technical Report No. 21.* Townsville: CRC.

UNESCO (1998). The World Heritage List. <http://www.unesco.org/whc/heritage.htm> Friday, 12 June, 1998.

Packaging a Resort:
An Analysis of Japanese Ski Holiday Package Tour Brochures

Daisaku Yamamoto

SUMMARY. This paper examines the characteristics of contemporary Japanese package tourism, through an analysis of tour brochures. The brochures are analyzed in terms of functional components of the tours, as well as the visual images that are represented. Drawing on a sample of 15 brochures that contain winter ski package holidays for Japanese travelers in Whistler, British Columbia (Canada), this study identifies several key elements in the promotion of Japanese package tourism. These elements include the lean and flexible nature of the functional components of package tours, and the use of both concrete, and abstract images of tourists and tour experiences in the brochures. *[Article copies available for a fee from The Haworth Document Delivery Service: 1-800-342-9678. E-mail address: <getinfo@haworthpressinc.com> Website: <http://www.haworthpressinc.com>]*

KEYWORDS. Japanese tourists, ski holidays, travel brochures, resorts

The rapid growth of Japanese outbound tourism in the 1980s has been "one of the most spectacular success stories" in the modern history of inter-

Daisaku Yamamoto is affiliated with the Department of Human Geography, Graduate School of Arts and Sciences, University of Tokyo, Tokyo, Japan. (E-mail: dai@humgeo.c.u-tokyo.ac.jp).

[Haworth co-indexing entry note]: "Packaging a Resort: An Analysis of Japanese Ski Holiday Package Tour Brochures." Yamamoto, Daisaku. Co-published simultaneously in *Journal of Travel & Tourism Marketing* (The Haworth Hospitality Press, an imprint of The Haworth Press, Inc.) Vol. 9, No. 1/2, 2000, pp. 115-127; and: *Japanese Tourists: Socio-Economic, Marketing and Psychological Analysis* (ed: K. S. (Kaye) Chon, Tsutomu Inagaki, and Taiji Ohashi) The Haworth Hospitality Press, an imprint of The Haworth Press, Inc., 1999, pp. 115-127. Single or multiple copies of this article are available for a fee from The Haworth Document Delivery Service [1-800-342-9678, 9:00 a.m. - 5:00 p.m. (EST). E-mail address: getinfo@haworthpressinc.com].

115

national tourism (Hall, 1994, p. 25). In the last few years, over 15 million Japanese have traveled overseas each year, and despite the recent economic downturn in Japan, outbound tourism is expected to grow further in the forthcoming years. Along with other tourist markets in advanced capitalist nations, the expansion of Japanese outbound tourism has in large been supported by mass package tours. Although it was recently identified that there appeared to be a shift away from mass packaged tourism for the Japanese, the importance of package tours remains higher in the Japanese tourist market than in other national markets such as Australia or the Netherlands (Canadian Tourism Commission, 1995). In spite of the persisting importance of package tours in this market, few researchers have specifically studied the nature of Japanese package tourism, and satisfactorily answered the reason behind its prosperity. The aim of this paper is to identify key elements in the promotion of contemporary Japanese package tourism through an examination of promotional brochures for the ski resort of Whistler, British Columbia. However, before proceeding to the analysis, the study must be placed in a theoretical and methodological context.

CONTEMPORARY TOURISM CONSUMPTION AND BROCHURE ANALYSIS

Urry (1990) argues that an important characteristic of modern tourism lies in its symbolic meaning to the tourist, where tourism functions as a type of status signifier, or as a means of "self-actualization." In this light, it is critical to comprehend tourism consumption not simply as various travel products and services, but also as signs and images, while this is where the tour brochure serves as a potentially useful research subject.

In the previous studies on tour brochures, some primarily focused on functional elements of brochures such as itineraries and prices, while others focused on image-related elements such as photographs and written messages. For example, the former type of studies were conducted by van der Borg (1994), who developed an inventory of destination cities in European package tours, and by Enoch (1996), who undertook a cross-cultural comparison of package tour itineraries based on British, Dutch, and Israeli tour brochures. This type of analysis is concerned with a tourism product of functional components, and tends to be descriptive in nature, although a certain degree of subjective interpretation may be involved.

The analysis of image-related elements may be further divided into two categories: content analysis and semiotic analysis (Albers & James, 1988). Content analysis emphasizes the quantification of data, and seeks some kind of emerging patterns (distribution, frequency, cluster, etc.). For example, Dilley (1986) conducted a frequency count analysis of brochure illustrations (based on the main theme of each illustration), by using Canadian tourist brochures for over twenty destination countries. Using a similar analytical technique, Albers and James (1983) examined the process of cultural stereotype image creation, by focusing on postcard photographs of the American Indian.

Instead of breaking down pictures (or written messages) into their constituents and then reassembling to identify emerging patterns, semiotic analysis treats each picture as a totality and attempts to interpret the meaning and ideology behind the picture (Albers & James, 1988). Adams (1984), by interpreting the image and language in brochures examined, the role of travel agents that elaborate and create marketable ethnic stereotypes of a host community (people and place) with a case study of the Toraja of Sulawesi, Indonesia. A similar type of semiotic study was conducted by Mellinger (1994) on the racist portrayal of African Americans on postcards around the turn of this century. Rather than focusing on the cultural stereotypes of ethnic groups, Uzzell (1984) focuses on the meaning of images in resort-oriented tour brochures, which are particularly relevant to this study. He concludes that contemporary (resort-oriented) tour brochures function to portray at least three types of images: (a) *image of experience*–the projection of superficial, but powerful images of the "sun, sea, sex and sand"; (b) *image of destination*–a focus on the attributes of a place, which contributes toward the enhancement of a customer's self image, rather than presenting features of the actual destination itself; and, (c) *image of self*–promotion of not only a product, but also the image of ourselves as being both in the reality and fantasy worlds of meaning.

It must be noted that, although the analysis of brochures is systematically categorized, an overlap in methodological perspectives and techniques exist, and one may adopt two or more different research methods in an integrated manner. For instance, Dann (1996) examined the image of hosts and guests in U.K. package tour brochures, by combining both quantitative content analysis and qualitative semiotic analysis.

Based on the above theoretical and methodological foundations, this paper uses package tour brochures to focus on key elements of the functional structure, and the symbolic image representation of Japanese package tours. The regional focus of this study is Japanese winter package tours to Whistler, British Columbia. Whistler is an international resort destination, with two of the largest ski hills in North America, and is one of the most popular overseas ski/snowboard vacation destinations among the Japanese today.

METHOD

Data

This study focuses on 15 Japanese ski/snowboard package holiday brochures for the 1995/96 winter season. Every brochure contains at least one tour package plan for Whistler. All 15 brochures were obtained at various retail travel agencies in the vicinity of Nagoya City, Aichi prefecture, which has the third busiest international airport in Japan after Narita (Tokyo) and Osaka. Although there is the possibility of regional variations in tour brochures within Japan (e.g., different image representations in Nagoya and Tokyo), such variations were expected to be minimal, and are not taken into account in the present study. In addition, due to the relatively small number of sample brochures, the result of the analysis must be regarded as a preliminary, to a more extensive examination of Japanese package tour brochures.

All examined brochures were created by Japanese tour operators, and consist of detailed information about the tours such as: travel schedules, services included, and prices. In terms of the geographical regions that are promoted in the brochures, one brochure exclusively promotes a ski vacation at Whistler. The remaining 14 brochures include various other destinations. Among the 14 brochures, 3 include other Canadian destinations (e.g., Banff), 3 include U.S. destinations (e.g., Utah and Colorado), and 8 include Europe and/or South Korean destinations. The volumes of brochures also widely vary, from a double-sided sheet of paper, to a 47-page comprehensive travel catalog.

Procedure

First examined, was the general structure of tour packages. Elements of investigation were travel schedules, service components (transportation, accommodations, meals, guides, and attractions) and prices. The frequency of various components in each brochure was recorded and summarized in tables, while the price range was graphically presented. The analysis of tour composition was followed by the analysis of images. The examined subjects were (a) 15 photographs and illustrations of front cover pages, and (b) 142 photographs of Whistler-related images. The images were classified by the primary content (people, place, and other objects). The 142 photographs were further divided into two categories: "concrete" and "abstract" images. "Concrete" images are defined as those that show some specific traits of Whistler as a destination. Such indications include the central commercial area (called "Whistler Village"), accommodation facilities, and signs and scenery that are distinctive to Whistler. On the other hand, the "abstract" photographs are those which do not have such an indication of the destination. For example, many brochures have close-up pictures of skiers in powder snow (usually, very advanced), but they do not present any distinguishable features of Whistler as a destination region.

This distinction is related to what Albers and James (1988) call image as a sign (metonym), and image as a symbol (metaphor), in the context of ethnographic photographs. Nevertheless, it must be noted that the distinction between the two types of images is not necessarily clear-cut. A documentary picture may be given some meaning and become metaphorical in quality, or metaphoric and metanymic qualities may coexist within a single picture (Albers & James, 1988). Thus, the distinction made in this study, between concrete and abstract images, should not be considered as unequivocal. Rather, this part of the analysis involves a degree of subjective interpretation, and must be considered preliminary to serve as a basis for further research.

JAPANESE TOURISTS IN WHISTLER, BRITISH COLUMBIA

The tourism industry in Whistler has dramatically expanded within the last few decades. The volume of skiers increased by over four fold, from less than 400,000 in the 1980/81 winter season to 1.75 million (skier days) in the 1994/95 winter season (Whistler Resort Association, 1996). The Japanese tourist market consists of a significant segment of the resort business, making up 15% of the total overnight guests to the resort in the 1995/96 winter season–the second biggest international market after the U.S. (32%). Some of the major characteristics of Japanese tourists in Whistler include: extensive use of package tours, short stay (average 3-4 days), the preference of a hotel for accommodation, a travel group of two people (often couples), and a high proportion of repeat guests (based on visitor research conducted by the resort's tourism agency in the 1995/96 winter season).

RESULTS

Product Structures and Components of the Package Tour

Components of package tours studied in the brochures are summarized in Table 1. All 15 tour packages provide somewhere between five and nine day trips as their standard package components, although extended stay is readily available upon request. Six, seven, and eight-day tour plans, appear to be the most common travel length. Typically, three days will be spent on transportation. Thus, in the seven-day tour schedule, there are three days of skiing in

Whistler and one day (practically a half day) of free time in Vancouver. This schedule is almost universal in all the examined Whistler packages.

All packages include air travel from Nagoya to Vancouver, accommodations in Whistler and Vancouver, bus service between the airport and Whistler, and an on-site escort service (a Japanese escort meets customers at the Vancouver Airport, and explains the tour schedule and other necessary issues during the tour.) No package has escort services from Japan. The minimum number of participants required to initiate the tour ranges from just one person to three persons.

Canadian Airlines, Delta Airlines, or Korean Air is used in the studied tours as the airline carrier (Canadian = 13, Delta = 7, and Korean = 3–some tours offer more than one airline company). No charter flights are used in any of the studied brochures. A total of 17 different accommodation facilities in Whistler were identified (11 hotels and 6 condominiums). Occasionally, unspecified accommodations in a brochure may be used in the event when all advertised facilities are filled (as indicated with expressions such as "stay at Hotel X, or the same class hotel" in the brochure). In 7 brochures, both hotel and condominium options are offered, while the other 7 provide only hotel options. One hotel provides only condominium options. In 6 brochures, a customer has 4 to 7 hotel options to choose from. The rest have 1 to 3 hotel options available. Four hotels are common in the 15 Japanese package tours. These are namely, Chateau Whistler (11 brochures), Delta Mountain Resort (10 brochures), Fairways Hotel and Resort (8 brochures) and Listel Whistler (7 brochures). The first three hotels are the three largest hotels in Whistler (Resort Municipality of Whistler, 1995).

In terms of package components besides airlines and accommodations, 10 tour packages include half-day ski guiding service (by Japanese staff) in their tours. Two packages include lift tickets as their standard package component. One package includes some meals (breakfast and dinner), while others do not have any meals during the tour. As optional components, 8 brochures indicate various options that one can purchase in addition to the basic tour itinerary. These tour options include: a helicopter skiing tour, a snowmobile excursion, video taping service and a "wedding at a log-house" option for honeymooners.

The price of each package tour varies by length, Airline Company, choice of accommodation, and also by the time of departure. Generally, the period around Christmas and New Year's Day is the most expensive time to take the trip. Also, around the beginning of May is an expensive time because of the Japanese national holiday week (April 28-May 5, "Golden Week"). The comparison of individual tour products is shown in Figure 1. Among those 14 packages that offer a hotel option, three general price categories are identified. These categories are: (a) the standard price group; (b) the limited time,

TABLE 1. Components of 15 Japanese Package Tours to Whistler (1995/1996 Season

Package Components	Number of Brochures
Standard Tour Length (Multiple Answers)	
5 days (4 nights)	8
6 days (5 nights)	12
7 days (6 nights)	12
8 days (7 nights)	12
9 days (8 nights)	2
Flight Arrangement	
Canadian Airlines	13
Delta Airlines	7
Korean Air	3
Hotel Arrangement in Whistler	
4-7 hotels offered	6
1-3 hotels offered	8
No hotel offered	1
Total Number of Hotels Identified	11
Condominium Arrangement in Whistler	
1-2 condominiums offered	8
No condominium offered	7
Total number of condominiums identified	6
Minimum Number of People Required	
Three	1
Two	10
One	4
Escort from Japan	0
Escort upon arrival (Vancouver)	15
Standard Components (Multiple Answers)	
All meal	0
Some meal	1
Lift ticket	2
Half-day ski guiding	8
Optional Components (Multiple Answers)	
Helicopter skiing	8
Snowmobile	4
Freshtrack[a]	2
Others[b]	4

Note. [a]Optional tour in which the participants are guided to the mid-mountain restaurant for breakfast and ski down in (supposedly) better, early morning snow condition. [b]Include snowboard lesson, video taping, cross country skiing, and wedding. From the 15 sample Japanese tour brochures for winter vacation in Whistler.

discounted price group; and (c) the high-end, inclusive price group. Most tours (10 tours) offer the minimum package price at the range between 110,000 and 160,000 yen, and the maximum price over 200,000 yen (group a: 1 US dollar was approximately 110 yen in 1996). Tour D and F are not offered during the peak Christmas season, and their maximum prices are under 200,000 yen (group b). Tour G and L are priced over 190,000 yen, partly due to lift tickets included in the package (group c).

Cosmetics of the Package Product: Image of Place and People

Front cover page. The 15 tour brochures are classified based on the front cover design (Table 2). In terms of image types, 11 brochures have photographs, and 4 have illustrations. In terms of portrayed objects, 9 brochures illustrate human figure(s) as the main image object(s), 3 illustrate scenery (without any human figures or with very small human figures) as the main image, and 2 illustrate animal(s) as the dominant image.

Among the nine brochures with human figures, one of the most evident characteristics is the absence of Japanese figures, except for one front cover of a young Japanese female. All other front page covers with human figure(s) have pictures of either non-Japanese figures, young white male and/or female figures (six brochures), or the illustration of comic figures (nationality/race unidentified: two brochures). Among the eight non-Japanese front cover images, four front page covers present a couple, and three show a picture of group figures. Among the three front cover designs that portray scenery, two brochures show a specific destination (Banff, Canada and Zermatt, Switzerland). Both brochures show popular landmarks (the township of Banff, and the Matterhorn) which not only represent the image of a specific place, but also portray a dominant image of an overseas winter vacation itself. It is noteworthy that Whistler does not appear in a distinguishable form in any brochure cover design. Neither image of animals in the two brochures is a photograph. One brochure displays a computer illustration of a Bugs Bunny-like figure jumping with skis. The other brochure shows a fancy picture of a rabbit and a squirrel in snow. Both images are abstract and show no indication of any specific destination regions.

Besides photographs and illustrations, nine brochures have some English words (excluding the name of the tour company or of the tour) on their front pages. Most of these English words are rather simple, being names of places (e.g., Canada, Canadian Rockies, and Whistler), or other words such as "ski," "open," or "aesthetic". One brochure has a long paragraph in English, with almost unreadable small letters, and also with a few spelling mistakes. This implies that this English paragraph is probably not placed to serve any functional purpose. Eight brochures indicate the prices of select "discounted" tour packages on the front page. Out of the eight brochures,

FIGURE 1. Prices of 14 Japanese Package Tours to Whistler Based on Eight Day Tour Plan with Hotel Option (1995/96 Season). (Minimum and maxium prices are shown. Tour O is not shown because it did not offer any hotel as an accommodation option.)

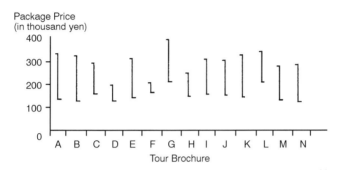

TABLE 2. Types of Front Cover Images on 15 Japanese Package Tour Brochures (1995/96 Season)

Tour Brochure	Type of Image	Main Image Object(s)[a]	Use of English	Price Shown
A	Non-photo	Animals		Yes
B	Photo	Group (NJ)	Yes	Yes
C	Photo	Scenery	Yes	Yes
D	Photo	Travel goods		
E	Photo	Scenery (Banff)	Yes	
F	Photo	Group and Individual (NJ)	Yes	
G	Photo	Couple (NJ)	Yes	
H	Photo	Individual (NJ)	Yes	
I	Non-photo	Couple (UI)		
J	Photo	Couple and Group (NJ)		Yes*
K	Non-photo	Animal		Yes*
L	Photo	Scenery (Zermatt)		
M	Photo	Individual (J)	Yes	Yes
N	Photo	Couple (NJ)	Yes	Yes*
O	Non-photo	Individual (UI)	Yes	Yes*

Note. * indicates that Whistler's package tour price is shown.
[a] J = Japanese figure, NJ = non-Japanese figure, UI = nationality unidentified.

four have the price of a package tour to Whistler among other tour destinations.

Whistler-page photographs. One hundred forty-two photographs in the pages that advertise tours to Whistler are categorized based on their main content, and the type of the image: concrete and abstract (Figure 2).

FIGURE 2. Types of Photographic Images in Whistler-Related Pages of 15 Japanese Package Tour Brochures (1995/96 Season). A total of 142 Photographs Were Identified.

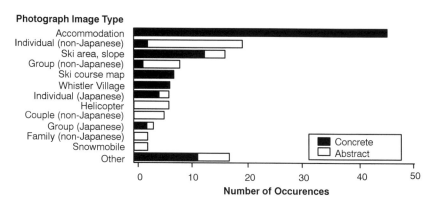

Photographs of accommodations are the most frequently used (31.6%) among all the photographs examined.

Photographs of non-Japanese figures (individual, group, couple and family combined) are also common, accounting for a total of 24.6%. Note that here, most non-Japanese figures are portrayed as tourists (guests), rather than as local residents or employees (hosts). As is the case in the front cover analysis, Japanese figures are largely absent, consisting of a mere 6.3%. Among the pictures with Japanese figures, 4.2% consist of an individual, 2.1% consist of a group, and none consist of a couple. Although most of the Japanese figures are portrayed as tourists (guests), a few pictures show on-site Japanese tour coordinators or tour guides (hosts). Pictures reflecting skiing/snowboarding as the main tourist activity in Whistler, while ski-area photographs and ski-area course maps of the Whistler or Blackcomb ski areas are commonly portrayed, consisting of 16.1%. Whistler Village, one of the most distinguishable landmarks of Whistler, accounts for six photographs (4.2%). No other photographs present places besides the ski areas and Whistler Village. Pictures of helicopters and snowmobiles are occasionally shown, reflecting their popularity as an optional tour.

"Concrete" images account for a little less than two thirds of all photographs displayed (63.4%). All of the photographs depicting the accommodation facilities, ski-course maps and Whistler Village are considered "concrete," because these pictures show some descriptive traits or metanymic signs of Whistler as a particular destination. In particular, photographs of the accommodation facilities account for nearly half of the "concrete" images. However, as already mentioned, one can argue that some of these pictures of accommodations carry a metaphoric message by showing a romantic image of castle-like hotels. Similarly, ski area course maps, although descriptive in nature, may function to enhance the exoticism of foreign ski resorts among the Japanese. In any case, what is promoted in these photographs is almost exclusively an image of the place as a resort. There is little sign of the local community outside the resort area (i.e., commercial area and ski area).

"Abstract" photographs consist of about one third of all the images examined (36.6%). Many photographs in these brochures are literally accompanied with small text "Image photograph," implying that these photographs are not necessarily taken in Whistler, and just refer to symbolic images of the tourist experience. One of the most extreme examples is the photograph that shows a group of people (non-Japanese) in a hot tub drinking wine, and warns in text below, "Image: You cannot eat or drink in the hot tub." Other photographs show a close-up of skiers (mostly non-Japanese) in the air, in fresh snow or on deep moguls. Most images with non-Japanese figures do not show any trait that would indicate that they were actually taken in Whistler. These pictures are used simply to show symbolic images, which carry the ambience of great skiing, foreignness, romance, or fantasy.

DISCUSSION

In this paper, Japanese package tour products to Whistler were examined in regard to their functional and image-related components. As far as the functional quality is concerned, the studied Japanese package tour products to Whistler typically have a very similar tour schedule, and contain minimal tour components (airline, accommodation, on-site coordinator, and local transportation), with a few airlines and hotels being particularly dominant components. Only a few tour packages contain tour components beyond these basic components (e.g., included meals and lift tickets). As a result, most tours appear quite undistinguishable from each other, with the emphasis on price, in terms of the functional tour components. This is not to say, however, that there is no flexibility within the tour package. Rather, many tours do offer a range of choices in the core tour components (e.g., airlines and accommodations), as well as in the optional components so that the tours can be "customized" to some extent. Thus, the concepts of standardization and customization may co-exist within a given tour product, which may result in "flexible mass production" of tourism.

In terms of image-related components, the analysis of front cover design of the package tour brochures has revealed a fairly diverse range of images and messages such as: cost advantage, romance, fantasy, having fun, excellent skiing, or outstanding nature. In this regard, to some extent the mass production of Japanese package tours to Whistler is disguised by superficial cosmetic design variations in the advertisement as Britton (1991) has argued. However, it must be noted that the photographs portrayed in the studied brochures indicate some common patterns suggested by Uzzell (1984)–images of experience, images of destination, and images of self.

In the Japanese tour brochures for winter vacations in Whistler, many pictures of extraordinary skiing have been identified. These images often portray semi-professional skier(s) enjoying the perfect powder snow condition under a sunny blue sky, although such an experience would not occur to everyone who takes the package tour. It must be noted that there is no way of knowing whether some of these skiing photographs were in fact taken in Whistler. For the tourists, it matters little whether it is Whistler or somewhere else, as long as the great skiing experience is promised.

It is evident that the vast majority of images, in which, specific attributes of Whistler could be identified, were either from ski slopes, or from the main commercial area. Few images show visual information about the destination community other than about the resort. This is an expected outcome because Whistler is almost exclusively a winter resort destination for the Japanese. Their primary consideration is not to understand or become familiar with a different place, culture, history or peoples. Rather, they are simply purchasing the intangible qualities of convenient recreational experiences.

In regard to the image of "self," the most evident is the lack of "Japaneseness" throughout the analysis of the front cover, as well as Whistler-related pages. Instead of Japanese figures, who are obviously the main participants in these packages, young white figures are the most predominantly used images in these brochures. It is especially noteworthy that there is one photograph of a Japanese couple in the brochures, although this is one of the most common type of Japanese visitors to Whistler. These images are used to enhance the self-image of the Japanese, which reflects their strong adoration of Western culture and people.

The projection of non-Japanese figures as tourists in the brochures has further theoretical implications. Often, the image of host-guest relationship is presumably equated with the image of the local indigenous population as the host, and non-local visitor population as the guest. However, in the case of Japanese tourism, the image of the guest (tourist) is frequently portrayed by the local (non-Japanese) population–almost exclusively Caucasians. This apparently complicated representation of the host-guest relationship in Japanese tour brochures deserves more attention and requires re-thinking the host-guest relationship concept in a future study.

Finally, it is critical for destination tourism suppliers to have a firm understanding of how their products are portrayed to consumers. Examining tour brochures provides a means of monitoring what the visitors anticipate in the destination, and supporting the further development and improvement of the tourism product. The destination suppliers may also need to make a decision whether a current image of the destination (e.g., the image of a "discounted" resort) is desirable for the long-term development of tourism business in the region.

In conclusion, the basic structure of Japanese package tours to Whistler is very lean, containing minimal necessary components. Thus, competitions among these packages appear to be mostly based on price. Yet, one may call such a lean package highly "flexible" because, there is considerable opportunity for consumers to build their own travel arrangements. Japanese package products are further complemented by a range of product images from adventurous ski experience to romantic resort stay. Images are often presented in a way so that readers of the brochures actively reflect, and construct their self-image and expected experience with the photographs. In this regard, part of the competition between different tours also lies in such superficial product differentiation based on product designs, and styles of image presentation.

REFERENCES

Adams, K. M. (1984). Come to Tana Toraja, 'Land of the Heavenly Kings': Travel agents as brokers in ethnicity. *Annals of Tourism Research, 11*, pp. 469-485.

Albers, P. C., & W. R. James. (1983). Tourism and the changing photographic image of the Great Lake Indians. *Annals of Tourism Research, 10*, pp. 123-148.

Albers, P. C., & W. R. James. (1988). Travel photography: A methodological approach. *Annals of Tourism Research, 15*, pp. 134-158.

Britton, S. (1991). Tourism, capital, and place: Towards a critical geography of tourism. *Environment and Planning D: Society and Space, 9*, pp. 451-478.

Canadian Tourism Commission (CTC). (1995). *Pleasure Travel Markets to North America: Japan Final Report* (prepared by Coopers and Lybrand Consulting). Ottawa: CTC.

Dann, G. (1996). The people of tourist brochures. In T. Selwyn (Ed.), *The Tourist Image: Myths and Myth Making in Tourism* (pp. 62-74). London: John Wiley and Sons.

Dilley, R. S. (1986). Tourist brochures and tourist images. *The Canadian Geographer, 30*, pp. 59-65.

Enoch, Y. (1996). Contents of tour packages: A cross-cultural comparison. *Annals of Tourism Research, 23*, pp. 599-616.

Hall, C. M. (1994). *Tourism in the Pacific Rim*. Melbourne: Longman Cheshire.

Mellinger, W. M. (1994). Toward a critical analysis of tourism representations. *Annals of Tourism Research, 21*, pp. 756-779.

Urry, J. (1990). *The Tourist Gaze*. London: Sage Publications.

Uzzell, D. (1984). An alternative structuralist approach of tourism marketing. *Annals of Tourism Research, 11*, pp. 79-99.

van der Borg, J. (1994). Demand for city tourism in Europe: Tour operators' catalogues. *Tourism Management, 15*, pp. 66-69.

Journeys for Experiences:
Japanese Independent Travelers in Scotland

Vivien Andersen
Richard Prentice
Kazumasa Watanabe

SUMMARY. This paper reviews the motives of Japanese independent travelers and offers a conceptualization–Journeys for Experiences. A desegregation of the independent traveler market is broken down into the three effected segments: *Careerists, Collectors* and *Mainstreamers.* These segments are compared to generic segments of the Japanese market, and the effectiveness of Japanese tourism policy reviewed in terms of this segmentation. Also identified is the need for target marketing and image differentiation in promotion, in order to match the differential importance of motives by each segment toward the product offered both in terms of perceived and consumed experiences. *[Article copies available for a fee from The Haworth Document Delivery Service: 1-800-342-9678. E-mail address: <getinfo@haworthpressinc.com> Website: <http://www.haworthpressinc.com>]*

Vivien Andersen is Lecturer in Tourism Management and member of the Scottish Centre for Cultural Management and Policy at Queen Margaret University College, Edinburgh. Richard Prentice is Head of the Department of Hospitality, Tourism and Leisure Management and Director of the Caledonian Centre for Cultural Services Management at Glasgow Caledonian University. Kazumasa Watanabe is Researcher at Queen Margaret University College, Edinburgh.

Address for correspondence: Vivien Andersen, Queen Margaret University College, Department of Business and Consumer Studies, Clerwood Terrace, Edinburgh EH12 8TS, United Kingdom (E-mail: v.andersen@mail.qmced.ac.uk).

[Haworth co-indexing entry note]: "Journeys for Experiences: Japanese Independent Travelers in Scotland." Andersen, Vivien, Richard Prentice, and Kazumasa Watanabe. Co-published simultaneously in *Journal of Travel & Tourism Marketing* (The Haworth Hospitality Press, an imprint of The Haworth Press, Inc.) Vol. 9, No. 1/2, 2000, pp. 129-151; and: *Japanese Tourists: Socio-Economic, Marketing and Psychological Analysis* (ed: K. S. (Kaye) Chon, Tsutomu Inagaki, and Taiji Ohashi) The Haworth Hospitality Press, an imprint of The Haworth Press, Inc., 2000, pp. 129-151. Single or multiple copies of this article are available for a fee from The Haworth Document Delivery Service [1-800-342-9678, 9:00 a.m. - 5:00 p.m. (EST). E-mail address: getinfo@haworthpressinc.com].

KEYWORDS. Motives, imagery, segmentation, cultural tourism, Japan, Scotland

INTRODUCTION

In 1997, Japanese outbound tourism was officially estimated to constitute 16.8 million trips (JNTO, 1998), of which 7.2 million were to Asia, 5.8 million to North America and 2.2 million to Europe. Within Europe, according to the number of visitors recorded in relation to destinations visited, the most visited countries in 1997 consisted of destinations characterized by their cultural attractions: namely, Italy (506,000 visitors), the United Kingdom (408,000), France (355,000) and Germany (265,000) (JNTO, 1998). Of these destinations, Italy and the United Kingdom are the only cultural destinations which managed to retain their market share, compared to that of 1989 (Baláz, 1998).

The importance of the Japanese market to Scottish tourism has been in the value of expenditure, rather than volume, as Japanese visitors to Scotland only comprise 2% of the total 1.96 million overseas arrivals who visited Scotland in 1995 (STB,1997). Scotland's main overseas markets are the United States (21%), Germany (12%), the Irish Republic and France (8%). However, the average spending of Japanese tourists in 1995 was estimated as £729 per trip, compared to £518 for tourists from the USA and £268 from France (STB, 1997). If the current economic problems in South East Asia can be resolved, the Japanese market will have a potential long-term increase in importance for Scotland. Offering a product comprised of cultural and landscape beauty, Scotland can potentially benefit from future repeat visits by Japanese tourists, wishing to broaden their experience away from London. With a hotel and attraction infrastructure dominated by small and medium-sized enterprises, Scotland can also benefit from increases in both fully independent travel, and gateway tours, which combine security with the independence of accommodation choice and routing after initial arrival. As Japanese tourists display a substantially seasonally unvaried pattern of visiting the United Kingdom (BTA, 1997a), they are of potential interest in attempts to reduce the marked seasonality of Scottish tourism (STB, 1994).

MOTIVES FOR TRAVEL

Tourists' 'motivations' include push factors and *pull* factors. *Push* factors are motives indicating a fundamental reason for behavior. These include ego-enhancement, exploration and evaluation of self, relaxation, escape, regression, kinship, social intercourse, novelty and education (Crompton, 1979; Yuan and McDonald, 1990; Cha, McCleary & Uysal, 1995). *Pull* factors are situational to specific destinations and are threefold: the imagery of a destination likely to meet motives (Crompton, 1979; Chon, 1991; Andersen, Prentice & Guerin, 1997), activities sought from visitation, or the benefits sought from the activities (Manning, 1986; Beeho and Prentice, 1995; Prentice, Witt and Hamer 1993; Gitelson and Kerstetter, 1990; Loker and Perdue, 1992; Prentice, 1993; Crompton and McKay, 1997). Segmentations have been developed from benefit analyses, identifying typologies of tourists (Cha et al., 1995; Prentice, Witt and Hamer, 1998).

Pearce and Caltabiano (1983) postulated that individuals develop their tourist experiences as "careers upward" through a ladder, primarily taking holidays to secure relaxation, but once experienced, seeking to meet higher order motives. Loker-Murphy (1996) and Kim (1997) have both used the travel career ladder to derive descriptive segments of tourists. However, Ryan (1997) has criticized this model as over-simple, in that it assumes that motives are single, rather than multiple for any holiday. The model may also be criticized for failing to recognize the importance of socialization in holiday taking, with individual tourists gaining lower order experiences as indirectly learned experiences from others. For example, in mature markets, young tourists may never have experienced a holiday for relaxation only, as they may have been directly socialized into vacationing for self-esteem and fulfillment through the influence of their parents. Equally, in developing markets, the ladder may have greater explanatory pertinence, as the socialization effect will be much less.

JAPANESE INDEPENDENT AND CULTURAL TRAVEL

Japan has been described as a society with a strong collectivist character of thinking and behavior, fueled by a workaholic culture, which spills over from working life into leisure (Ahmed & Krohn, 1992; Horne, 1998). Japanese workers have traditionally not taken their full holiday entitlement (Burns, 1996). This is despite initiatives such as the "10 Million Program" launched in 1987 to double overseas travel, in order to encourage the substitution of worktime for leisure. Although numerically successful, Burns has argued that the wider objectives of the program, such as the facilitation of cultural change, were not achieved. The combination of a collectivist and workaholic culture has traditionally been thought to constrain independent travel for cultural appreciation. However, the great emphasis placed upon careers by males, may by itself inspire cultural travel as a means of demonstrating internationality to one's superiors when seeking promotion.

Despite generalizations of the Japanese character to be inherently collectivist, the late 1980s heralded a significant development in independent travel. For example, in 1987 it was estimated that 14.9% of Japanese outbound was by individual arrangement, while by 1992, this had risen to 19.9% (Devas, 1993; Morris, 1994). Changes in the organization of package travel also occurred in this period, with the introduction of skeletal-type (airfare and accommodation) tours and gateway tours (airfare and one or two night accommodations), targeted towards the independent travel market. Consequent of these changes, by 1996 it was estimated by the BTA that 25% of all Japanese travelers to Britain were independent travelers (BTA 1997b).

In the 1990s, along with a changed emphasis in the purpose of vacationing, the Japanese government was also promoting independent travel. In 1991, the "Two-Way 21 Tourism Program" (Two-Way 21) was launched, with the objective of promoting mutual understanding and goodwill between Japan and the rest of the world, through the medium of tourists developing person to person contacts (Devas, 1993). This was a shift in policy by the Japanese government, from expanding the quantity of outbound tourism to refining its quality. The message of the program was that taking a holiday was not a frivolous or irresponsible activity, but on the contrary, a conscious act of self-development to benefit Japan as a nation, by contributing to world harmony. Among the objectives of this program were those of expanding individual, greater contact with people in overseas destinations, and the inclusion of cultural issues in guidebooks about overseas countries. As a result, Two-Way 21 set challenges regarding the extent and quality of independent travel, cultural appreciation as a motivational tool and post-travel outcome, and as a source of information used for travel decision-making.

Previous studies of Japanese outbound tourists, either potential or actual, primarily have not focused on independent cultural tourists. In 1986, an early analysis of Japanese outbound tourism was undertaken by the United States Travel and Tourism Administration (USTTA) and Tourism Canada (Yuan and McDonald, 1990). In this survey, culture and history were ranked as higher *pull* factors than wilderness. A further study was conducted by the Japanese Government in 1987 (Nozawa, 1992). This survey partly contradicted the findings related to the relative importance of culture against landscape for the outbound Japanese market. The survey identified overseas travel as primarily dominated by a desire to see aesthetic landscape and historical sites, rather than travel to understand local cultures. Nozawa described the first of these objectives of travel as pertaining to 58% of outbound tourists, whereas the latter only pertained to 21% of tourists. If the latter profile is more substantial, it sets a greater challenge for the Japanese government in its "Two-Way 21 Tourism Program." However, for certain market segments, these objectives may be more readily realized.

A further USTTA and Tourism Canada survey of potential Japanese tourists was undertaken in 1989 and analyzed by Cha et al. (1995). This survey used 30 push motivational items to produce six factors, summarizing half of the variance found between the motivational items measured. The principal factor summarizing push motivations was proven to be Relaxation, which accounted for 41.2% of the variance explained. However, Knowledge formed a second factor, explaining 18.1% of the explained variance, and was principally described as "seeing," rather than understanding. Cha et al. used these factors as a basis for a cluster analysis to segment the Japanese market, producing three segments, which were described as *Sports seekers, Novelty seekers* and *Family/relaxation seekers*. The segment of Novelty seekers represented 35% of the Japanese market, and was disproportionately older, less educated, and less well paid in comparison to the other two segments. This segment may be interpreted as disproportionately seeking to "view" the world as a novelty experience.

The Japanese market traveling to Britain also changed in the 1990s. The British Tourist Authority (BTA), produced a segmentation based on demographics, values, behavior, leisure and travel habits (BTA 1997b), which may be compared to that reported by Devas (1993), which was produced by the Japanese Travel Bureau (JTB) in 1990. Three segments were identified by the BTA as pertinent to the British market. Firstly there are the *Candols*, whom are couples and so-called 'office ladies,' aged 25-44. This segment is characterized as innovators with histories of past travel, making them discerning, sophisticated and informed consumers. Activities such as shopping, cultural pursuits and following fashion were identified as important to this segment. The segment includes the cohort of 18-29 year-old office ladies of the previous decade, as well as contemporary office ladies. In total, the BTA estimates that *Candols* represent 21% of all tourism related trips. The second Japanese segment considered pertinent to the British market by the BTA was termed as *Rewarders,* accounting for 25% of all Japanese tourism related trips. These were travelers aged 55-74, where travel for these individuals is a reward for having helped Japan rebuild itself during the post-war years. This segment includes the cohort of middle aged travelers of the previous decade, now freed from work obligations, and therefore, are more able to travel for leisure purposes. Most *Rewarders* travel as married couples. Demonstrating further aging of the traveling segments, the *Rewarders* represent a more extensive category than the former JTB full-mooners of the 1980s, as they also include elderly couples. The BTA expects that as the present cohort of *Rewarders* ages, it will be replaced not by a similar segment, but by aged *Candols* (experienced tourists). The third BTA category was termed as *Searchers,* young travelers aged 18-24, representing 14% of all trips. This segment is described as being made up of tourists looking for safe adventures, and trendy experiences. They are described by the BTA as "butterflying around, collecting experiences." The BTA *Searchers* are essentially a new segment, compared to the JTB segmentation of 1990.

The new BTA segments reflect a maturing of the Japanese market, beyond the pleasure mass market more pertinent to Pacific destinations patronized by Japanese tourists. This implies enhanced demands for cultural insight and opportunities to develop independent travel: "Japanese travelers want more opportunities to observe local culture, history and daily life–a shift from 'visual' tours to 'journeys of experiences' " (BTA 1997b p. 8). This would imply that the novelty-seeking segment of the Cha et al. segmentation will change from viewing to seeking more meaningful experiences. However, studies of other South East Asian countries such as Korea (Kim, 1997; Cho, 1998) and Taiwan (Lang et al., 1997) do not suggest such cohesive development as in Japan. Instead, it is suggested that the continued pre-eminence to escape from routine, and the seeking of security will be *push* and *pull* motivations for these neighboring markets respectively.

PROMOTING SCOTLAND IN JAPAN

In part, Scotland is a constructed image to the Japanese market, as both the BTA and the Scottish Tourist Board (STB) have actively advertised in Japan for over thirty years. Whilst the STB is still focusing mainly on direct or overt promotion to create imagery, it is also attempting to penetrate the covert information sources (Gunn, 1972; Gartner, 1993; Andersen and Prentice, 1998) such as travel writing, which enjoys a higher credibility amongst the potential market.

The imagery of Scotland to the Japanese market is also formed from the promoted content of package tours to Scotland. In the promotion of many package tours, Scotland is seen as part of a wider British tour in the Japanese market. An analysis of the itineraries of the package tours offered by 12 wholesalers to the potential Japanese leisure visitor to Britain during the first half of 1997 (BTA, 1997b), reveals the popularity of Scotland as part of the Great Britain product offering. Of the 46 tours offered, only 2 were exclusive to Scotland, while 30 of these tours included stays in Scotland, predominantly in the Edinburgh area. Twenty tours had their point of departure in Scotland, although the average length of stay in Britain was 9.47 days, compared to an average of 3.6 days spent in Scotland. With some of the tours even carrying English titles such as *Afternoon Tea and Rose Country*; and *Let's Go to Cotswolds,* Scotland's strength as a separate brand in Japan is questionable. Likewise, what the tourist is seeking by means of benefits from traveling to Scotland is by no means apparent from the overall Britain-wide content of the tours.

THE STUDY

Within the context of the changing Japanese market pertinent to Scotland, and in particular, the officially recognized importance of what has now been termed as *Candols* and *Searchers,* the study is designed to profile and segment independent tourists from Japan. The study primarily focuses on *push* factors as motivational factors, the fundamental reasons for travel, and the extent of 'independence' characterizing the different market segments. However, consequent of the varied importance attributed to culture and history in past studies as motives for Japanese outbound travel, as well as the importance of these in the promoted attraction base as *pull* factors for Scotland, particular attention was given to these motives in the design of the survey. With the "Two-Way 21 Program," emphasizing understanding and self-realization as travel objectives, the survey design seeks to investigate both the extent to which learning as opposed to viewing is considered important as a motive, and the extent to which tourists are seeking cultural appreciation from their visit to Scotland. The collectivist and workaholic culture, often used as a descriptor of the Japanese, is further investigated in terms of motivation. In view of the disputed usefulness of the travel career ladder in understanding travel development in developing tourism markets, the extent to whether the different motivations for travel according to the different market segments are reflective of different levels of the career ladder, is also investigated.

Analysis of motives alone gives only a partial picture of why tourists visit a particular destination. Motives enable us to understand the propensity of travel, but not why they actually arrive at a specific destination. To fully understand this process, *pull* factors also need to be considered. Accordingly, in this study, reasons for having chosen Scotland are also investigated. As imagery is also part of the pull of a destination, this study seeks to understand the images of Scotland held by Japanese tourists. The extent to which these images reflect the officially constructed and promoted images of Scotland are particularly investigated. Since the study surveys Japanese tourists who have arrived in Scotland, rather than establishing a full profile of outbound tourists from Japan, it must be noted that both *push* as well as *pull* factors are potentially contextualized.

Preliminary, semi-structured, in-depth interviews were held in Japanese with thirteen Japanese tourists by one of the authors (a Japanese national), in the late summer and fall of 1995, to explore their motives for travel, and their experiences related to Scotland. A focus group was held with Japanese nationals working as tour guides in February 1996. Similarly, discussions with STB officials, and discussions with both government officials and outbound travel agents in Japan were conducted. The purpose of these interviews and discussions was to determine the qualitative parameters of Japanese travel to

Scotland. From these parameters, an interview schedule was constructed and piloted by which, the study's objectives could be operationalized.

In total, 408 interviews using this schedule were carried out in the Japanese language, by the same co-author who had undertaken the preliminary interviews with independent Japanese tourists, in the main Scottish tourism season of spring and summer in 1996. These completed interviews slightly exceeded in number of the 400 intended, to enable multi-variate segmentation into clusters of robust size. The interviews were undertaken in Edinburgh. The city was chosen due to its position as the primary destination for Japanese visitors to Scotland. Potential interviewees were identified at the city's main tourist locations. They were approached in Japanese on a next to pass basis, and having agreed to be interviewed, these interviews were held in an adjacent cafeteria, or later that day at the tourists' chosen accommodation.

The interviews were conducted using a schedule of questions which were a mixture of open-ended and structured questions, with the latter devised as a mixture of Likert scales, bi-polar semantic differential and multidimensional scales. As fundamental to the segmentation by motives, the former was scaled using a five point ordinal Likert scale, with responses ranging from strongly agree, agree, neither, disagree, and strongly disagree. Five point semantic differential scales were used to retrospectively measure imagery, as pull factors. Piloting demonstrated that the alternative of using seven point scales was both confusing and unreliable, despite a preference for their use to enable a greater differentiation of the positive side of the scale, aiming to provide politeness to the Japanese respondents (Iverson, 1997). Some open-ended questions were also included, designed to elicit opinions on destination image and on satisfaction levels.

A PROFILE OF THE JAPANESE INDEPENDENT TRAVELER

The projected importance of *Candols* and *Searchers* to the British market, has focused official attention on younger adults as tourists from Japan. Of those Japanese independent tourists interviewed in Edinburgh for the present study, 77.9% were adults under 40 years of age, most of whom were in their twenties. This profile is similar to that recorded for all Japanese visitors to the UK, in a study of the International Passenger Survey in 1996, where 71.9% of respondents were between 16-44 years of age (BTA, 1997a). However, the gender profile of the independent Japanese tourists interviewed in Edinburgh was skewed more towards females than found by the IPS in 1996. Of those surveyed in Edinburgh, 65.2% were female, compared to 51% of all Japanese tourists interviewed by the IPS in Britain. From the present survey, Edinburgh would appear to be attractive to independent tourists, with a noteworthy disproportionate number of students among its visitors. However, the

BTA segment of *Searchers* (18-24 years old) was estimated to represent 14% of the Japanese market (BTA 1997b), while 42.2% of all independent Japanese tourists to Edinburgh consisted of students. The age profile of the independent travelers is reflected in their choice of accommodation, with guest houses, bed and breakfasts and youth hostels (i.e., the cheaper forms of accommodations) being the most popular choices by 53.2% of those surveyed. The use of guesthouses and bed and breakfast accommodation in particular implies contact between the Japanese visitors and members of the host community, as these small enterprises tend to be either managed by families or their owners.

In terms of the travel career ladder, few of the tourists interviewed could be considered naive tourists, as only 13% were on their first trip abroad. Indeed, these independent tourists were largely experienced travelers, with 25.7% having been abroad six times or more in the previous five years, and a further 47.3% having traveled between two to five times. More than half of the respondents (51.2%) had been to Britain before, although only 17.2% had previously been to Scotland. This emphasizes the secondary nature of Scotland as a destination within the UK. The short length of stay in Scotland by Japanese independent tourists further confirms this. Of those surveyed, the median frequency of total intended stays in Scotland was 3 to 4 days, whereas the median projected total stay abroad was 8 to 14 days, largely in other parts of Britain. This would imply that Japanese independent tourists are seeking to amass diverse experiences in Britain, rather than developing a deeper understanding of Scotland.

MOTIVES AND MOTIVATIONS

The domains of motives identified by Crompton (1979) and Fodnes (1994) were combined to form a composite system interpretable within the context of cultural tourism and independent travel.

These domains were operationalized from the qualitative interviews, which preceded the main survey to produce seven composite domains which may be offered as describing journeys for experience (Table 1). It will be noted that for Journeys for Experiences, *Independence* and *Development* are inverse equivalents of the earlier typologies. The Journeys for Experiences domains are not hypothesized in the form of a ladder, but rather, as a basket of domains, varying in importance by segments.

The domain of *Novelty* contained one of the two most supported motives, namely that new experiences were very important (Table 2), with 67.9% of those interviewed strongly agreeing that such experiences were very important. Experiencing new foods and staying in unique accommodations formed second order novelty motives. The other most widely supported motive

TABLE 1. Composite Domains of Motives Identified for *Journeys of Experiences*, Derived from Those of Crompton (1979) and Fodnes (1994)

Crompton (1979)	Fodnes (1994)	*Journeys for Experience*
Novelty		Novelty
Socialization Kinship	Social adjustment	Independence
Prestige	Value expression	Prestige
Relaxation	Punishment minimization	Relaxation
Education/Knowledge	Knowledge	Understanding
Regression		Development
	Reward maximization	Utility

formed part of the *Understanding* domain, namely, learning about new culture. Of the respondents, 63.4% held this motive strongly. The other motive within the *Understanding* domain of meeting local people, was also widely supported, although less strongly than that pertaining to culture. Of the respondents, 40.0% held this motive strongly. Taken together, the importance of the *Understanding* domain to independent travelers in Scotland suggests both the applicability of the recent BTA re-segmentation of the Japanese market, and the success of the "Two-Way 21 Program."

The domain of *Utility* contained two motives that were comparatively strongly supported by those interviewed. Both pertained to career development in the form of gaining new inspirations, and the importance of traveling widely. Respectively, 45.3% and 43.6% of those interviewed held these motives strongly. The enhanced appreciation of life on returning home was also commonly supported, but less strongly than career development. This would support both the workaholic interpretation of Japanese culture, and the ethos of "Two-Way 21," that through vacationing, one was contributing to the development of Japan. For these independent Japanese tourists, the distinction between work and leisure was clearly inapplicable, despite the youthfulness of the sample and their presumed exposure to Western youth norms of a leisure-based society.

The three motives within the domain of *Independence,* did not attract such extensive support as some of the motives already discussed for the other domains. However, a majority of respondents demonstrated independence in all three *Independence* motives, and in particular, 76.9% of respondents either strongly or otherwise agreed with the need to get away from the Japanese environment.

TABLE 2. Motives for Holiday-Taking Amongst Japanese Independent Travelers, by Domains, in Response to the Question: "In Connection with Going on Holiday, to What Extent Do You Agree with the Following Statements?"

	1	2	3	4	5
	strongly agree %	agree %	neither %	disagree %	strongly disagree %
Novelty					
New experiences are very important.	67.9	27.5	4.2	0.5	0
It is important to try out new sporting activities.	3.0	6.9	54.9	21.7	13.5
I like trying out new foods.	39.2	41.9	15.2	2.7	1.0
I like to stay at unique accommodation.	24.3	38.7	26.0	7.6	3.4
Independence					
I need to get away from the Japanese environment.	35.0	41.9	16.4	3.9	2.7
I like being on my own.	26.8	38.2	30.3	3.4	1.2
I like being with other Japanese people when on holiday.	7.4	15.3	51.0	18.0	8.4
Prestige					
It is prestigious to visit famous sport venues.	4.2	13.5	43.8	23.6	14.8
I avoid visiting famous places.	2.5	7.1	37.3	37.5	15.7
It is imperative to receive good quality accommodation and services.					
I like to buy goods in the country of origin.	23.2	40.9	28.3	5.9	1.7
I like to show friends at home pictures and souvenirs of new places.	19.7	35.7	31.8	9.6	3.2
Relaxation					
I want to relax completely on holiday abroad.	28.5	35.9	31.2	3.7	0.7
Understanding					
I like learning about new culture.	63.4	31.2	5.4	0	0
I like to meet the local people.	40.0	42.9	15.9	1.0	0.2
Development					
I enjoy going to concerts.	10.8	20.1	46.7	14.3	8.1
Plays and shows provide me best evening entertainment.	11.8	28.7	41.3	12.8	5.4
Utility					
I appreciate life at home more when I return.	33.0	49.3	14.5	2.2	1.0
It is important for my career to get new inspirations on holiday.	45.3	34.7	16.7	1.7	1.5
It is important for my career to have a rest on holiday.	23.5	30.7	34.7	8.2	3.0
It is important for my career to travel widely on holiday.	43.6	33.5	18.2	2.7	2.0

N = 408
Note: The motives listed in the table have been re-ordered into their pertinent domains, from the intermixed order used in the interview schedule

Of the remaining domains, *Relaxation* was the most important. However, *Prestige,* in terms of buying goods in the country of origin, and showing friends at home pictures and souvenirs, was also supported by a majority of those interviewed. It is perhaps noteworthy, that these are the tangible dimensions of prestige, compared say to memories as the basis of social discourse. *Development* as a domain was comparatively poorly supported. This domain had been operationalized in terms of concerts and plays, which form a substantive part of living the formal culture of Edinburgh. This disparity between motives and attractions may in part result from the promotion of Scotland to Japan as primarily a landscape and heritage attraction, rather than a performing arts attraction and in part from the existence of a language barrier for many Japanese visitors.

The present analysis of motives may also be expressed in terms of domains of motives proposed by Yuan and McDonald (1990) and Cha, McCleary and Uysal (1995). Of the six distinct domains identified for Japanese travelers by these authors, five, namely Relaxation, Knowledge *(Understanding),* Adventure *(Novelty),* Travel Bragging *(Prestige)* and Family *(Independence)* can be demonstrated as pertinent to greater or lesser extents, to the present sample. However, Family is pertinent only in the inverse, *Independence,* and *Sports* was found to be unimportant. Of the three 'types' derived by Cha et al., namely *Sports Seekers, Novelty Seekers* and *Family/Relaxation Seekers,* only *Novelty Seekers* would seem pertinent to the independent travelers to Scotland.

Similar to the travelers having multiple motives for traveling, they also have multiple motivations for visiting Scotland. Of the fourteen suggested motivations for choosing Scotland as a destination, 60.1% of the sample identified the scenery and countryside, 40.0% an interest in the culture and 31.8% showing an interest in history as "very important." These reasons clearly reflect the prevalent motives for new experiences *(Novelty)* and learning about new cultures *(Understanding)* identified above. However, they also demonstrate that for independent Japanese travel to Scotland, the viewing of scenery is of far greater importance than cultural understanding, reflecting the ranking reported by Nozawa (1992) rather than that of Yuan and McDonald (1990). No other motivations were considered to be important by the majority of the respondents, despite the emphasis placed on activity holiday promotions by the STB.

IMAGERY AND EXPERIENCE

Overt sources of official promotion were featured poorly in the sources of information reported by the independent travelers, other than those subsequent to their decision-making. Instead, organic sources of information predominated the decision to visit Scotland such as friends and relatives, and guide books. Of the sample, 44.3% considered friends and relatives to be very important or moderately important in the decision-making process. The next most important influences were guide books; both unspecified books, cited by 38.3% of respondents, as well as the most popular series "Chikyu-no-Arukikata", cited by 29.4% of respondents. Chikyu-no-Aruki-kata literally means "how to walk the earth (or the world)." This is the most popular series of guidebooks for all kinds of Japanese travelers. Currently, three books cover Scotland. These are "Europe," "Britain" and "Scotland."

The open-ended questions at the beginning of the interview provided the opportunity for respondents to reveal their initial, unprompted images of Scotland. Landscape related questions were most commonly featured as landmark images, as did the cultural icons of Scotland, tartan and bagpipes (Table 3), as reinforced by the STB and other Scottish promotional organizations (McCrone et al., 1995). Furthermore, 15.4% of the respondents identified Scotland as historically and culturally distinct from England, despite the common promotion of the two countries and other survey evidence suggesting a lack of differentiation of Ireland from England by the Japanese (Bord Fáilte, 1992). Overall, the image was diffuse, with no single attribute being cited by more than one quarter of respondents, apart from the severe climate, which commanded the highest number of (negative) mentions. Despite the attraction of Edinburgh as a destination, the images described were largely Highland (rural), and not of city images. Tartan and bagpipes are also traditional and related to military images, rather than images of contemporary Scottish culture.

Changes in the imagery of Scotland as a result of visitation were also investigated. Few of those interviewed described their experience of Scotland as different from what they had expected, except in respect to the weather. Respondents (90.1%) had expected Scotland to be cold or very cold, and 45.3% of respondents experienced the weather as different or very different from what they expected. A number of respondents (49.9%) expected the countryside to be more untouched than developed. The cities were expected to be more old-fashioned than modern by 74.8% of the respondents and more quiet than busy by 63.6% of the respondents. Art and historical museums were expected to be interesting or very interesting by 58.0% and 55.5% of respondents. However, substantial minorities of those interviewed reported not having experienced art galleries (36.6%), museums (37.2%), entertainment (47.0%) or sporting activities (55.3%) in Scotland. For these substantial minorities, the formal cultural offerings of Scotland would appear to have been totally missed, although 78.8% were including at least one visit to a heritage site in their itinerary. In reply to the open-ended question on their

TABLE 3. Responses to Initial Open-Ended Questions About Scotland, by Japanese Independent Travelers

What did you think was special about Scotland before you came?		
Rank		Mentioned %
1	scenery/lochs	26.0
2	tartan	23.8
3	bagpipe	23.5
4	independence/culture/tradition stubborn/against England	15.4
5	whisky	14.0
6	kilt	13.5
7	castle	8.3
8	sheep	4.9
9.5	friendly people	2.9
9.5	Braveheart	2.9
11	other history	2.5
12.5	shortbread	2.2
12.5	Loch Ness	2.2
14	cashmere	2.0
15	golf	1.5
16	Scottish songs	1.0
17	Candy Candy (Japanese animation featuring Scotland)	0.7
18	other (relaxed, part of England, remote, football/rugby, rock groups)	12.3
Was there anything you thought you would not like about Scotland before you came?		
1	severe climate/cold/dark/much rain	31.4
2	Scottish accent	8.3
3	People are mean	2.7
4	other (dangerous, IRA terrorism, inconvenient, bad food, poverty, no shopping, empty countryside)	10.3

N = 408

satisfaction with their experience of Scotland, it was the informal cultural settings of towns and landscapes, which received the most references. The townscape (of Edinburgh), its well-preserved buildings and the overall historical character of the city were noted by 27.5% of respondents, with the beautiful scenery mentioned by 22.8% of respondents.

SEGMENTATION BASED UPON MOTIVES

Implicit in the foregoing, has been the assumption that Japanese independent tourists to Edinburgh do not form sub-markets in terms of their travel motives. This is not the case. The Japanese independent traveler market to Edinburgh can be differentiated into useful segments as sub-markets in terms of motives. Equally, this market is currently dominated by one segment.

The market segments were derived by hierarchical cluster analysis, using a furthest neighbor (complete linkage) method and a chi-square measure of dissimilarities run under SPSS windows. The ordinal nature of the data did not permit preliminary factor analysis of the motives, or subsequent testing of the dissimilarities of the clusters using discriminant analysis. The respondents were clustered on the twenty-one motives, which they had generally rated as important in their vacation.

Three robust clusters were derived: Segment 1 consisting of 56 tourists, Segment 2 of 94 tourists and Segment 3 of 239 tourists. Nineteen individuals clustered separately, and due to the trivial size of this cluster, it has been omitted from further analysis. In summary, Segment 1 may be termed *'Careerists'*, Segment 2 *'Collectors'* and Segment 3 *'Mainstreamers'*. As the large cluster was formed at the penultimate stages rather than in the final stages in the agglomeration, its desegregation was problematic. This was especially so, as it was formed from the amalgamation of two large clusters at penultimate stage 13 of the agglomeration (two clusters of 141 and 98 respondents respectively). Due to the problems presented by the large segment of 239 tourists in generalizing over half the market as alike, where pertinent, this large segment is split into its two component groups (sub-segments 3A and 3B).

Careerists were the most distinct of the three segments, while *Mainstreamers* were the least distinct. *Careerists* displayed patterns of motives disproportionately emphasizing the domains of Utility, Understanding, Novelty and Independence (Table 4). Three-quarters of the sample strongly agreed that it was important for their career to gain new inspirations on holiday, and a similar proportion strongly agreed that it was important for their career to travel widely. *Careerists* displayed the strongest motives for Understanding with a percentage of 83.9%, and 75.0% strongly agreed with the motives of learning about new culture and liking to meet local people. *Careerists* also displayed the strongest agreement that new experiences were very important, with 87.5% strongly agreeing with this motive for vacationing. *Careerists* were the most independent of the three segments, with 58.9% of this segment strongly expressing likelihood to be on their own.

As a whole *Careerists* were younger than members of the other two segments, with 71.4% under 30 years old (Table 5). In consequence, a higher proportion of this segment was unmarried. They were also much more likely

TABLE 4. Motives for Vacationing by Japanese Independent Travelers, by Clusters, in Response to the Question: "In Connection with Going on Holiday, to What Extent Do You Agree with the Following Statements?"

Percentages of the segments strongly agreeing (1) or agreeing (2) with the question:

	Careerists		Collectors		Mainstreamers			
	Segment 1 N = 56		Segment 2 N = 94		Segment 3a N = 141		Segment 3b N = 98	
	1	2	1	2	1	2	1	2
	%	%	%	%	%	%	%	%
New experiences are very important.	87.5	5.4	78.7	19.1	65.2	32.6	48.0	41.8
It is important to try out new sporting activities.	5.4	0	4.3	6.4	2.9	9.4	1.0	8.2
I like trying out new foods.	44.6	38.6	55.3	33.0	33.3	51.1	29.6	45.9
I like to stay at unique accommodations	33.9	10.7	42.6	27.7	14.2	50.4	11.2	50.0
I need to get away from the Japanese environment.	44.6	35.7	52.1	27.7	21.4	46.8	24.5	57.1
I like being on my own.	58.9	26.8	46.8	25.5	10.7	50.0	4.1	45.4
I like being with other Japanese people when on holiday.	5.4	8.9	13.8	18.1	0	16.4	3.1	14.4
It is prestigious to visit famous sports venues.	8.9	8.9	2.1	8.5	5.0	16.5	3.1	18.4
I avoid visiting famous places.	0	7.1	3.3	5.8	1.4	7.1	0	10.2
It is imperative to receive good quality accommodations and services.	25.0	8.9	25.5	25.5	5.0	26.4	7.2	33.0
I like to buy goods in the country of origin.	3.6	28.6	50.0	27.7	11.4	57.9	16.5	39.2
I like to show friends at home pictures and souvenirs of new places.	8.9	21.4	43.6	29.8	5.7	50.7	14.4	29.9
I want to relax completely on holiday abroad.	44.6	32.1	24.7	30.1	24.8	35.5	19.4	48.0
I like learning about new culture.	83.9	10.7	72.0	21.5	57.4	39.0	50.0	42.9
I like to meet the local people.	75.0	19.6	64.9	28.7	31.2	51.8	10.2	58.2
I enjoy going to concerts.	5.4	26.8	34.0	20.2	4.3	15.0	3.1	25.5
Plays and shows provide me best evening entertainment.	3.6	32.7	35.1	22.3	5.0	29.8	5.1	34.7
I appreciate life at home more when I return.	71.4	23.2	39.4	41.5	25.7	59.3	12.4	62.9
It is important for my career to get new inspirations on holiday.	75.0	16.1	56.4	24.5	48.6	42.1	7.2	46.4
It is important for my career to have a rest on holiday.	60.7	21.4	18.1	23.4	18.7	37.4	8.3	34.4
It is important for my career to travel widely on holiday.	75.0	17.9	54.3	23.4	46.4	42.9	5.2	40.2

N = 389.
Note: The motives listed in the table have been re-ordered into their pertinent domains, from the intermixed order used in the interview schedule

TABLE 5. Socio-Demographic Profile of Japanese Independent Travellers in Scotland by Clusters

	Careerists	Collectors	Mainstreamers	
	Segment 1 N = 56	Segment 2 N = 94	Segment 3a N= 141	Segment 3b N = 98
Gender	%	%	%	%
Male	37.5	18.1	45.4	34.7
Female	62.5	81.9	54.6	65.3
Marital Status				
Single	73.2	62.8	67.4	66.3
Married	26.8	37.2	32.6	33.7
Age				
16-29 years old	71.4	62.8	60.3	64.3
30-39 years old	10.4	10.6	17.7	15.3
40 years and over	17.9	26.6	22.0	20.4
Occupation				
Professional and managerial	19.6	11.7	21.3	13.3
Office worker	10.7	6.4	16.3	23.5
Housewife	7.1	18.1	5.7	14.3
Student	42.9	45.7	42.6	36.7
Other	19.6	18.1	14.2	12.2

N = 389

to be well traveled, with 37.5% having made more than 5 trips abroad in the preceding 5 years. This segment contained the highest proportion of Japanese residents within Europe, with 23.6% living in Europe. Over half (53.6%) of the *Careerists* were traveling by themselves, and were more likely to be staying in youth hostels. This form of accommodation was used by 25.5% of the segment. Previous visits to Scotland were much more important to *Careerists*, as an influence on having selected Scotland as a destination, compared to the overall sample. *Careerists* (26.8%) cited a previous visit as either an important or very important influence, compared to only 15.6% of the overall sample.

Collectors were characterized by motive domains such as Prestige, Novelty, Understanding, Independence and Development (Table 4). *Collectors* may be characterized as *collecting* experiences, partly in the tangible form of souvenirs. For example, exactly half of this segment strongly agreed that they liked to buy goods in the country of origin, and many liked to show souvenirs to friends at home. *Collectors* also demonstrated the highest proportion strongly agreeing with the preference to stay in unique accommodations. Although this was used as a measure of *Novelty*, it may also be interpreted as a basis for travel bragging, and therefore, for this segment, may also be an aspect of *Prestige*. *Collectors* were also characterized by the importance they gave to new experiences, and, unlike the other segments, a majority of *Collectors* enjoyed going to concerts, plays and shows. Learning about new cultures, and liking to meet local people were also strongly held motives for travel by *Collectors*.

The *Collectors* segment contained the largest proportion of females (Table 5). As a whole, the segment was also older than the other two. In terms of recent travel, *Collectors* were a mixed group, but contained a disproportionate number of non-recent travelers, with 20.2% on their first visit abroad for at least the past five years. *Collectors* were the least likely to be traveling by themselves, and the most likely to be in a group of six or more persons, with 19.8% traveling in a group of this size. *Collectors* were the segment most likely to be touring and, mirroring this motive, including concert and theater visits in their itineraries. The percentage (40.4), compared to 29.6% of the full sample said they were touring generally, and exactly one third, compared to 19.8% of the full sample, said that they were attending a concert or theater performance.

Their comparative lack of need for independence, and a generally weaker endorsement of other motives (Table 4) characterized the remaining segments, the *Mainstreamers*. Few of either sub-segments liked being by themselves. Sub-segment 3B was also characterized by an extremely weak endorsement of utility motives and a liking to meet local people.

Mainstreamers contained the highest proportion of white-collar workers (Table 5). Sub-segment 3B was particularly characterized by office workers, who formed 23.5% of this group. This sub-segment was the least likely group to be on business, and contrasted in this respect particularly with sub-segment 3A, which was the most balanced in gender terms. Sub-segment 3B contained the lowest proportion of tourists including a concert or theater visit in their itinerary.

Although different in their profile of motives and socio-demographics, the three segments did not substantially differ in their activities undertaken. With the exception of concert and theater going, it would seem that the Japanese independent travelers are engaging in a comparative standardized product, irrespective of their diverse motives. Either independent tourists to Scotland are interpreting this product in different ways, dependent upon the segment which best describes them, or their motives are not necessarily being realized. If the latter is the case, as the Japanese market further matures, and travelers becomes more discriminating through wider experience, Scotland may be vulnerable to a loss of market share where motives are unmet. Further, irrespective of segment, as the Japanese independent traveler to Scotland seemed dependent on the same sources of information, awareness of the wider Scottish product is unlikely to be achieved.

The segmentation demonstrates that Japanese independent travelers to Scotland do vary significantly by segment in terms of their relative independence, with *Careerists* and *Collectors* distinctive from *Mainstreamers* in their desire for independence. The understanding of foreign cultures, pertinent to the "Two-Way 21 Program," also varies by segment, again with the *Careerists* and *Collectors* distinguishable from the *Mainstreamers*. The cultural understanding objective of the "Two-Way 21 Program" is clearly being most readily achieved among the *Careerist* and *Collectors* segments. The workaholic culture of Japan is most strongly evident among the *Careerist* travelers, for whom *Utility* is fundamental to their travel motives, although this is also prevalent among other segments, too. These travelers are effecting the "Two-Way 21 Program" in the almost literal manner of traveling individually, to aid the collective continued economic development of Japan.

The travel career ladder cannot be unambiguously substantiated via these segments. It would be easy to rank the segments in terms of this ladder, with *Mainstreamers* positioned lower down than *Careerists* and *Collectors*. In terms of the ladder, *Mainstreamers* may be allocated mid-way, principally in terms of their relationship (*Non-Independence*) and stimulation (*Novelty*) needs. *Careerists* and *Collectors* could be ranked higher in terms of their Understanding, self-esteem (*Prestige*) and Development needs. However, the present analysis is only a snapshot of tourists during one holiday, and therefore, positioning on the career ladder has to be temporal. Any progression implicit in a career has therefore to be inferred, if the career ladder is to be accepted as an appropriate contextualization of the three segments identified.

CONCLUSIONS: JOURNEYS FOR EXPERIENCES

The "Two-Way Tourism 21 Program" has emphasized cultural understanding as an objective of foreign travel. This study suggests that this objective still remains to be fully achieved. However, suggesting some success, it has demonstrated the prevalence of the desire for new experiences by Japanese independent travelers. Understanding was found to be a generic motive for travel by those interviewed, but developmental motives for cultural travel, to experience formal culture were far less commonly expressed. Principal among the reported motivations for choosing Scotland was scenery and countryside, with culture and history being second order motivations. The very short stay in Scotland intended by many of the travelers, means that much cultural experience was almost of informal necessity, and perhaps, incidental, gained from touring to view scenery and visiting historic structures. Expectations of tartan, bagpipes and scenic lochs are essentially a

Highland image, and one also associated with military history. The surprise of many at the historical urban quality of Edinburgh, with its dominant castle and palace, extend this military image into the urban form. For many Japanese visitors, Scottish culture may be in effect, equated with Scottish military history, staged in a predominantly rural setting.

In terms of motives, the Japanese independent traveler market to Edinburgh in spring and summer is not homogenous, although it is currently dominated by one segment. Three segments may be identified. The *Careerists,* seeking to improve their careers through foreign travel, *Collectors,* seeking prestigious and developmental experiences, and a large segment, the *Mainstreamers.* The latter can be desegregated into at least two sub-segments. These segments differ in the emphasis given to independence in travel, with *Mainstreamers* least emphatic about liking to be alone. For this large segment, care is needed in not conveying images of being alone, while also soliciting care not to convey imagery of being with other Japanese.

The fact that these segments are formed from motive domains that transcend Japanese travel, suggests that in terms of independent travel, the Japanese out-bound market is comparable to other markets in terms of motives for travel, if not in the manner that these motives are commonly held by subgroups. However, where the Japanese outbound independent market differs notably from Western markets, is in the presence of a minority segment of non-trivial size, for which, utilitarian motives are very important while traveling. These *Careerists* particularly embody the Japanese workaholic culture of blurring leisure and work, with their holiday taking strongly motivated by career advancement. However, it is not just this segment where such motives are held. Members of all segments hold such intentions, although in some aspects it can be prioritized less strongly, clearly differentiating Japanese travel motives from Western markets.

With the Japanese independent traveler market to Scotland clearly segmented by motives, a challenge is offered to tourism promoters to interpret their resources in ways these segments may identify with. At present, standard information sources, dominated by the guidebooks, prescribe largely similar activities and itineraries for the Japanese independent traveler, replicating those of the package tour market to Scotland. As a minimum, the promotion of Scotland to the Japanese independent travel market requires differentiation around the motive domains associated with the three segments identified, but with a common experiential emphasis. Only in the latter manner, can 'Journeys for Experiences' be made fully meaningful.

Despite traditional images dominating information sources, they are not likely serving to construct or at least reinforce a generic image to be consumed. This traditional image may not only act as an inhibitor to growth amongst the cultural tourism market, but may prevent the allocation of time for the undertaking of the cultural immersion and 'Journeys for Experiences,' which motivate the visit. Emphasis upon cultural differentiation away from tartan and bagpipes is also essential if the *Understanding* domain is to be met. A further challenge is to make potential *Mainstreamers* more emphatic and differentiated, by capturing them with the unique Scottish product that could be offered. Otherwise, as the Japanese market becomes increasingly more experienced in international travel, it may deem standardized products inappropriate, and move to destinations able to offer more specialist opportunities and information. This is especially so, due to the politeness of Japanese tourists, who may simply not complain even when dissatisfied with a product offering when at a destination. Satisfaction ratings from exit surveys are simply inappropriate to the Japanese market, therefore making Journeys for Experiences methodology, or its equivalent, essential.

Furthermore, while this study was limited to one specific destination, it may usefully provide a model for other destinations similarly placed at the periphery of Japanese awareness, both for the examination and alignment of motives and experiences, and for identifying a basis of product repositioning. Also, as the survey was limited to spring and summer visitors, replication of the survey in the low season, may warrant some attention in Scotland or elsewhere. For example, students may form a different proportion of visitors during the summer half-year, thereby potentially changing the segmentation basis. Wherever a standard product is being consumed, irrespective of motive, a need for product development and promotion, in terms of distinctive mixes of travel motives is implied. The present study offers a basis by which motives can be conceptualized and used to differentiate the market. The practical challenge for Scottish tourism is to differentiate its product in ways appropriate to the segments identified. The challenge for other destinations is to see how far a comparable analysis not only replicates the present segments, but enables competitive product offerings to meet those motives which transcend place.

REFERENCES

Ahmed, Z. U., and Krohn, F. B. (1992). Understanding the Unique Consumer Behavior of Japanese Tourists. *Journal of Travel & Tourism Marketing*, 1 (3): pp. 73-86.

Andersen, V., Prentice, R. C., and Guerin, S., (1997). Imagery of Denmark among visitors to Danish fine arts exhibitions in Scotland. *Tourism Management*, 18 (7): pp. 453-464.

Baláz, V., and Mitsutake, M. (1998). Japanese tourists in transition countries of Central Europe: Present behavior and future trends. *Tourism Management*, 19 (5): pp. 433-443.

Beeho, A. J., and Prentice, R. C. (1995). Evaluating the experiences and benefits gained by tourists visiting a socio-industrial heritage museum, *Museum Management and Curatorship*, 14: pp. 229-251.

Bord Fáilte (1992). *Japan–Know Your Market* Dublin. Bord Fáilte.

British Tourist Authority (1997a). *Japanese Visitor Traffic to the UK: A Market Summary.* London, BTA/ETB Research Services.

British Tourist Authority. (1997b). *A BTA Market Guide; Japan 1997/98.* London, British Tourist Authority.

Burns, P. M. (1996). Japan's Ten Million Program: The Paradox of Statistical Success. *Progress in Tourism and Hospitality Research*, 2: pp. 181-192.

Cha, S., McCleary, K. W., and Uysal, M. (1995). Travel Motivations of Japanese Overseas Travellers: A Factor-Cluster Segmentation Approach *Journal of Travel Research*, 34 (1): pp. 32-39.

Cho, B-H. (1998). Segmenting the Younger Korean Tourism Market: The Attractiveness of Australia as a Holiday Destination. *Journal of Travel and Tourism Marketing*, 7 (4): pp. 1-18.

Chon, K.S., (1991) Tourism destination image modification process. Marketing implications. *Tourism Management*, 12 : pp. 68-72.

Crompton, J. (1979). Motivations for pleasure vacation. *Annals of Tourism Research*, 6 (4): pp. 408-24.

Crompton, J., and McKay, S. L., (1997). Motives of visitors attending festival events. *Annals of Tourism Research*, 24 (2): pp. 425-439.

Devas, E. (1993) *The Japanese Tourist Outbound: A Market Profile.* London Tourism Planning and Research Associates.

Fodnes, D. (1994) Measuring Tourist Motivation. *Annals of Tourism Research*, 21 (3): pp. 555-581.

Gartner, W.C., (1993). Image Formation Process, in F. Uysal Muzaffer (Ed.) *Communication and Channel Systems in Tourism Marketing* (pp. 191-216) New York: The Haworth Press, Inc.

Gitelson, R. J., and Kerstetter, D. L. (1990). The Relationship Between Sociodemographic Variables, Benefits Sought and Subsequent Vacation Behavior: A Case Study. *Journal of Travel Research*, 28 (3): pp. 24-29.

Gunn, C., (1972), *Vacationscape, Designing Tourist Regions*, Bureau of Business Research, Austin, University of Texas.

Horne, J., (1998). Understanding leisure time and leisure space in contemporary Japanese society. *Leisure Studies* 17: pp. 37-52.

Iverson, T. J., (1997). Japanese visitors to Guam: Lessons from experience. *Journal of Travel & Tourism Marketing*, 6 (1): pp. 41-54.

Japan National Tourist Organization, (1998). *1997 Visitor Arrivals & Japanese Overseas Travelers*, Japan National Tourist Organization.

Kim, E. Y. (1997). Korean Outbound Tourism: Pre-Visit Expectations of Australia. *Journal of Travel & Tourism Marketing*, 6 (1): pp. 11-19.

Lang, C-T., O'Leary, J. T., and Morrison, A. M., (1997). Distinguishing the Destination Choices of Pleasure Travelers from Taiwan. *Journal of Travel & Tourism Marketing*, 6 (1): 21-40.

Loker, L. and Perdue, R. (1992). A Benefit Segmentation of a Nonresident Summer Travel Market. *Journal of Travel Research*, 31 (1): pp. 31-35.

Loker-Murphy, L., (1996) Backpackers in Australia: A Motivation-Based Segmentation Study. *Journal of Travel & Tourism Marketing*, 5 (4): pp. 23-45.

Manning, R. E., (1986). *Studies in Outdoor Recreation*. Corvallis, Oregon State University Press.

McCrone, D., Morris, A., and Kiely, R. (1995). *Scotland the Brand: The Making of Scottish Heritage*. Edinburgh. Edinburgh University Press.

Morris, S. (1994). Japan Outbound. *EIU Travel and Tourism Analyst 94*, 1 : pp. 40-64.

Nozawa, H. (1992). A marketing analysis of Japanese outbound travel. *Tourism Management*, 13 (2): pp. 226-234.

Pearce, P. L., and Caltabiano, M. L., (1983), Inferring Travel Motivations from Travelers' Experiences. *Journal of Travel Research*, 3: pp. 16-20.

Prentice R. C. (1993). *Tourism and Heritage Attractions*. London, Routledge.

Prentice R. C., Witt, S.F., and Hamer, C. (1993). The experience of industrial heritage: The case of Black Gold. *Built Environment*, 19: pp. 137-146.

Prentice R. C., Witt, S.F., and Hamer, C. (1998). Tourism as Experience: the case of heritage parks. *Annals of Tourism Research*, 25 (1): pp. 1-24.

Ryan, C. (ed.) (1997). *The Tourist Experience*. London. Cassell.

Scottish Tourist Board (1994). *Strategic Plan*, Edinburgh. Scottish Tourist Board.

Scottish Tourist Board (1997). *International Marketing Plan*. Edinburgh, Scottish Tourist Board.

Yuan, S., and McDonald, C., (1990). Motivational Determinants of International Pleasure Time. *Journal of Travel Research*, 29 (1): pp. 42-44.

Understanding the Cultural Differences in Tourist Motivation Between Anglo-American and Japanese Tourists

Chulwon Kim
Seokho Lee

SUMMARY. There is considerable evidence to suggest that differences in cultural characteristics exist across the world. Among them, individualistic societies emphasize "I" consciousness, autonomy, emotional independence, pleasure seeking and universalism. On the other hand, collectivistic societies stress "we" consciousness, collective identity, group solidarity, sharing, and particularism. A comparative research on the motivation of tourists from different cultures may challenge current tourism research, which mainly focuses on individualism and rationalism. These values of individualism and rationalism result in underestimation of the influence of groups, norms, culture, and emotion or impulse on tourist behavior. There have been few studies which attempt to directly measure cultural characteristics and identity across culture, and to explain how these cultural characteristics play a role in creating distinctive

Chulwon Kim and Seokho Lee are affiliated with the Department of Recreation, Park and Tourism Sciences, Texas A&M University.

Address correspondence to: Chulwon Kim, Department of Recreation, Park and Tourism Sciences, Texas A&M University, 354 Francis Hall, College Station, TX 77843-2261 (E-mail: ckim@rpts.tamu.edu).

The authors acknowledge great help from Junko Matsukawa, Texas A&M University for translation, Eunkyung Suh and Hyungsook You, Rikkyo University, Tokyo, Japan, and Mr. Sibuya, Chugai Pharmacy Co. Tokyo, Japan for data collection.

[Haworth co-indexing entry note]: "Understanding the Cultural Differences in Tourist Motivation Between Anglo-American and Japanese Tourists." Kim, Chulwon, and Seokho Lee. Co-published simultaneously in *Journal of Travel & Tourism Marketing* (The Haworth Hospitality Press, an imprint of The Haworth Press, Inc.) Vol. 9, No. 1/2, 2000, pp. 153-170; and: *Japanese Tourists: Socio-Economic, Marketing and Psychological Analysis* (ed: K. S. (Kaye) Chon, Tsutomu Inagaki, and Taiji Ohashi) The Haworth Hospitality Press, an imprint of The Haworth Press, Inc., 2000, pp. 153-170. Single or multiple copies of this article are available for a fee from The Haworth Document Delivery Service [1-800-342-9678, 9:00 a.m. - 5:00 p.m. (EST). E-mail address: getinfo@haworthpressinc.com].

differences in tourist motivation. Thus, this study explores (1) cultural differences underlying individualism-collectivism between Anglo-American and Japanese tourists; (2) examines the relationship of two cultural dimensions to tourist motivation, and (3) suggests management implications facing tourism industry. *[Article copies available for a fee from The Haworth Document Delivery Service: 1-800-342-9678. E-mail address: <getinfo@haworthpressinc.com> Website: <http://www.haworthpressinc.com>]*

KEYWORDS. Japanese tourists, travel motivation, American tourists, cross-cultural marketing

INTRODUCTION

Cross-cultural research on the motivation of tourists from different cultures may challenge the current tourism research, which mainly focuses on individualism and rationalism–important values that Western researchers use without conscious awareness (Hogan & Emler, 1978). These values of individualism and rationalism result in the underestimation of influence groups, the norms, culture, and emotion or impulse on human behavior (Triandis, 1988). The popular motivation theories in North American literature (which have been mostly embedded in Western values) are: achievement motivation (McClelland, 1965), hierarchy of human needs (Maslow, 1943), two factor theory of motivation (Herzberg, Mausner, & Snyderman, 1959), and expectancy theory (Vroom, 1964).

It is noteworthy that there is great potential for variability among the different cultures in terms of their travel behavior, preferences, and motivation. Regrettably, there has been lack of study which attempts to directly measure cultural characteristics and explains how these cultural characteristics play a role in creating distinctive differences in tourist motivation.

There is considerable evidence to suggest that differences in cultural characteristics and values exist across the world (Hofstede, 1980; Markus & Kitayama, 1991; Rosenthal & Bornholt, 1988; Schwartz & Bilsky, 1990; Schwartz, 1990; Triandis & Vassiliou, 1972). In a survey of IBM workers in 40 countries, Hofstede (1980) found that he could classify the countries along four cultural orientations including power distance, individualism-collectivism, masculinity-femininity, and uncertainty avoidance. Power distance is defined as the amount of respect and deference between those in superior and subordinate positions. Masculinity-femininity refers to the relative emphasis on achievement and interpersonal harmony which characterizes gender differences in some national cultures. Individualism-collectivism has to do with whether one's identity is defined by personal choices and achievements or by the character of the collective groups to which one is more or less permanently attached.

Uncertainty avoidance has to do with the amount of planning people undertake to deal with life's uncertainties. A group of mostly European and North American countries would emerge as high on individualism and low on power distance, whereas another group of mostly Latin American and Asian countries would emerge as low on individualism and high on power distance. Hofstede's four cultural orientations are widely accepted and have been used by many researchers to locate and compare cultural groups (Bond & Forgas, 1984; Leung, 1989).

Among these four cultural orientations, however, Triandis (1990) proposed that the distinction between individualism and collectivism promises to explain much of the variance of social behavior. Individualism and collectivism constructs have been discussed in many contexts in the social sciences, including values (Hofstede, 1980; Kluckhohn & Strodtbeck, 1961), social systems (Parsons & Shils, 1951), morality (Miller, Bersoff & Harwood, 1990; Shweder & Bourne, 1982), religion (Bakan, 1966), cognitive differentiation (Berry, 1976), economic development (Adelman & Morris, 1967), modernity (Inkeles & Smith, 1974; Taylor, 1989), and cultural patterns (Hsu, 1983).

The dimension of individualism and collectivism may lead to the development of hypotheses concerning the relationship of culture and tourist motivation. Thus, this paper examined a fundamental dimension of cultural identity and postulated its implication for tourist motivation and management of international tourism industry. Specifically, this paper examined matters pertaining to individualism and collectivism in terms of multicultural perspectives toward tourism.

INDIVIDUALISM AND COLLECTIVISM

The term "individualism" is defined as the emotional independence from groups; organizations, or other collectivities (Hofstede, 1980). On the other hand, collectivism, can be characterized by associative, intimate relations with in-groups, conformity, solidarity, and duties and obligations (Hui & Triandis, 1986).

Individualism-collectivism is not a new concept in social theory. Its evolution can be traced back at least as far as nineteenth-century classical sociology, when Tonnies (1887) proposed the distinction between *Gesellschaft* (society developed through complementary, self-interested exchange), and *Gemeinshaft* (community nurtured through shared, group-oriented kinship or tradition). Later, Durkheim (1930) noted the existence of two distinctly different forms of social cohesion: *mechanical solidarity*, based on the complementary satisfaction of differing interests, and *organic solidarity*, based on the collective satisfaction of shared interests. In a similar tone, Weber (1947) observed the presence of both voluntary, temporary interpersonal relationships motivated by self-interested gain, and more permanent group relationships supported by traditions fostering a sense of joint obligation. The distinction between individualism and collectivism was introduced to contemporary theorists by Parsons and Shils (1951), whose dimension of self-orientation versus collectivity-orientation was appropriated from Weber.

According to Waterman (1984), individualism symbolizes four psychological qualities. The first one is a sense of personal identity, which is the knowledge of who one is and what one's own goals and values are. A sense of personal identity is related to the philosophical concept of the true self. which specifies "what an individual reckons personally expressive and therefore what is to be actualized" (p. 30). The second one is Maslow's self-actualization, which, in brief, is the driving to be one's true self. The third quality is Rotter's (1966) internal locus of control, which reflects one's willingness to accept personal responsibility for life's happiness and sorrows. The final one is principled (postconventional), moral reasoning (Kohlberg, 1969), which reasoning involves consistency with general and abstract principles.

On the other hand, Hui and Triandis (1986) argued that collectivism is a syndrome of feelings, emotions, beliefs, ideology, and actions related to interpersonal concern, reflected in seven categories: consideration of implications (costs and benefits) of one's own decisions and/or actions for other people, sharing of material resources, sharing of material resources (such as time and effort), susceptibility to social influence, self-presentation and face-work, sharing of outcomes, and feeling of involvement in others' lives. The sense of "we-ness" is salient. A person's identity is derived from the social system rather than from individual attributes. Privacy is diminished owing to interaction between the individual and the collective.

Individualism is very high in the United States, England, and British-influenced countries, such as Australia. On the other hand, Africa, Latin America and Asia have a high tendency of collectivism, as a contrasting cultural syndrome to individualism.

In particular, Japanese collectivism has been attributed to characteristics that are assumed to be unique to the Japanese. Hamaguchi (1977) stresses the importance of personal relationships (*Kanjinshugi*) in Japanese culture. According to Hamaguchi (1982), *Kanjinshugi* is characterized by three features: interdependence, mutual reliance, and respect for person-to-person relationships without consideration of costs and benefits.

TOURIST MOTIVATION

McIntosh and Goeldner (1990) proposed four basic tourism preference dichotomies to help explain travel behavior: dependence versus autonomy; activity versus relaxation; order versus disorder; and familiarity versus novelty. This model of basic tourism preferences appears to be similar to the four cultural dimensions of Hofstede's study. McIntosh and Goeldner (1990) explained that order (i.e., high power distance or authority ranking) in most Western societies is becoming less important, and a desire for disorder (i.e., low power distance or authority ranking) in the tourism experience is becoming more important. McIntosh and Goeldner (1990) described that Western tourists do not feel inhibited about what to wear and how to behave when on holiday. For example, opportunities for unplanned action, and freedom from institutionalized regulations are distinctive characteristics of the Western tourists. On the other hand, people in collectivistic cultures think of themselves less as individuals and more as being members of some group. A long vacation away from the group means painful separation and a danger to psychic well being. Group interaction, which is closely associated with dependence on others to provide satisfaction in the experience, is also an important component of the tourism experience.

Nonetheless, the popular motivation theories in the U.S. tourism management literature are expectancy theory (Vroom, 1964) and hierarchy of human needs (Maslow, 1943). To specify, Parrinello (1993) and Gnoth (1997) have studied tourism motivation in terms of expectation and anticipation, which see people as pulled by the expectancy of outcomes, mostly consciously. The expectancy theory of motivation has been refined and expanded by Deci (1975) and Deci and Ryan (1987). According to Deci and Ryan (1987), motivation is formed by autonomous initiation or self-determination of behavior and is expected to lead to personally satisfying experiences. Consistent with this theory, Iso-Ahola (1 982) suggests that novelty-seeking and escaping are the basic motivational dimensions of travel behavior. And Cohen (1972) suggests that all tourist roles can be based on a typology of several distinct novelty-seeking experience levels. In a subsequent work. Bello and Etzel (1985) have well documented the importance of "novelty" to the tourism experience.

Novelty-seeking has something to do with the cultural dimension of high individualism, combined with fairly high masculinity and low uncertainty avoidance, which corresponds with the U.S. pattern. This explains the popularity in expectancy theories of motivation. Cultures high in collectivism often have very clear norms for proper behavior in social situations and avoid new situations with no clear norms. Evidently, Philipp (1994) found that there is a racial difference between black and white Americans in seeking novelty in their tourism preferences. In his findings. whites are significantly more likely than blacks to agree with the statement" When I travel I like to be on streets I don't know" and "When I travel I like to stay at motels and hotels which I have never heard about." Although Philipp (1994) considers the main reason to be a preconception of the possibility of prejudice and discrimination in unfamiliar settings, it implies that there are differences of cultural characteristics in their motivation.

The combination of high individualism, low uncertainty avoidance, and masculinity in the United States explains the theory of Maslow's hierarchy of human needs (Maslow, 1943). Maslow's highest category, self-actualization, is highly individualistic. Pearce and Caltabiano (1983) explored a travel motivation applied by Maslow's hierarchy of human needs. Moreover, Dann (1977) examined "anomie" and "ego-enhancement" with respect to tourism motivation. Anomie. according to Dann, represents the desire to transcend the feeling of isolation inherent in everyday life and to simply "get away from it all." Ego-enhancement, on the other hand, derived from the need for recognition, which is obtained through the status given by travel. Markus and Kitayama (1991) maintain that the self-enhancement value is primarily a Western phenomenon. In a collectivistic society, other-enhancement is more desirable than self-enhancement, because the latter risks isolating the individual from the network of reciprocal relationships. Markus and Kitayama argue that individualistic formulations of self-values, such as expectancy motivation, self-actualization as well as self-emotions (e.g., shame, guilt, pride) need modification when considered in the context of the interdependent self-paradigm (collectivism).

RESEARCH QUESTIONS

The cultural characteristics and identity lead to the development of research questions concerning the relationship of cultural attitudes to tourist motivation. The general research questions for this study were:

1. Anglo-American and Japanese tourists show different cultural attitudes. (i.e., Anglo-Americans tend to express a high individualism, while Japanese tourists tend to express a high collectivism).
2. Anglo-American and Japanese tourists express different motivations in their travel behaviors.
3. Seven cultural attitudes, including composite measures of individualism and collectivism have relationships with five dimensions of tourist motivation.

METHODS

A self-administered questionnaire was used to collect data from two international airports in the United States and Japan during the month of February,

1998. Data were collected from 165 Anglo-American and 209 Japanese tourists at two international airports in Los Angeles, CA, U.S, and Tokyo, Japan during the month of February 1998. The survey was conducted during morning, afternoon, and evening periods in order to improve the representativeness of the sample. International tourists who completed the check-in process were approached by the interviewers and asked if they were traveling for pleasure. Those who indicated a purpose of travel other than pleasure were identified and excluded from further consideration. Pleasure travelers were then asked to participate in the survey. Upon agreeing to participate, tourists were given a questionnaire to fill out. A convenient sampling technique was employed due to the limitations of time. However, the demographic profile of this sample corresponds with the population of actual tourists in gender and age.

Table 1 contains the frequencies and percentage distributions of Anglo-American and Japanese respondents on the demographic variables of gender, marital status, age, and level of education. Approximately half of the Japanese respondents were male (54.5%) and half were female (45.5%). According to Japan National Tourist Organization (1997), 51.8% of actual Japanese overseas pleasure travelers (international travelers) were male and 48.2% were female. Japanese respondents were mainly between the ages of 25 and 44(59.9%). In this sample, the age group of 25 to 44 was over-represented and the age group of 45 to 64 was under-represented. Actual percentage of those groups were 41.8% and 30.9% respectively (JNTO, 1997). Approximately half of the Japanese respondents were single (47.3%) and half were married (51.2%), while others comprise the remaining 1.5%. The majority of Japanese respondents (59.2%) reported an education level of college degree or higher.

Anglo-American tourists closely approximate a cross-section of the population of American overseas tourists in terms of demographic characteristics. Females comprised 34% of respondents (approximately 38% of the U.S. resident overseas travelers). According to 1996 Survey of International Air Travelers (Travel Industries, 1998), 46% of the U.S. resident overseas travelers were between the ages of 25 to 44. In this study, 50% of respondents were between the ages of 25 to 44.

Twenty-seven percent of respondents were high school graduates. Approximately 60% of respondents had graduated from college or had either an advanced or professional degree. More than 50% of the U.S. resident overseas travelers had college, advanced or professional degrees.

Half the respondents said they were married, 47% said they were single, 2% said they were divorced or separated, and less than 1% said they were widowed. These proportions are very similar to those for the U.S. resident overseas travelers.

TABLE 1. Socio-Demographic Characteristics of Respondents

	Anglo-American Tourists		Japanese Tourists	
	Number	%	Number	%
Gender				
Male	108	65.9	114	54.5
Female	56	34.1	95	45.5
Age				
18 years old or younger	7	4.4	10	4.8
19 to 24 years old	21	13.0	37	17.9
25 to 44 years old	81	50.3	124	59.9
45 to 64 years old	21	13.0	27	13.0
65 years old or older	31	19.3	9	4.4
Marital Status				
Single	77	47.2	98	47.3
Married	81	49.7	106	51.2
Divorced	4	2.5	2	1.0
Widowed	1	0.6	1	0.5
Level of Education				
High school	42	27.1	36	17.9
Some college	4	2.6	13	6.5
College student	14	9.0	33	16.4
College graduate	64	41.3	78	38.8
Some graduate school	4	2.6	5	2.5
A graduate degree or higher	27	17.4	36	17.9

For Japanese tourists, the questionnaire was translated into Japanese. The process of translation was very carefully done, adopting the method of "back translation." Bilinguals were asked to translate English passages into Japanese language, and then other bilinguals (working independently) translated back to English. The two versions were compared for the successful translation.

The questionnaire for this study was constructed in two parts: the first part for measuring cultural construct of individualism and collectivism of subjects, and the second part for investigating differences of travel motivation within two cultural dimensions. The questionnaire for the first part of this paper was mainly based on individualism and collectivism scales (16 items) introduced by Triandis and his associates. The scale gives this paper validity and generalizability about cultural constructs of individualism and collectivism. The second part is the Tourist Motivation Scale (24 items), which is adapted and modified from Fodness's (1994) self-report scale to measure leisure travel motivation.

First, this paper compared Japanese and American tourists on cultural attitudes that reflect individualism and collectivism, and travel motivation. A multivariate analysis of variance (MANOVA) design was formulated to test differences between the groups with regard to attitudes toward two cultural dimensions and motivation toward tourism. Two sets of dependent variables were included: (a) cultural dimensions, including two composite measures of individualistic and collectivistic attitudes, which were factor analyzed; and (b) motivation variables toward tourism explored by factor analysis. The independent variables consisted of two levels: Anglo-American and Japanese tourists. Second, this study investigated relationships of travel motivation and two cultural contexts. Intercorrelation matrices among all the variables were computed.

RESULTS

The 16-item INDCOL scale that reflects individualism and collectivism was factor analyzed. When a principal factor analysis was computed within each culture and varimax rotation was used, the individualism and collectivism were found to be analyzable into four factors. Individualism consists of three factors: self-reliance, emotional detachment, and separation from in-groups. Collectivism has two factors: family integrity and social interdependence. The five factors are orthogonal to one another. While previous studies (Hofstede, 1980; Triandis, McCusker, and Hui, 1990) yielded four factors instead of five factors, this instrument appears to have moderately high convergent validity since this paper had relatively high alpha reliability coefficients of .76.

Table 2 shows that the alpha reliability coefficients for the five factors were: .75 for social interdependence, .71 for self-reliance, .70 for family integrity, .69 for separation from in-groups, and .62 for emotional detachment. The total variance explained was 61.1%.

Next, this paper identified five dimensions of travel motivation within two culture, computing principal component factor analysis: knowledge, prestige/status, family togetherness, novelty, and escape. Principle component factors with an eigenvalue of one or greater were rotated by varimax analysis. As can be seen in Table 3, the five extracted motivation factors explained 64.9% of the total variance, of which "knowledge" explained 31.9%, "prestige/status" explained 12.2%, "family togetherness" explained 8.4%, "novelty" explained 6.8%, and "escape" explained 5.5%.

Table 3 also presents Cronbach' s alphas for each travel motivation factor and shows that they varied from a high of .88 (first factor) to a low of .65 (fifth factor). The five factors had relatively high coefficients of internal consistency.

To compare the Anglo-American and Japanese tourists on cultural attitudes and travel motivations, MANOVA was tested. Then correlational anal-

TABLE 2. Items Loading on Same Factor in Cultural Attitudes of Individualism and Collectivism

Factors and Items	Factor Loading	Mean	S.D.
Factor 1: Social Interdependence (α = .746)			
16. One does better working in a group than alone	.81	3.3	1.5
11. When faced with a difficult personal problem, one should consult one's friends and relatives widely	.67	3.2	1.3
5. One of the pleasures of life is to be related interdependently with others	.65	2.9	1.6
3. I like to live close to my good friends	.60	3.0	1.6
1. I would help within my means if a relative told me that he or she is in financial difficulties	.57	3.0	1.6
(Eigenvalue = 5.0463 Variance Explained = 20.0%)			
Factor 2: Self-Reliance (α = .714)			
15. It is important to me that I perform better than others	.78	4.2	1.6
14. I tend to do my own thing and most people in my family do the same	.69	4.9	1.5
10. The most important thing in my life is to make myself happy	.62	5.3	1.6
6. What happens to me is my own doing	.55	4.2	1.6
(Eigenvalue = 2.9962 Variance Explained = 13.5%)			
Factor 3: Family Integrity (α = .703)			
9. Aging parents should live at home with their children	.74	3.2	1.7
6. Children should live at home with parents until they get married	.63	5.9	3.5
13. One of the pleasures of life is to feel being part of a large group of people.	.59	4.2	1.9
(Eigenvalue = 1.5441 Variance Explained = 10.2%)			
Factor 4: Separation from In-Groups (α = .691)			
2. When faced with difficult personal problems, it is better to decide what to do yourself rather than follow the advice of others	.78	4.9	1.5
8. I would struggle through a personal problem by myself rather than discuss it with my friends.	.62	4.6	1.7
(Eigenvalue = 1.3099 Variance Explained = 9.5%)			
Factor 5: Emotional Detachment (α .= 621)			
12. One should live one's life independently of others as much as possible	.68	5.0	1.5
4. It does not matter to me how my country is viewed in the eyes of other nations	.53	2.8	1.7
(Eigenvalue = 1.0588 Variance Explained = 7.9%)			
Total Variance Explained = 61.1%			

TABLE 3. Items Loading on Same Factor in Travel Motivation

Factors and Items	Factor Loading	Mean	S.D.
Factor 1: Knowledge (α = .8843)			
7. To experience custom, culture, and nature different from those in my own environment	.82	5.87	1.35
8. To explore new things	.82	5.69	1.42
17. To learn new culture and custom	.80	5.56	1.34
6. To expand my interest	.70	5.84	1.30
19. To meet new and different people	.65	4.79	1.57
16. To learn about things around me	.64	5.06	1.53
14. To interact with others	.59	4.46	1.72
23. To satisfy my curiosity	.54	5.43	1.49
15. To learn about myself	.51	4.60	1.72
(Eigenvalue = 7.3452 Variance Explained 31.9%)			
Factor 2: Prestige/Status (α = .8602)			
10. To gain others' respect	.83	2.22	1.51
22. To reveal my thoughts, feelings, or physical skills to others	.81	2.94	1.64
13. To influence others	.78	2.56	1.59
3. To demonstrate my ability to travel	.77	2.60	1.55
24. To share what I have learned with others	.57	3.96	1.59
9. To gain a feeling of belonging	.56	3.25	1.59
(Eigenvalue = 2.7991 Variance Explained = 12.2%)			
Factor 3: Family Togetherness (α = .7841)			
1. To bring my family closer together	.85	4.57	1.59
4. To do something with my family	.85	4.62	1.72
18. To make things more meaningful to my family	.68	4.11	1.83
(Eigenvalue = 1.9246 Variance Explained = 8.4%)			
Factor 4: Novelty (α = .6822)			
11. To experience something different from my ordinary life	.72	4.33	2.06
12. To have a chance for something unexpected to happen	.71	4.26	1.88
(Eigenvalue = 1.5748 Variance Explained = 6.8%)			
Factor 5: Escape (α = .6089)			
5. To escape from my ordinary life	.74	5.87	1.20
20. To reduce tension, anxiety, and frustration	.66	4.85	1.66
21. To relieve boredom	.59	4.61	1.77
(Eigenvalue = 1.2762 Variance Explained = 5.5%)			

Total Variance Explained = 64.9%

ysis was utilized to examine and compare the relationships of travel motivation with the cultural dimensions expressed within the two different cultural contexts. In a MANOVA test, the dependent variables were seven cultural attitudes, including two composite measures of individualism and collectivism, and five types of travel motivation. The five cultural attitude variables included scores of self-reliance, separation from in-groups; emotional detachment, family integrity, and social interdependence. The five travel motivation variables were: knowledge, prestige/status, family togetherness, novelty, and escape. The independent variable contrasted the two cultural groups, Japanese and American tourists. The multivariate test for effects of groups was significant (Wilks' V = .409, F = 39.97, p < .000). Because the multivariate test revealed significant difference between Japanese and American tourists, the corresponding univariate F-tests were further performed to investigate which variables contributed to the overall multivariate significance.

Means and standard deviations of seven cultural attitudes, including the composite measures of individualism and collectivism. For Anglo and Japanese tourists and the results of univariate F-test are shown respectively in Table 4 and Table 5. Findings in Table 5 indicate that Anglo-American and Japanese tourists differed significantly on "separation from in-groups," "emotional detachment," "family integrity," and "social interdependence." There was no significant group difference on the variable of "self-reliance." This result reveals that Japanese culture represents traits of collectivism, while American culture is characterized by individualism. The findings are also important in understanding Japanese tourists' collectivism, because group harmony bolstered by healthy interpersonal relationships among in-group members is an important ingredient of collectivism (Triandis, 1990).

Means and standard deviations of five dimensions of travel motivation [or Anglo-American and Japanese tourists are displayed in Table 6. Means of knowledge, prestige/status, and family togetherness variables for Japanese tourists are bigger than those for Anglo-American tourists, while means of novelty and escape variables for Anglo-American tourists are bigger than means of the same factors in travel motivation for Japanese tourists.

The univariate comparisons of travel motivations between Anglo-American and Japanese tourists are given in Table 7. There were no significant differences in two dimensions of travel motivation: knowledge and escape. However, two groups differed significantly on travel motivation toward prestige/status, family togetherness, and novelty. Japanese tourists manifested more favorable feeling toward family togetherness and prestige/status than Anglo-American tourists did. Anglo-American tourists expressed more motivation toward novelty than Japanese tourists did. It implies that Japanese tourists demonstrated collectivism in expressing their travel motivation, while Anglos exhibited individualistic characteristics.

TABLE 4. Means and Standard Deviations of Five Cultural Attitude Variables for Anglo-American and Japanese Tourists

Cultural Attitudes	Anglo-American Tourists (N = 165)		Japanese Tourists (N = 209)	
	Mean	S.D.	Mean	S.D.
Self-reliance	20.64	3.55	19.92	5.46
Separation from in-groups	9.59	2.13	8.51	8.99
Emotional detachment	8.90	2.19	6.73	2.11
Individualism composite	**39.13**	**5.08**	**35.16**	**6.85**
Family integrity	12.25	3.19	15.36	2.77
Social interdependence	17.58	3.49	21.43	3.04
Collectivism composite	**29.83**	**5.57**	**36.79**	**4.87**

TABLE 5. Univariate Analysis of Anglo-American and Japanese Tourists on Seven Cultural Attitudes

Variance Source	MS	F	P-value
Self-reliance	48.30	2.173	.141
Separation from in-groups	107.94	23.593	.000***
Emotional detachment	434.07	94.280	.000***
Individualism composite	1457.23	38.802	.000***
Family integrity	892.04	101.638	.000***
Social interdependence	1365.87	129.837	.000***
Collectivism composite	4465.54	165.687	.000***

Pearson correlations between total two cultural dimensions of individualism and collectivism and five dimensions of travel motivation are identified in Table 8. When it compared five factors of travel motivation with seven factors of cultural dimensions, this paper found that the "collectivism composite" is significantly and positively correlated to all variables of knowledge, prestige/status, and family togetherness in dimensions of motivation. while the "individualism composite" is significantly and positively related to variables of novelty and escape. More specifically, self-reliance in cultural attitudes is positively correlated to novelty and escape in travel motivation. Separation from in-groups is negatively related to knowledge and novelty in travel motivation. Emotional detachment is negatively related to knowledge,

TABLE 6. Means and Standard Deviations of Five Travel Motivation Variables for Anglo-American and Japanese Tourists

Travel Motivation	Anglo-American Tourists (N = 165)		Japanese Tourists (N = 209)	
	Mean	S.D.	Mean	S.D.
Knowledge	46.47	10.44	47.60	9.27
Prestige/status	16.38	7.32	18.39	7.09
Family togetherness	12.15	4.60	14.16	3.81
Novelty	9.21	3.26	7.79	3.50
Escape	15.42	3.65	14.93	3.59

TABLE 7. Univariate Analysis of Anglo-American and Japanese Tourists on Five Travel Motivations

Variance Source	MS	F	P-value
Knowledge	115.405	1.201	.274
Prestige/status	370.753	7.174	.008**
Family togetherness	365.861	20.995	.000***
Novelty	184.647	16.278	.000***
Escape	22.111	1.684	.195

prestige/status, family togetherness, and novelty. Family integrity is positively correlated to prestige/status and family togetherness. Finally, social interdependence in cultural attitudes is positively related to three motivation variables, including knowledge, prestige/status, and family togetherness.

DISCUSSION

This paper examined cultural differences between Japanese and American tourists with respect to cultural attitudes that reflect individualism and collectivism, and travel motivation. A further analysis was to investigate relationships of travel motivation within two cultural contexts. Results from this study suggest that the two cultures do differ with regard to specific attitudes. Also, certain aspects of travel motivation are strongly correlated to two cultural dimensions.

First, five cultural attitude dimensions in this study were examined, in-

TABLE 8. Pearson Correlation of Five Travel Motivations with Cultural Attitudes for Anglo-American Tourists

Variables	Knowledge	Prestige/ Status	Family Togetherness	Novelty	Escape
Self-reliance	.071	.164*	.064	.216*	.122*
Separation from in-groups	−.110*	.037	.077	−.129*	−.069
Emotional detachment	−.134*	−.116*	−.157*	−.218*	−.058
Individualism composite	−.035	.017	.088	.242*	.290*
Family integrity	.074	.152*	.408*	.044	.030
Social interdependence	.205*	.210*	.315*	.034	.093
Collectivism composite	.164*	.208*	.409*	−.302*	−.126*

cluding self-reliance, separation from in-groups, emotional detachment, family integrity, and social interdependence. Among these dimensions, Anglo-American tourists showed more preference for separation from in-groups and emotional detachment than Japanese tourists did. Japanese tourists expressed more cultural attitudes toward interdependence and family integrity. The findings manifest there is cultural difference between Anglo-American and Japanese tourists in terms of individualism and collectivism. Individualism emphasizes "I" consciousness autonomy, emotional independence, pleasure seeking and universalism. Collectivism, on the other hand, stress "we" consciousness, collective identity, and emotional interdependence, solidarity, sharing, and particularism (Hofstede, 1980).

Second, in an examination of travel motivation within two cultural contexts Japanese and American tourists differ in prestige/status, family togetherness, and novelty, while they are insignificantly different in knowledge and escape. This paper found that Japanese tourists tends to show more collectivistic characteristics in seeking travel motivation, while American tourists tends to show more individualistic characteristics.

In fact, the group difference between Japanese and American tourists was not bigger in two cultural contexts than would be expected. It seems that a plausible explanation may be that individualist and collectivist orientations coexist within Japanese and American culture. In particular, due to increased exposure to Western cultural influences, the Japanese appear to be moving toward a more individualistic society. For example, the young Japanese people have contributed greatly to the cultural changes of the past 10 years. These children of the affluent society prefer enjoying life to working hard. Loyalty not to a business company but to their own interests is their motivating force. The desire of the young for self-realization and individualism or privatism has made an undeniable impact on the life-styles of Japanese adults as well.

This fact will be explained by two psychological dimensions of allocentrism and idiocentrism. It is likely that a majority of people in collectivist cultures will be allocentrics and a majority in individualistic cultures will be idiocentrics. It implies that within one culture, there are various social worlds, which refers to a culture space in which people and organizations orient their behavior in some identifiable way (Sibutani, 1955). Thus, this study should be expanded to investigate these two psychological dimensions of allocentrism and idioncentrism at each cultural dimension, collectivism or individualism.

Understanding of cultural differences in tourist motivation across cultures may enhance both efficiency and effectiveness in international tourism management. Furthermore, within the tourism managers' understandings about different culture may encourage more participation of diverse cultural groups in their tourism facilities. Tourism management practices dealing with tourism resources should embrace a wider range of users and their cultural values, preferences, and behavior, looking beyond Western cultural boundaries. Crompton and Lamb (1986) argue that people within one target market may vary in their predisposition to use service offerings. An old aphorism among research chemists quoted by Crompton and Lamb," Those who understand the barriers will make the breakthrough," is equally applicable to utilization of tourism services by certain cultural groups. An understanding of groups' cultural orientations (i.e., individualism and collectivism) may facilitate this new perspective.

REFERENCES

Adleman, I. & Morris, C. T. (1967). *Society, Politics and Economic Development: Quantitative Approach*. Baltimore: John Hopkins University Press.

Bakan, D. (1966). *The Duality of Human Existence*. Chicago: Rand McNally.

Bello, D. C. & Etzel, M. J. (1985). The role of novelty in the pleasure travel experience. *Journal of Travel Research*, 24, 20-26.

Berry, J. W. (1976). *Human ecology and cognitive style: Comparative studies in cultural and psychological adaptation*. New York: Halsted.

Bond, M. H. & Forgas, J. P. (1984). Linking person perception to behavior intention across culture: The role of cultural collectivism. *Journal of Cross-cultural Psychology*, 15, 337-352.

Cohen, E. (1972). Towards a sociology of international tourism. *Social Research*, 39, 164-182.

Crompton, J. L. & Lamb, C.W. (1986). *Marketing Government and Social Services.* New York: John Wiley & Sons.

Dann, M. S. (1977). Anomie, ego-enhancement and tourism. *Annals of Tourism Research,* 4 (4), 184-194.

Deci, E. L. (1975). *Intrinsic motivation.* New York: Plenum Press.

Deci, E. L. & Ryan, R. M. (1987). The support of autonomy and the control of behavior. *Journal of Personality and Social Psychology,* 53, 1024-1037.

Durkheim, E. (1930). *The division of labor in society.* Glencoe, IL: Free Press.

Fondness, D. (1994). Measuring tourist motivation. *Annals of Tourism Research,* 21, 555-581.

Gnoth, J. (1997). Tourism motivation and expectation formation. *Annals of Tourism Research,* 24 (2), 283-304.

Hamaguchi, E. (1977). *"Nihonrashisa" no saihakken.* Tokyo: Nihon Keizai Shinbunsha.

Hamaguchi, E. (1982). Nihonteki shudan shugi towa nanika. In IF. Hamaguchi & S. Kumon (Ed.), *Nihonteki shudan shugi.* Tokyo: Yuhikau.

Herzberg, F., Mausner, B. & Snyderman, B. (1959). *The motivation to work.* New York: John Wiley.

Hofstede. G. (1980). *Culture's Consequences: International Differences in WorkRrelated Values.* Beverly Hills. CA: Sage.

Hogan, R. & Emler. N. (1978). The biases in contemporary social psychology. *Social Research,* 45, 478-534.

Hsu, F. L. K. (1983). *Rugged individualism reconsidered.* Knoxville: University of Tennessee Press.

Hui, C. H. & Triandis, H. C. (1986). Individualism-collectivism: A study of cross-cultural researchers. *Journal of Cross-cultural Psychology,* 17, 225-248.

Inkeles, A. & Smith, D. H. (1974). *Becoming modern: Individual change in six developing countries.* Cambridge, MA: Harvard University Press.

Iso-Ahola, S. E. (1982). Towards a social psychology theory of tourism motivation: A rejoinder. *Annals of Tourism Research,* 9, 256-262.

Japanese National Tourist Organization (1997). *Annual Japan Tourism Statistics.* JNTO.

Kluckhohn, F. & Strodtbeck, F. (1961). *Variations in Value Orientations.* Evanston, IL: Row Peterson.

Kohlberg, L. (1969). Stage and sequence: The cognitive-developmental approach to socialization. In D.A. Goslin (Ed.), *Handbook of Socialization theory and research.* Chicago, IL: Rand McNally.

Leung, K. (1989). Cross-cultural differences: Individual-level vs. cultural level analysis. *International Journal of Psychology,* 24, 703-719.

Markus, H. & Kitayama, S. (1991). Culture and the self: Implications for cognition, emotion, and motivation. *Psychological Review,* 98, 224-253.

Maslow, A. H. (1943). A theory of human motivation. *Psychological Review,* 50, 370-396.

McClelland, D. C. (1965). Achievement motivation can be developed. *Harvard Business Review,* 43 (6) 6-24 and 178.

McIntosh, R. & Goeldner, C. (1990). *Tourism: Principles, Practices, Philosophies.* New York: John Wiley & Sons. Inc.

Miller, J. G., Bersoff, D. M. & Harwood R. L. (1990). Perceptions of social responsibilities in India and the United States: Moral imperatives or personal decisions? *Journal of Personality and Social Psychology*, 58, 33-47.

Parrinello, G. L. (1993). Motivation and anticipation in post-industrial tourism. *Annals of Tourism Research*, 20, 233-249.

Parsons, T. & Shils, E. A. (1951). Values, motives, and systems of action. In T. Parsons & E. A. Shils (Ed.), *Toward a general theory of action*. Cambridge, MA: Harvard University Press.

Pearce, P. L. & Caltabiano, M. L. (1983). Inferring travel motivations from travelers' experience. *Journal of Travel Research*, 3, 16-20.

Philipp, S. F. (1994). Race and tourism choice: A legacy of discrimination? *Annals of Tourism Research*, 21 (3), 479-488.

Rosenthal, D. A. & Bornholt, L. (1988). Expectations about development in Greek-and Anglo-Australian families. *Journal of Cross-cultural Psychology*. 19, 19-34.

Rotter, J. B. (1966). Generalized expectations for internal vs. external locus of reinforcement. *Psychology Monographs*, 80 (1, Whole No. 609).

Schwartz, S. H. (1990). Individualism-collectivism: Critique and proposed refinements. *Journal of Cross-cultural Psychology*, 21, 139-157.

Schwartz, S. H. & Bilsky, W. (1990). Toward a theory of the universal content and structure of values: Extensions and cross-cultural replications. *Journal of Personality and Social Psychology*, 58, 878-891.

Shibutani, T. (1955). Reference groups as perspectives. *American Journal of Sociology*, 60, 562-568.

Shweder, R. A. & Bourne, E. J. (Ed.). (1982). *Does the concept of the person vary cross-culturally*? New York: Reidel.

Taylor, C. (1989). *Sources of the self: The making of modern identity*. Cambridge, MA: Harvard University Press.

Tonnis, (1887). *Community and society*. New York: Harper & Row.

Tourism Industries (1998). *1996 Profile of U.S. resident travelers visiting overseas destinations-outbound reported from: Survey of international air travelers (IFS)*. Trade Development, International Trade Administration, U.S. Department of Commerce.

Triandis, Il. C. (Ed.). (1988). *Cross-cultural contributions to theory in social psychology*. Newbury Park: Sage.

Triandis, H. C. (1990). Cross-cultural Studies of Individualism and Collectivism. In J.Berman (Ed.), Nebraska Symposium on Motivation (pp. 41-133). Lincoln: University of Nebraska Press.

Triandis, H. C. & Vassiliou, V. (1972). A comparative analysis of subjective culture. In H. C. Triandis (Ed.), *The analysis of subjective culture*. New York: Wiley.

Triandis, H. C., McCusker, C. & Hui, C. H. (1990). Multimethod probes of individualism and collectivism. *Journal of Personality and Social Psychology*, 59, 1006-1020.

Vroom, V. H. (1964). *Work and Motivation*. New York: John Wiley & Sons.

Waterman, A. S. (1984). *The psychology of individualism*. New York: Praeger.

Weber, M. (1947). *The Protestant ethic and the spirit of capitalism*. New York: Scribneis.

Travel-Related Behavior
of Japanese Leisure Tourists:
A Review and Discussion

Connie Mok

Terry Lam

SUMMARY. Japan has emerged as a leading generator of international tourism in the past decade. Given the importance of Japanese tourists to the global tourism industry, understanding of their travel-related behavior has become an essential item in the tourism research agenda. A review of literature revealed that a number of studies related to various aspects of Japanese tourists' behavior was reported. However, these studies did not follow any systematic themes of research and the information generated by these studies has not been well conceptualized. Therefore, this paper aims to present a comprehensive review of the literature which pertains to the travel-related behavior of Japanese leisure tourists and to conceptualize the major behavioral attributes and findings of reported research. *[Article copies available for a fee from The Haworth Document Delivery Service: 1-800-342-9678. E-mail address: <getinfo@haworthpressinc. com> Website: <http://www.haworthpressinc.com>]*

KEYWORDS. Japanese tourists, travel behavior, cross-cultural differences

---

Connie Mok is Associate Professor, Conrad N. Hilton College of Hotel and Restaurant Management, University of Houston, 4800 Calhoun Street, Houston, TX 77204-3902 (E-mail: cmok@UH.EDU). Terry Lam is Lecturer, Department of Hotel & Tourism Management, The Hong Kong Polytechnic University, Hunghom, Kowloon, Hong Kong.

[Haworth co-indexing entry note]: "Travel-Related Behavior of Japanese Leisure Tourists: A Review and Discussion." Mok, Connie, and Terry Lam. Co-published simultaneously in *Journal of Travel & Tourism Marketing* (The Haworth Hospitality Press, an imprint of The Haworth Press, Inc.) Vol. 9, No. 1/2, 2000, pp. 171-184; and: *Japanese Tourists: Socio-Economic, Marketing and Psychological Analysis* (ed: K. S. (Kaye) Chon, Tsutomu Inagaki, and Taiji Ohashi) The Haworth Hospitality Press, an imprint of The Haworth Press, Inc., 2000, pp. 171-184. Single or multiple copies of this article are available for a fee from The Haworth Document Delivery Service [1-800-342-9678, 9:00 a.m. - 5:00 p.m. (EST). E-mail address: getinfo@haworthpressinc.com].

INTRODUCTION

Japan, which is slightly smaller than the state of California, is one of the most densely populated countries in the world. Its population (125 million) is almost one-half of the United States (Nishiyama, 1996). During the 1980s, Japan achieved the highest growth in the world in outbound international tourism (Ahmed and Krohn, 1992), and became recognized as Asia's leading generator of international tourism (Polunin, 1989; Murakami & Go, 1990; Cha, McCleary, & Uysal, 1995). In the early 1990s, the number of Japanese who traveled abroad exceeded 10 million per year (see Table 1). The downturn in Japan's economy in the last few years may have taken the boom out of the travel market but it hasn't exactly turned it into a bust. In both 1996 and 1997, the Japan National Tourist Organization (JNTO) (1998) reported over 16 million outbound Japanese tourists. In 1995, Cha, McCleary, and Uysal reported major causes for the boom in Japan's out bound travel market. These causes included: Japan's strong and stable economy, the strength of the yen, increasing allowances on the amount of foreign currency for tourist use, change of lifestyles, the contemplated reduction in work hours causing people to explore recreation facilities, overseas investment in the hospitality industry, and the deregulation of the Japanese airline industry in 1986.

Ahmed and Krohn (1992) lamented that "Serving Japanese tourists sometimes poses severe problems for domestic suppliers of tourism products due to differences in expectations, ideologies, perspectives, and visions of Japanese clients" (p. 75). Japanese tourists have been characterized by their unique travel behavior (Sternberg, 1993). In all the great cities of the world, one can see large groups of obedient Japanese tourists, cameras slung around their necks following a flag-bearing tour leader from duty free shop to famous site to hotel and back home. Given the importance of Japanese tourists to the global tourism industry, understanding of their travel-related behavior has become an essential item in tourism research agenda. The goal of a behavior analysis approach to travel studies is to understand the psychological motives of an individual traveler which influence various travel-related decisions and the level of satisfaction with destination region (Chon, 1989). A review of the literature revealed that a number of studies related to various aspects of Japanese tourists' behavior was reported. However, these studies did not follow

TABLE 1. Outbound Tourism from Japan

	1964	1969	1974	1979	1984	1989	1994	1995	1996
Japanese outbound travelers	127,749	492,880	2,335,530	4,038,298	4,658,833	9,662,752	13,578,934	15,298,125	16,691,769

Source: Japan National Tourist Organization, 1998; Travel Journal, 1994: 242

any systematic themes of research and the information generated by these studies has not been well conceptualized. Thus, the aim of this paper is three-fold. First, this article presents a comprehensive review of the literature which pertains to the travel-related behavior of Japanese leisure tourists. Second, based on the findings of the literature review, major behavioral attributes are conceptualized; and third, recommendations are made for future research.

A REVIEW OF LITERATURE

The growth of Japanese outbound tourism in the last decade has sparked considerable interests among travel and tourism researchers to study the travel-related behavior of Japanese tourists. A comprehensive review of the literature on travel-related behavior of Japanese tourists was conducted in early 1998 and the key behavioral attributes and findings are summarized in Table 2. The literature reviewed reported findings which could be conceptualized into the following behavioral attributes:

1. preferred destinations
2. travel motivation
3. preferred activities at destinations
4. travel mode
5. length of stay
6. tourist photography
7. shopping
8. vacation planning

Findings related to these attributes are reported in the following section.

Preferred Destinations

A number of studies investigated Japanese tourists' preferred destinations. Morris (1988) and Polunin (1989) studied the boom in Japanese international travel and reported that the Japanese have become more leisure and service oriented. Morris (1990) summarized a selection of data from numerous Japanese consumer surveys, and concluded that Japanese travelers preferred places with natural scenery and good beaches, as well as cities rich in historical spots and modern culture. Good shopping and 'crime free' reputations are extremely important to them. Dybka (1988) concluded from the findings of his joint Canada-U.S. study that an ideal overseas destination for the Japanese would combine the main elements that make for an enjoyable touring-type experience which included sightseeing in cities, shopping, dining out, guided tours, and visiting scenic landmarks. Sheldon and Fox (1988) con-

TABLE 2. Behavioral Attributes of Japanese Leisure Tourists

Attribute	Literature Reviewed	• Major Findings
Preferred Destinations	Morris (1988), Dybka (1988), Sheldon and Fox (1988), Polunin (1989) Murakami and Go (1990), Morris (1990), Picola (1992), Nozawa (1992), Jansen-Verbeke (1994), Focus Japan (1994), JNTO (1994).	• Popular destinations: USA, Hawaii, Hong Kong, South Korea, Australia, Canada, Europe. • Destination choices influenced by demographic factors and travel motives. • More leisure and service oriented. • Safety conscious about destinations. • Preferred places with natural scenery, good beaches, historical spots, modern culture, and good shopping. • Destination choice influenced by existing dining facilities.
Travel Motivations	Woodside and Jacobs (1985), Cha, McCleary and Uysal (1995).	• Relaxation and rest were major motivations. • Honeymoon was also cited as important motivation. • Push factors were relaxation, knowledge, adventure, travel bragging, family, sports.
Preferred Activities at Destinations	Lin (1990), Ahmed and Krohn (1992), Lang, O'Leary and Morrison (1993), Jansen-Verbeke (1994), Iverson (1997b).	• Preferred activities by market segments: "office ladies" were attracted to shopping; "silver market" were generally passive and avoided outdoor recreation activities. • Five distinct activity-sets were found: outdoor sports, sightseeing, life-seeing, activity combo, naturalist. • Playing golf at overseas destinations.
Travel Mode	USTTA (1987), The Economist (1988), Ahmed and Krohn (1992), Nazawa (1992), Lang, O'Leary and Morrison (1993), Stemberg (1993), Jansen-Verbeke (1994), Dace (1995), Carlile (1996), Pizam, Jansen-Verbeke, and Steel (1997).	• Traveling mostly in groups by joining package tours because of cultural value for collectivism. • Attitude towards package tours slowly changing when Japanese travel market becomes more mature.
Length of Stay	The Economist (1988), Kurokawa (1990), Nazawa (1992), Lang, O'Leary and Morrison (1993), Jansen-Verbeke (1994), Carlile (1996).	• Preferred shorter stay in overseas destinations. • Length of stay influenced by age. • The short length of stay may be attributed to difficulty in taking holidays and long working hours.
Tourist Photography	Ahmed and Krohn (1992), Pizam, Jansen-Verbeke, and Steel (1997).	• Highly involved in photography at destinations. • Custom of *kinen shashin* or memorial photo to share with members of the collective.
Shopping	Grabum (1983), Moeran (1983), Dybka (1988), Keown (1989), Morris (1990), Bailey (1991), USTTA (1991), Ahmed and Krohn (1992), Nazawa (1992), Jansen-Verbeke (1994), Dace, (1995), Pizam, Jansen-Verbeke, and Steel (1997), HKTA (1998).	• Excessive love for shopping at destinations. • Big spenders, sophisticated, and clever shoppers. • Customs of *senbetsu-omiyage*.
Preferred Shopping Items	Morris (1988), Keown (1989), Jansen-Verbeke (1994).	• Interested in products of'ethnic', brand name, and high quality. • Drew up shopping list before departure. • Price conscious. • Shopping in duty/tax free stores, and gift shops. • Top six purchases: liquor, tobacco, cosmetics, chocolate, leather goods, clothing.
Vacation Planning	Iverson (1997a)	• Japanese tourists took longer time in vacation planning to avoid uncertainty.

ducted a survey to investigate the role of dining facilities in choosing vacation destinations on a cross-cultural basis, and found that Japanese were more strongly influenced by food services when choosing destinations than Americans and Canadians. These authors also reported that the Japanese were reluctant to try new cuisine, but strongly preferred "higher-end" restaurants.

Given the preferences of Japanese travelers as stated earlier, it is not surprising to find that the U.S., Hawaii, South Korea and Hong Kong were the preferred destinations (JNTO, 1994). Australia and Canada became most popular in recent years, followed by New Zealand and Switzerland. The UK, France and Italy were rated highly as desirable destinations for their 'historical,' 'major cities for sightseeing,' and 'folklore' tours (Morris, 1990). Due to geographical closeness to Japan, it appears that, besides Hong Kong, South Korea and Singapore, other Asian countries such as Taiwan, Thailand, and China have also become popular destinations for Japanese travelers (Picola, 1992). Table 3 summarizes the major destinations of Japanese outbound tourists from 1964 to 1994.

Focus Japan (1994) reported interesting observations on characteristics of Japanese tourists. Age and gender seemed to be related to destination choice. Middle-aged and elderly Japanese travelers favored Asian countries, while

TABLE 3. Major Destinations of Japanese Overseas Tourists

	1964	1969	1974	1979	1984	1989	1994	1995	1996
Asia									
China					386,169	358,828	1,141,200	1,305,190	1,548,849
(Hong Kong)	47,251	143,746	423,098	508,011	575,428	1,176,189	1,440,632	1,691,283	2,382,890
Macau		74,990	207,547	225,882	168,740	342,576	979,283	416,168	516,002
Malaysia	2,404		63,627	102,673	107,800	199,661	271,916	319,344	340,905
Philippines	7,478	16,101	150,939	253,717	160,109	215,634	277,825	323,199	350,242
Singapore		24,546	109,266	250,255	383,305	841,371	1,109,350	1,179,007	1,171,899
South Korea	2,280	31,381	299,756	649,707	576,394	1,379,523	1,644,097	1,667,203	1,526,559
Taiwan	21,519	143,624	438,911	695,575	632,481	96,4691	823,882	914,325	917,690
Thailand	15,237		132,660	203,333	221,945	555,638	691,705	814,706	931,111
Oceania									
Australia					87,884	349,600	721,100	782,673	813,113
New Zealand					41,888	97,922	148,162	151,543	165,014
Europe									
France			211,000	422,000	447,843	770,000	950,000	920,000	855,000
Germany	65,447	117,345	203,638	302,787	410,296	762,554	743,693	912,654	800,810
Italy		694,600	212,600	383,200	340,209	456,700	823,965	997,427	926,369
Switzerland	41,982	80,118	177,908	230,040	280,914	472,268	553,182	561,324	553,252
U.K.	22,800	59,100	148,000	140,000	200,600	504,800	578,000	619,000	595,000
North America									
Canada		18,525	77,543	158,582	162,246	387,000	481,300	591,200	650,100
U.S.	43,454	136,528	763,215	1,095,000	1,430,000	3,080,396	3,804,551	4,598,354	5,182,555
(Guam)			27,777	170,103	190,810	301,499	555,748	996,219	1,028,673
(Hawaii)		65,000	381,000	577,491	803,000	1,319,340	1,756,100	1,998,650	2,099,760

Source: Travel Journal, 1994: 229-230. Figures in the 1989 to 1996 columns are from Japan National Tourist Organization, 1998.

young single working women and housewives opted for the beaches of Hawaii, Guam, and Indonesia. Europe was also popular with elderly couples while honeymooners favored Australia and New Zealand. Leisure travelers accounted for about 85% of the Japanese outbound market, with business travel accounting for most of the remainder (Focus Japan, 1994).

Travel Motivation

Different segments of consumers may seek different benefits from using a product or service. Tourism research studies (Woodside and Pitts, 1976; Crompton, 1977) confirmed the proposition that travel-related benefits sought affect leisure travel behavior variables such as primary motivation for travel on vacation and choice of destinations. Two studies were reported in the tourism literature which were related to travel motivations of Japanese tourists. Woodside and Jacobs (1985) studied the benefits experienced by vacation tourists traveling to Hawaii, and found that 56% of their Japanese respondents reported rest and relaxation was a major purpose of their trips, while 12% stated 'honeymoon' as a trip purpose. Cha, McCleary, and Uysal (1995) attempted to study the travel motivations (push factors) of Japanese overseas travelers by using a factor-cluster market segmentation approach. Their study revealed six distinct motivation factors: relax, knowledge, adventure, travel bragging, family, and sports; and they were segmented into three groups: sports seekers, novelty seekers, and family/relaxation seekers. The first factor, 'relax,' included eight variables such as feeling at home away from home, escaping from the ordinary, and doing nothing at all. 'Knowledge' included six items, such as seeing and experiencing a foreign destination, seeing as much as possible, and learning new things or increasing knowledge. The third factor, 'adventure,' included five variables such as finding thrills or excitement, being daring and adventuresome, and safe or secure travel. 'Travel Bragging' is an interesting and unique factor which included three push items such as talking about a trip after returning home, going places friends have not been, and indulging in luxury. 'Family,' the fifth factor, included two items: visitation of friends or relatives and places family came from. The last factor, 'sports,' included three items: sports participation, sports watching, and physical activity.

Preferred Activities at Destinations

A number of studies focused on identifying Japanese tourists' preferred activities based on various market segments. Jansen-Verbeke (1994) reported preferred activities of the younger market. The younger market, which covered the age group 20 to 29, accounted for 13 percent of the Japanese population. About 28 percent of them traveled abroad. A unique subgroup which belonged to this age group was the so called 'office ladies.' These are single career business women in well-paid jobs. They traveled in groups, were highly attracted to shopping facilities, and adopt a specific life style. They preferred four-or five-star hotels and spent most time during their trip on shopping. Ahmed and Krohn (1992) reported preferred activities of the 'silver' market which accounted for 29 percent of the total Japanese population. This was the generation of 50 years and older and it included many retired people and experienced travelers. These older Japanese tourists were generally passive. They avoided participation in outdoor recreation activities in unfamiliar cultures. However, they liked to watch others engaging in recreation activities such as surfing, water skiing, canoeing, etc. Lang, O'Leary, and Morrison (1993) segmented female Japanese tourists based on activity-type through cluster analysis. It was found that there were five distinct activity-set clusters formed: outdoor sports, sightseeing, life-seeing, activity combo, and naturalist. Tourists in 'outdoor sports' type showed tremendous interest in water-based activities such as swimming, sunbathing/beach activities, and water sports. They also like to participate in shopping and sampling local food. 'Sightseeing' represented the major activity in this cluster. These sightseers also enjoyed shopping, sampling local food, and short guided excursions. The 'Life-seeing' group preferred activities such as getting to know the host community, sampling local food, attending festivals, shopping, and sightseeing in cities. Tourists who belonged to the "activity combo' cluster were active and had broad interests in participating in many activities during their trip. The 'naturalists' had strong interests in visiting historically important places, commemorative places, archaeological places, and national parks/forests. However, they also engaged in shopping and sightseeing in cities. It is interesting to note that shopping activity was common to all clusters. Lin (1990) also reported that Japanese tourists traveled abroad not just for sightseeing but also for outdoor activities. Playing golf has become a social status symbol in Japan, but it is both limited by season and expensive to play at home. As a result, Japanese traveled to other Asian countries, such as Taiwan, for golf. Besides golf, Japanese also participated in fishing, cycling, and mountain climbing.

Travel Mode

One distinct travel-related characteristic of the Japanese tourists consistently reported in the tourism literature was their travel mode. It was generally agreed that the majority of Japanese leisure tourists traveled in groups by purchasing package tours and they stayed for shorter lengths of time than other international travelers (USTTA, 1987; Jansen-Verbeke, 1994; Lang, O'Leary, & Morrison 1993, Nazawa, 1992; Dace, 1995; Carlie, 1996; Pizam,

Jansen-Verbeke, & Steel, 1997). In 1988, *The Economist* reported that one-third of all tourist trips abroad were on package holidays, while other kinds of group tours accounted for most of the remainder. Independent travel was only fashionable among the young and wealthy. Both Ahmed and Krohn (1992) and Pizam, Jansen-Verbeke, and Steel (1997) postulated that because of the Japanese cultural value for collectivism, they found comfort in togetherness. This was interpreted as the main reason for not traveling individually. An interesting phenomenon reported by Ahmed and Krohn (1992) concerned newlyweds who traveled internationally on their honeymoon in groups of several dozen couples on organized tours. Carlile (1996) suggested that, given the fact that they were less confident in communicating in foreign languages Japanese preferred package tours through which they could obtain the services and security of a tour escort who could mediate between the Japanese tourist and the host community. In addition, Carlile (1996) also stated that package tours made possible the purchase of transportation, accommodation, and tour services at discounted rates, a practice that was essential in keeping tour costs within the reach of even the wealthier Japanese tourists.

Nishiyama (1996) discussed the influence the Japanese tour wholesalers have on the Japanese travelers. He stated that "Each major tour wholesaler in Japan organizes and markets a variety of package tours to hundreds of overseas destinations. These companies compete with each other by conducting research, planning, and organizing many different package tours by market segments, and by marketing them through an extensive network of retail outlets." Huge sums of money were spent on consumer research and the printing of extremely attractive catalogs on destinations to promote their package tours. Travel agencies provide "one-stop" convenient service which ranges from obtaining passports and visas for their customers to pre-arrangement of gift shipping from the places they plan to visit before their departure.

However, it was also reported that Japanese attitude towards package tours has been gradually changing in recent years. Ron Sternberg (1993) of *Asian Business* reported that in 1993, group tours accounted for about one-third of all outbound traffic from Japan. Nevertheless, Nozawa (1992) still thought that package tours will remain a major mode of travel among the Japanese, but they will become more sophisticated in their preferences when the number of experienced travelers increases and as the travel market becomes more mature.

Length of Stay

Another distinct characteristic of Japanese tourists is their preference for shorter stay in overseas destinations (Nozawa, 1992; Jansen-Verbeke, 1994; Carlile, 1996; Lang, O'Leary, & Morrison, 1993). Jansen-Verbeke (1994) reported that Japanese travelers usually stayed in one country for about two nights when they took a two-week trip to Europe. However, some argued that the elderly Japanese travelers in the 'Full Moon' market (mature married couples aged over 45 years) preferred to stay longer in a single destination (Nozawa, 1992), and they were more concerned about the content and the value of a tour than its price (Kurokawa, 1990). Rationalizations for their short stay were given in the literature including difficulty in taking holidays, and long working hours of Japanese workers (The Economist, 1988; Nazawa, 1992). Working hours were believed to be a Japanese cultural value that viewed long working hours as hard work, representing a virtue of loyalty to their employers. Thus, they do not take long holidays to travel overseas. Nozawa (1992) postulated that shorter stay abroad will remain a characteristic of the Japanese outbound travel market. However, he suggested that different types of stays, including longer stays in a single destination, will gain popularity at the expense of the traditional multi-destination tour packages, mainly due to the increasing maturity of the Japanese market.

Tourist Photography

Although tourists taking photographs in a destination is not uncommon, Pizam, Jansen-Verbeke, and Steel (1997) reported that Japanese tourists were perceived by the Dutch tour guides as highly involved in photography when compared to their French, Italian, and American counterparts. To the Japanese, taking a picture of oneself in front of a tourist site is called *kinen shashin,* or memorial photo. According to Ahmed and Krohn (1992), this was achieved in one of the following two ways:

> "For larger groups, official photographers are arranged at important sites to take formal group portraits, and for smaller groups, couples, and individuals, one hands one's own camera to someone else to take a similar photo." (p.84)

Pizam, Jansen-Verbeke, and Steel (1997) attributed this particular travel-related behavior to the Japanese cultural value for collectivism. They saw sending letter and post cards and showing photographs and videos a form of sharing the trip experience with the members of the collective.

Shopping

It was extensively reported in the tourism literature that Japanese tourists were characterized by their excessive love for shopping during their overseas trips. They were described as big spenders, sophisticated consumers, and enthusiastic but clever shoppers (Keown, 1989; Nozawa, 1992; Jansen-Verbeke, 1994; Dace, 1995; Pizam, Jansen-Verbeke, and Steel, 1997). Economically, the strong yen and high disposable income of Japanese travelers has helped them to earn such a reputation. This reputation has been substantiated by a number of studies asserting that Japanese travelers spent two to five times more than the average international travelers in tourist destinations (USTTA, 1991; Morris, 1990; Bailey, 1991).

Many studies examining the shopping behavior of travelers asserted that the high shopping propensity of Japanese was influenced by the *senbetsu-omiyage* custom (Graburn, 1983; Keown, 1989; Ahmed, & Krohn, 1992; Nozawa, 1992; Jansen-Verbeke, 1994). When a Japanese traveler is going to travel abroad, he/she is given a farewell party, where members of the family along with close friends and colleagues give money as a present (*senbetsu*) and wish him/her a pleasant vacation. Thus the tourist is obliged to reciprocate the regards by buying presents overseas of approximately similar value of the money received, and bring them back home. Such gift-buying might account for over three-fourths of the travelers' spending budget (Keown, 1989). This custom is known as *omiyage*. Furthermore, Japanese travelers preferred to purchase souvenirs (*kinen*) to legitimize and commemorate their visit to a particular tourist destination (Ahmed and Krohn, 1992). The customs of *senbetsu-omiyage,* and *kinen* created an avid attitude of Japanese travelers shopping abroad. Keown (1989) reported that one-third of the Japanese tourists to Hawaii spent between 5 to 8 hours shopping and another one-third spent between 9 to 16 hours. He also reported that they spent $251 per day which was about two and a half times that spent by American mainland tourists and about one-third of the total Japanese visitors' expenditures were for shopping. The Hong Kong Tourist Association ranked Japanese visitors its second top-spending tourist group after the Taiwanese with a per capita expenditure of US$956 (HKTA, 1998).

Preferred Shopping Items

Jansen-Verbeke (1994) asserted that Japanese travelers were interested in 'ethnic' products such as fashion products and perfumes from France. It was very customary for Japanese travelers to draw up a shopping list, and to decide where to buy which item of a particular brand name before departure (Jansen-Verbeke, 1994). Those items were likely to be 'authentic' brand products in the country of origin. When reporting Japanese shopping patterns in Amsterdam, Jansen-Verbeke (1994) asserted that their preferred shopping items were souvenirs, Chinaware, food, flower seeds or bulbs, diamonds and jewelry. In a study of a model for tourists' propensity to buy in a vacation destination, Keown (1989) found that Japanese tourists to Hawaii bought liquor, souvenirs, cosmetics, candy and chocolate, jewelry in descending order of percentage of total mentions by Japanese tourists. The popularity of these items was mainly because their prices were much lower than those in Japan. Price was a major concern of the Japanese which explained why they favored duty-free shops. In fact, Keown found that price, warranty, or store reputation were the major considerations when they decided which store to buy in, while the store clerk's attitude and store location were not important factors. Both Keown (1989) and Jansen-Verbeke's (1994) findings might be destination specific and cannot be generalized to other destinations. Morris (1988) reported that the top six purchases by Japanese were liquor, tobacco, cosmetics, chocolate, leather goods and clothing. From these findings, it can be seen that there is some consistency in the products that Japanese tourists preferred to purchase from overseas.

Vacation Planning

In his examination of vacation planning behavior, Iverson (1997) hypothesized that Korean travelers have a shorter decision time than Japanese tourists. He compared vacation planning characteristics of Korean and Japanese tourists using data available from exit surveys conducted in Guam. Having controlled the effects of demographic variables on decision time, Korean travelers were found to have significantly shorter decision time frames than Japanese tourists. This finding was attributed to Hofstede's (1980) characterization of Japanese as high in uncertainty avoidance, taking longer time to plan their vacations. It was also reported that marital status, travel experience, and age were found to be significantly related to decision timing.

Conclusion and Recommendations for Future Research

It is gratifying to see an increasing interest in Japanese tourist behavior research. In an effort to improve marketers' understanding of Japanese consumer behavior, researchers looked at various aspects of their travel-related behavior. This review was conducted to provide tourism practitioners and researchers a summary of research findings and guidelines for future research that would result in more rigorous theoretical progress. As evidenced by the preceding literature review, it was obvious that their travel-related behavior was believed to be influenced to a large extent by cultural values. However, it could be easily seen that past research was mainly descriptive in nature. There is still a lot more to be investigated before a fuller understanding of their behavior can be achieved. Based on the findings of previous studies, the authors identified seven major knowledge gaps and recommended the following areas for further research:

1. The effect of demographic and psychographic variables on shopping venues, product preferences, and expenditure patterns; and compare these effects based on destinations.
2. Push and pull motivations of Japanese travelers based on different market segments.
3. The effect of demographic and psychographic variables on travel-related behavior of Japanese tourists: destination preferences, trip planning horizon, sources of information, travel mode, and activities in destinations.
4. Complaint and feedback behavior of Japanese tourists.
5. Systematic theoretical linkage between Japanese travel behavior and Japanese cultural values.
6. Japanese tourists' expectations and perception of destination specific tourism product and/or service quality.
7. Changes in Japanese tourists' expenditure patterns as a result of the current economic downturn in Japan and the devaluation of the Yen.

Japanese consumers are unique in many ways and they are an interesting group to research. The authors hope that through this review more rigorous investigations will be stimulated which would lead to an increased understanding of Japanese tourists and hence better service provisions will be provided for them.

REFERENCES

Ahmed, Z. F., & Krohn, F. B. (1992). Understanding the unique consumer behavior of Japanese tourists. *Journal of Travel & Tourism Marketing*, 1 (3): 73-86.

Bailey, A. C. (1992). A yen for Travel. In *The Annual review of Travel*. American Express.

Bailey, M. (1991). A question of value. *Asian Business*, July, 43-45.

Carlile, L. E. (1996). Economic development and the evolution of Japanese overseas tourism, 1964-1994. *Tourism Recreation Research*, 21 (1): 11-18.

Cha, S., McCleary, K. W., & Uysal, M. (1995). Travel motivations of Japanese overseas travelers: A factor-cluster segmentation approach. *Journal of Travel Research*. Summer, 34 (1): 33-39.

Chon, K. S. (1987). An assessment of images of Korea as a tourist destination by American tourists. *Hotel and Tourism Management Review*, 3, 155-170.

Crompton, J. L. (1977). Motivations for pleasure vacations. *Annals of Tourism Research*, 7, 408-424.

Dace, R. (1995). Japanese tourism: How a knowledge of Japanese buyer behavior and culture can be of assistance to British hoteliers in seeking to develop this valuable market. *Journal of Vacation Marketing*, 1 (3), 281-288.

Dybka, J. (1988). Overseas travel to Canada: New Research on the perceptions and preferences of the pleasure travel market. *Journal of Travel Research*, 26 (Spring): 12-15.

Focus Japan. (1994). *Japan's outbound travel market*, April, 3.

Gallup Organization. (1989). *American express global travel survey: An international study of the traveling public conducted in the United States, West Germany, United Kingdom and Japan*. Princeton: NJ.

Graburn, N. (1983). *To Pray, Pay and Play*. Center des Hautes Etudes Touristiques Series B, No. 26.

HKTA (1998). A Statistical Review of Tourism 1997. Hong Kong Tourist Association: Hong Kong.

Hofstede, G. (1980). *Culture's Consequences: International Differences in Work-Related Values*. Sage: Beverly Hills, CA.

Iverson, T. J. (1997a). Decision timing: A comparison of Korean and Japanese travelers. *International Journal of Hospitality Management*, 16 (2), 209-219.

Iverson, T. J. (1997b). Japanese visitors to Guam: Lessons from experience. *Journal of Travel & Tourism Marketing*, 6 (1).

Jansen-Verbeke, M. (1994). The synergy between shopping and tourism: The Japanese experience. In W. F. Theobald (Ed.), *Global Tourism-The Next Decade* (347-362). Oxford: Butterworth-Heinemann.

Japan National Tourist Organization (1998). *Visitor Arrival and Japanese Overseas Travellers*. Japan National Tourist Organization, 14.

Keown, C. F. (1989). A model of tourists' propensity to buy: the case of Japanese visitors to Hawaii. *Journal of Travel Research*, Winter, 18 (3): 31-34.

Kurokawa, M. (1990). Furu Mun Marketto (Japanese full-moon travel market). *Weekly Travel Journal*, 30 July, 38.

Lang, C. T., O'Leary, J.T., & Morrison, A.M. (1993). Activity segmentation of Japanese female overseas travelers. *Journal of Travel & Tourism Marketing*, 2 (4): 1-22.

Lin, M. (1990). Taiwan: Magnet for Japanese tourists. *The Cornell H.R.A. Quarterly*, 31 (1): 96-97.

Moeran, B. (1983). The language of Japanese tourism. *Annals of Tourism Research*, 10: 93-108.

Morris, S. (1988). Outbound markets/market segment studies: Japanese leisure patterns. *Economist Intelligence Unit Travel and Tourism Analyst, 5: 32-53.*

Morris, S. (1990). *The Japanese Overseas Travel Market in the 1990s*, Economist Intelligence Unit, London.

Morris, S. (1991). Japanese travel to Europe. *Travel and Tourism Analyst*, 3: 145.

Murakami, K. & Go, F. (1990). Transitional corporations capture Japanese Market. *Tourism Management*, December, 348-352.

Nishiyama, K. (1996). *Welcoming the Japanese Visitor: Insights, Tips, Tactics*. University of Hawaii Press: Honolulu.

Nozawa, H. (1992). A marketing analysis of Japanese outbound travel. *Tourism Management*, 13 (2): 226-233.

Picola, G. 1992. *International travel market trends: Asia*. A speech addressed at the 6th Travel Review Conference, Arlington, 5 February.

Pizam, A., Jansen-Verbeke, M., & Steel, L. (1997). Are all tourists alike, regardless of nationality? The Perceptions of Dutch tour-guides. *Journal of International Hospitality, Leisure & Tourism Management*, 1 (1), 19-39.

Polunin, I. (1989). Japanese Travel Boom. *Tourism Management*, March, 4-8.

Sheldon, P. J., & Fox, M. (1988). The role of food service in vacation choice and experience: A cross-cultural analysis. *Journal of Travel Research*, Fall: 9-15.

The Economist. (1988). *Japanese Tourism: Broadening the Mind*. May 7, 64.

Tourism Canada. (1992). *Marketing Intelligence Brief–Japan*. United States Travel and Tourism Administration: Tokyo (1991). *Japanese Market Update*.

Travel Journal Inc. (TJI). (1989). *Japan Travel Blue Book '89/90*, Tokyo, 124.

Travel Journal Inc. (TJI). (1992). *The 24th survey on Japanese overseas travel*, 20 January, 14-18.

United States Travel and Tourism Administration (USTTA). (1987). *Highlights Report Pleasure Travel Markets to North America: Japan, United Kingdom, West Germany, France*. Washington: DC.

United States Travel and Tourism Administration (USTTA). (1990). *Pleasure Travel Market to North American: Japan*. Washington: DC, 8.

United States Travel and Tourism Administration (USTTA). (1991). *Japanese Market Update*, unpublished, Tokyo, 18 October.

Woodside, A. G., & Jacobs, L. W. (1985). Step two in benefit segmentation: Learning the benefits realized by major travel markets. *Journal of Travel Research*, Summer, 24 (1): 7-13.

Woodside, A. G., & Pitts, R. E. (1976). Effects of consumer lifestyles, demographics, and travel activities on foreign and domestic travel behavior. *Journal of Travel Research*, 14, Winter, 13-15.

Ziff-Levin, W. (1990). The cultural logic gap: A Japanese tourism research experience. *Tourism Management*, 11 (2): 105-110.

The Japanese Travel Life Cycle

Roger March

SUMMARY. This paper offers an alternative way of segmenting a non-western travel market, namely, the Japanese outbound market. The segmentation schema comprises several institutionalised forms of travel likely to be undertaken by a Japanese individual in the course of his or her life. Coined the 'travel life cycle,' the concept fits Japanese society well due to the highly organized and group-oriented patterns of travel that have emerged over the past one hundred years. While this form of segmentation is unlikely to be usefully applied to western travel markets, its application in the Japanese context may suggest that it has relevance when examining the travel patterns of other tradition-bound and group-oriented Asian travel markets such as Korea, China or Indonesia. The paper's conceptual contribution lies in the implicit suggestion that particular cultures may develop and exhibit unique forms of consumption behavior that lie outside the conceptual framework normally adopted by western academics and marketing practitioners. Managerially, the paper suggests ways by which tourism operators and tourism promotion bodies can more efficiently and effectively target Japanese travellers according to the stage of travel life cycle. *[Article copies available for a fee from The Haworth Document Delivery Service: 1-800-342-9678. E-mail address: <getinfo@haworthpressinc.com> Website: <http://www.haworthpressinc. com>]*

KEYWORDS. Japanese tourists, travel life cycle, Japanese outbound tourism

---

Roger March is affiliated with the School of Marketing, University of New South Wales, Sydney 2052 Australia. (E-mail: r.march@unsw.edu.au).

[Haworth co-indexing entry note]: "The Japanese Travel Life Cycle." March, Roger. Co-published simultaneously in *Journal of Travel & Tourism Marketing* (The Haworth Hospitality Press, an imprint of The Haworth Press, Inc.) Vol. 9, No. 1/2, 2000, pp. 185-200; and: *Japanese Tourists: Socio-Economic, Marketing and Psychological Analysis* (ed: K. S. (Kaye) Chon, Tsutomu Inagaki, and Taiji Ohashi) The Haworth Hospitality Press, an imprint of The Haworth Press, Inc., 2000, pp. 185-200. Single or multiple copies of this article are available for a fee from The Haworth Document Delivery Service [1-800-342-9678, 9:00 a.m. - 5:00 p.m. (EST). E-mail address: getinfo@haworthpressinc.com].

INTRODUCTION

Conventional marketing theory and discourse in the area of international marketing can be highly eurocentric (Douglas and Craig 1992). Consumption behavior, for example, is most frequently examined and interpreted through the cultural values, intellectual concepts and personal beliefs of individuals that have been educated and shaped by western culture. Ironically, even the most influential of all cross-cultural management researchers, Geert Hofstede, whose 1980 *Culture's Consequences* represents an enormous contribution to our understanding of the impact of national culture upon cross-cultural marketing management, was later obliged to amend his original thesis after 'discovering' a fifth dimension from Asian culture, namely, 'Confucian dynamism' (Hofstede 1991, Fang 1998). Eurocentricity extends also to the study of international tourism (March 1994), where little cross-cultural research has been undertaken (see Dimanche 1994 for a useful discussion of the field). The present study makes a contribution in this area of tourism by identifying segments in the Japanese travel market that are manifested though a combination of cultural and historical factors unique to Japan.

LIFE CYCLE THEORY IN THE MARKETING AND TOURISM LITERATURE

The evolutionary cycle of birth, growth, decline and death has been adapted by marketing scholars to explain various aspects of consumer behavior. In traditional marketing literature, the family life cycle is one such conceptual adaptation. First proposed by an economist, (Becker 1965), the life-cycle concept in marketing was pioneered by Wells and Gubar (1966), who classified the history of a family's consumption behavior into nine phases. The family life cycle (FLC) incorporated age–previously the main demographic variable used to distinguish consumer segments–into a broader bundle of attributes that included marital and employment status, age of children, size of travelling group, and amount of discretionary income.

By the late 1980s, the family life cycle had been adapted by marketing scholars as a useful multidimensional segmentation tool. The FLC allowed marketers to quantify the impact that different family composition variables–for example, couples with dependent children versus couples without children, age of couples–had upon discretionary income and ultimately upon consumption patterns and leisure time. The concept has been tested empirically in terms of allocation of income to consumption goods and leisure time (Douthitt & Fedyk 1990), and time-based factors such as growing older and transitions in family situations (Wilkes 1995). Schaninger and Danko (1993) conceptually and empirically compared several alternative family life cycle models.

In the field of tourism marketing, the concept was first applied by Lawson in his 1991 study of how the family life cycle reflects the type of vacation taken and financial expenditure made. Recent empirical studies indicate a growing interest in the application of the concept. Bojanic (1992) built upon the Lawson study by including two additional segments–single parent and middle-aged couples without dependent children–which he found were the two most frequent types of overseas travellers. Fodness (1992) focused on information search behavior and decision-making processes across the FLC. An interesting study was undertaken by Oppermann (1995), who incorporated the cohorts of destination choice, seasonality, choice of accommodation and transportation in his longitudinal investigation into the travel patterns that German citizens develop through their lives. (See Table 1 for a summary of these works.) The most famous conceptual contribution to the debate is Butler's seminal paper on the tourism area (destination) life-cycle, which extended the concept to describe the evolution of destinations (1980).

The most useful feature of the family life cycle in tourism is its ability to identify particular market segments that are best measured and targeted in terms of socio-economic and demographic variables of discretionary income, age, marital status and presence or absence of children. Beyond this, a number of theoretical problems emerge. Firstly, not all travel parties fit neatly under the banner of 'family' travel (Oppermann 1995). Many singles will travel alone or with friends; business people travel with other business people; and travellers with special interests such as art will travel with like-minded aficionados. Some segments are more likely to exhibit more homogeneous travel patterns than others; for example, newlyweds, full nesters (couples with dependent children) and empty nesters (couples whose children have left home). Other segments, such as the monogender 'bachelor' and single parents, are less likely to be predictable in terms of travelling desires and spending behaviour. Secondly, some segments are so large as to be meaningless. The age range of Bojanic's single parents segment is 18-49, a group hardly likely to be particularly homogeneous in either travel behavior or discretionary income. Thirdly, the characteristics of segments are likely to change from one generation to another (Oppermann 1995; Silvers 1997) and from one culture/society to another (see Kumagai's (1984) comparison of U.S., Canadian and Japanese family life cycles). A further concern with the FLC is the academic predisposition to place as many of the sample as possible into one of the stages. Such theoretical endeavors do not approximate the reality of today's business world. As Dibb and Simkin (1997) have pointed out,

> While the academic seeks to identify, statistically validate and test the existence of alternative [segmentation] schemes, for the practitioner the real test of a particular segment solution is the marketing program which must be developed. (p. 54)

TABLE 1. Family Life Cycle Studies in Tourism

	Lawson 1991	Bojanic 1992	Fodness 1992	Oppermann 1995
Final sample	3,426	2,001	3,565	86
Setting	Exit surveys of overseas visitors at New Zealand airports	U.S. residents who travelled to Europe in previous 3 years	Florida domestic tourism exit survey of Florida visitors (not residents)	Residents of German university town
Dependent variables	expenditure, type, of vacation, age, marital status, children's age, presence/ absence of children	age, presence/ absence of children, marital status, destination preference	married couples (only), age, presence/ absence of children	age, presence/ absence of child-ren, children's age
Life cycle stages	8	8	5	9
Classifiable respondents (%)	60%	89%	100%	100%

TRAVEL LIFE CYCLE AS SEGMENTATION TOOL

This paper proposes the Japanese Travel Life Cycle as a useful segmentation tool for analyzing and targeting the overseas Japanese traveller. This paper identifies eight stages of the Japanese Travel Life Cycle (JTLC): family trip, school excursion, language trip, graduation holiday, honeymoon, overseas wedding, in-company trip, and silver trip. What are these consumer segments and why have they been chosen?

The nine stages of the JTLC comprise various institutionalized forms of overseas travel that a Japanese individual is likely to undertake through his or her lifetime. The JTLC differs from the family life cycle in that the former encompasses travel patterns that are not necessarily influenced by the action or presence of family members. The JTLC is a useful segmentation approach for the Japanese travel market for three reasons. First, Japan is a group-oriented society in which travel, no less than other forms of social interaction, has traditionally been undertaken in groups rather than individually. In 1997, 70 percent of Japanese overseas travellers travelled in a group, rather than make their own independent arrangements (JTB 1998). Group-orientation also manifests itself in the influence that particular groups exert on others. In a report released a few years ago, Japan Travel Bureau (JTB) identified six market segments that represent the driving forces behind the growth of the

Japanese outbound market since travel was liberalized in 1964 (*JTB News,* September 1993). These are: (1) the wealthy class (immediately after liberalization in 1964), (2) honeymooners (from second half of the 1960s), (3) the "silver" (couples over sixty years of age) market (from the 1970s), (4) OL ('office lady', female office workers between 18-39) market (from early 1980s), (5) student market (from the mid-1980s), and (6) the family market (from the early 1990s). According to JTB, each of these segments has influenced the destination choices of contemporary and future Japanese overseas travellers. While this notion would be difficult to test empirically, it does suggest a benefit in taking into account sub-cultural groups when attempting to understand Japanese consumer patterns in travel.

Secondly, and related to the notion of group, many aspects of social behavior are institutionalized (Christopher 1984). From early age, the Japanese individual is obliged to adopt culturally prescribed behavioural patterns for particular social situations, whether at school, in the workplace or in interpersonal relationships. As we shall see, these patterns are particularly useful for marketers in the context of travel behaviour due to their relative uniformity in number of travelling companions, purchasing patterns and activities and experiences sought.

Thirdly, and most importantly from the marketing perspective of market share and channel power, the Japanese travel market is very much controlled by a small number of large wholesalers who are permitted to have their own retail networks (March 1997). The top eight wholesalers account for approximately 65 percent of the outbound market (based on interviews with Japanese travel industry participants). As a result, trade–not consumer–marketing is the critical factor that marketing enterprises and government promotion bodies must consider in formulating marketing strategies targeting these key segments. And since marketing to the travel trade is, by definition, less expensive and more focused than consumer marketing, the cost advantages to firms are obvious. This is good news for many participants in an industry that is composed predominantly of small enterprises which lack the financial resources and managerial capabilities to devise and implement extensive marketing activities. Mismatches often arise between organizational capabilities and resources when small firms attempt to segment and target particular consumer segments (Jenkins and McDonald 1997).

STAGES OF THE JAPAN TRAVEL LIFE CYCLE

This section explains the eight stages of the Japanese Travel Life Cycle (TLC). Table 2 summarizes the main indicators of each stage.

TABLE 2. Summary of Japanese Travel Life Cycle

Segment	Size (% of total market)	Proportion of customers buying group tours[4]	First	Top three destinations Second	Third
Family trip[1]	25%	75-80%	Hawaii	Guam	Australia
School excursion[2]	0.8%	90-100%	Korea	China	Australia
Language study	1.5%	75-85%	U.S. Mainland	U.K.	Australia
Graduation trip[3]	0.4%	50-70%	U.S. Mainland	Hawaii	Asia
Overseas wedding	0.5%	90-100%	Hawaii	Guam	Australia
Honeymoon	2.6%	75-80%	Hawaii	U.S. Mainland	Australia
In-company trip	12%	80-90%	Hawaii	Hong Kong	S.E. Asia
Silvers	16%	60-70%	Hawaii	Italy	Hong Kong
Overall market (1997)	16,803,000	70%	U.S. Mainland	Hawaii	Korea

Source: *JTB* Report '98, unless stated otherwise.
Notes: 1. Includes family and relatives as travel companions. 2. *"Kaigai Shugaku Ryokô no Jisshi Jôkyô"* [Situation of overseas school excursions] 3. 1995 figures (*Travel Journal*, Feb. 10, 1997) 4. Industry estimates based on interviews.

Family Trip (kazoku ryokô)

The family market (both parents and at least one child usually under the age of twelve years) represents about more than 20 percent of total outbound travel (JTB Report, 1998); this proportion increases in the summer season, when up to 40 percent of wholesalers' sales are derived from family-oriented travel products (JTB 1998). In a society that traditionally places a high priority on personal safety, the growth in the family segment reflects the increasing maturity and experience of the Japanese travel market in which parents children feel comfortable in taking their children on an overseas trip. It is also further proof of the extent to which overseas travel has become an integral part of many Japanese people's everyday lives. For parents with babies or very young children, short-haul destinations such as Guam and Saipan are the preferred choice (JTB unpublished data, 1997). Parents with teenagers will travel further, perhaps to destinations with cultural or historical sightseeing. An emerging trend is the three-generation family trip, with the grandparents joining the parents and kids.

Overall, the most preferred destination for family travel is Hawaii. Hawaii has become very successful at capturing a large part of the young family trip market. Hawaiian hotels offer special services such as baby-sitting and day-care facilities, as well as supervised playgrounds. According to a 1995 industry survey, 69 percent of parents who have travelled on an overseas family trip prefer Hawaii, followed by North America (27 percent), Oceania (26 percent) and Europe (25 percent) (*Travel Journal*, September 14, 1996). Over 95 percent of respondents expressed a desire to travel overseas with their children. The two major reasons cited for family trips abroad were the low cost of these trips and the opportunity for their children to experience things outside Japan.

School Excursion (shugaku ryokô)

School excursions refer to organized school travel by junior-and senior high school students to places of historical and cultural interest. Funded by parents, it dates back to the 1880s when it was introduced as a means of physical (they mostly walked) and spiritual training for Japan's youth. In 1996, over 131,000 students from 706 schools travelled abroad, spending a total of γ21.9 billion, or $182 million (US 1 $ = γ120) (Japan Shugaku Ryokô Association 1997); 95 percent of students were from senior high schools. While domestic *shugaku ryokô* are still more prevalent, more and more schools are opting for an overseas school excursion.

In the past, overseas *shugaku ryokô* were limited to private schools since Japan's Ministry of Education traditionally "discouraged" government schools from using aircraft for *shugaku-ryokô,* even inside Japan (Minagawa 1991). This is now changing, with many local government education boards giving the "green light" to overseas travel by government schools. In 1996, overseas *shugaku-ryokô* were undertaken by six percent of private junior high schools and 25 percent of private senior high schools, compared to less than one percent of government junior high schools and six percent of government senior high-schools. Unlike private schools, which have no restrictions on their travel arrangements, government schools require the approval of the prefectural or city education board to undertake overseas travel. As of June 1997, thirty-two (of 47) prefectures and three cities had given such approval, representing roughly sixty-five percent of all government schools in Japan (Japan Shugaku Ryokô Association 1997). Average expenditure per student in 1996 was γ202,375 for senior high school students, with students in some tours spending over γ660,000 (Japan Shugaku Ryokô Association 1997).

The school excursion market is a lucrative market for wholesalers and for the overseas destinations the students descend upon. Moreover, it is not a one-off trip. Schools will choose a destination at least twice, usually three years in succession, because of the time and money necessary to arrange a new destination every year. Though there are no figures available for the amount of spending money students carry with them, Japanese travel agents believe it is not uncommon for a student to carry between γ50-100,000 ($420-840) (based on interviews with industry sources). JTB and Kinki Nippon Tourist (KNT), Japan's second largest travel company, account for about 70 percent of the entire school excursion domestic and overseas market (based on interviews with industry sources). Of the overseas market alone, a

1996 Japan Airlines survey found that the top five wholesalers controlled some 78 percent of the market (*Asahi Shimbun Newspaper,* 8/9/1996).

Graduation Trip (sotsugyo ryokô)

Graduation travel, or *sotsugyo ryokô,* refers to overseas travel taken by university students after completing their final year studies and before beginning full-time employment. Since the tradition in Japan is to begin work on April 1 each year (but commence in-company training a couple of weeks beforehand), graduation trips peak in mid to late February, with some departures in early March. Industry analysts estimate the market is worth some $40 million annually (*Travel Journal,* March 21, 1997). Typically, students will travel with one or more close friends, book the first couple of nights hotel accommodations and then make their own arrangements. They travel around using a cheap rail pass, such as a Eurorail Pass in the case of Europe. Main destinations in Europe are London, Paris and Rome; in Mainland USA, the west coast destinations of San Francisco and Los Angeles, as well as New York are the most popular. The average price of a trip was γ158,300 ($1,319), down from γ211,000 ($1,758) in 1992; while the average number in a group was 3.0 persons. The average length of graduation trip in 1995 was eight days (Travel Journal, March 21, 1997).

Overseas Weddings

One of the fastest growing new market segments in recent years is the overseas wedding market. According to research by industry provider Watabe Wedding Company, approximately 40,000 couples (5.5 percent of all marriages) were married overseas in 1996, double the figure of three years earlier (*Asahi Shimbun,* January 9, 1997). At a wedding show organized in Tokyo attended by some 1200 engaged couples, one in seven couples said they wanted to have their wedding overseas (*Travel Journal,* May 11, 1997).

Hawaii captures over 60 percent of the overseas wedding market, according to Watabe Wedding (*Asahi Shimbun,* January 9, 1997) followed by Australia with 14 percent. In fiscal 1996, JTB alone arranged over 6,000 weddings in Hawaii. The main advantages of an overseas wedding are the relatively lower cost and easier arrangements, a more intimate and relaxed atmosphere and the heightened romance. The average cost of a domestic wedding is $27,000. Substantial savings in time and money can be made by opting for an overseas ceremony which reduces the number of guests to be invited and a number of ancillary costs, such as the hire of an expensive wedding hall. A lot of time, effort and stress are also saved. Decisions about the guest list, about seating arrangements (in a society in which hierarchy is a sensitive issue), and even about the order of speeches can be exhausting for the couple involved.

Another great advantage lies in the ability of the couple to escape the social demands of a domestic wedding. In deciding to get married overseas, the couple is not obliged into inviting large numbers of relatives and co-workers, many of whom they would rather do without. Instead of inviting the people that they have to, they can invite the people they really want to share their wedding day with. These would include the immediate relatives, close friends, and perhaps a couple to serve as the go-between at the ceremony and reception. On average, 7.4 people accompanied a couple to Hawaii and 10 people travelled to Guam/Saipan with a blissful couple (*Travel Journal,* May 11, 1997). Most Japanese couples are open-minded when it comes to choosing an overseas location for their wedding. According to Watabe Wedding Company research (Asahi Shimbun, January 9, 1997), only about one in three couples have decided where they want to go before they enter the travel agency to make arrangements. The major wholesalers now offer a variety of overseas wedding plans. For many couples, having a wedding reception in one destination does not mean they will honeymoon there. Some couples prefer, for example, to have their wedding in Hawaii, followed by a honeymoon visiting the theme parks of California.

The overseas wedding market is expected to maintain its healthy growth into the future. Though only about five percent of all marriages in 1996 were held overseas (*Travel Journal,* May 11, 1997), some industry experts confidently predicted this to double to around 10 percent (of an estimated 900,000 couples marrying) by 2000. In the coming years, about eight million Japanese belonging to the second generation of the post-war baby boom will reach marriageable age. Given the strong interest in overseas travel by Japan's youth combined with the high cost of domestic weddings we could expect more and more Japanese to tread the 'virgin road' in a foreign country in the years to come.

Honeymoon Travel

Marriage in Japan is an expensive business–for couples, parents, and wedding guests alike. The average cost of getting married is γ5.4 million ($45,000): $10,000 for the engagement, $27,000 for the wedding and $8,000 for the honeymoon (*Daily Yomiuri,* August 2, 1996). Against these costs, a newlywed couple will receive, on average, a total of γ600,000 ($5,000) from wedding guests, since cash is the traditional form of wedding gift. Tradition dictates that the couple reciprocate the kindness by using a portion of the money to buy *omiyage* (souvenirs) for their friends, relatives and work colleagues.

Approximately 750,000 couples are married each year, of which 60-80 percent (depending on the year) opt for an overseas honeymoon. Since the honeymoon was the traditional 'once-in-a-lifetime' event, no expense was spared. Although spending has declined in recent years on a per person and per day basis, Japan's newlyweds still spend more on accommodations, on meals, on tours, and on shopping than any other market segment (JTB 1998). Honeymooners account for well over fifty percent of the large wholesalers' luxury package product customers. In short, honeymooners are the most lucrative and sought-after segment in the Japanese package market and for that reason wholesalers and foreign tourism operators (especially five-star hotels) devote considerable resources to capturing and maintaining market share. The average length of a honeymoon is six nights/eight days, since most couples are reluctant to take off from work more than one week, or five working days.

Overseas honeymoons have been the preferred option for newlyweds since the early 1980s. Though it was not until 1977 that a foreign destination (Hawaii) became one of the three most popular honeymoon destinations, by 1984 all the top three destinations were overseas. Though Australia and Hawaii competed for the No.1 spot in the honeymoon market from the late 1980s through the late 1990s, Australia was displaced in the Top Three for the first time in 1998 (see Table 3 for a summary of the most popular destinations in recent years).

In-Company Trip (shokuba ryokô)

A custom in Japanese corporate life is for company workers to take a vacation with their co-workers once a year. Called *shokuba ryokô*, the trip lasts between a couple of days and a week. It became popular around the mid-1960s with one-or two-night visits to famous hot springs being the most

TABLE 3. Main Spring Honeymoon Destinations and Average Spending, 1995-1998

	First	Second	Third	Ave. budget per couple
1995	Hawaii	Australia	Europe	¥632,000
1996	Hawaii	Australia	Mainland USA	¥596,000
1997	Mainland USA	Hawaii	Australia	¥582,000
1998	Mainland USA	Hawaii	Europe	¥552,000

Source: JTB News quarterly newsletters

common pattern. The rise in the value of the yen in the mid-1980s saw a gradual increase in overseas *shokuba ryokô*.

Funding for the trip is shared between the worker and the company, with the company usually paying a greater proportion. The Japanese government encourages the custom by offering workers tax relief in the form of a non-taxable threshold (presently, 4-nights/5-days). This allows companies to sub-sidize company employees for a trip up to 4-nights in length without the employees being taxed for the amount of money they received as a subsidy. To be eligible for the tax benefit, companies must contribute at least half the cost of the trip. The most popular travelling seasons are the autumn months of October and November, followed by June.

Japan's economic downturn during the 1990s sparked a decline in *shokuba ryokô*–both overseas and domestic. In 1996, 74 percent of firms sponsored company trips, down from 90 percent in 1994, according to a survey by the Sanro Research Institute (*Nikkei Weekly,* February 14, 1997). In general, about one third of companies offer their employees overseas trips. Despite the decline, about 7-10 percent of overseas travellers each year reportedly travel with company colleagues. The top overseas destinations in 1996 were Hawaii, Hong Kong/Macau and Southeast Asia, followed by Guam/Saipan, Korea and Australia. The majority of overseas trip lasted just 2-3 nights. The average cost per person was γ128,774 ($1,073), with the lowest being γ48,000 ($400) and the highest γ340,000 ($2,833) (*Travel Journal,* November 28, 1996).

Silver Market

The 'silver' market refers to travellers over the age of sixty. Japan is the most rapidly ageing society in the world, with 25 percent of the population expected to be over the age of sixty by 2020 (Ministry of Labor, 1997). The silver market is an aggressively targeted market by Japanese wholesalers and overseas destination marketers alike. In 1995, 1.75 million Japanese over the age of 60 travelled abroad, a rise of 14.2 percent over the previous year, and accounting for 11.5 percent of total outbound travellers. (The proportion aged 50 and over was 26.8 percent, representing one in four of all Japanese travellers.) According to JTB (1998) research, almost nearly four out of ten 'silver' travellers are accompanied by their spouses, 24 percent travel with family members and 20 percent with friends and acquaintances. About two-thirds of senior travellers buy full package tours (JTB 1997). Their most popular destinations for 'silver' travellers were the United States, followed by South Korea, China, Taiwan, and Hong Kong. More elderly married couples are travelling and as the family travel grows in popularity the number of two and three-generational travel parties will rise.

Recent trends show that senior travellers are staying longer in overseas destinations, which explains the strong interest in this segment by the travel industry. Longer stays are growing because 'silver' travellers have more experience and greater appreciation of the value of the overseas travel. Another reason for the longer stay is that the older consumer, supposedly with higher disposable income, is willing and able to pay more for overseas travel. The greater propensity to pay may be the result of the crippling burden of inheritance taxes–20-25 percent–that Japanese are forced to pay. Many elderly parents will spend up on an overseas trip and reduce the future tax burden.

LIMITATIONS

While much of the foregoing discussion was based on the author's interviews with industry participants in Japan (and in Australia), a considerable proportion of the thesis was based on secondary data. While the degree of confidence in the conclusions is high, future longitudinal research would validate the extent to which Japanese individuals continue to conform to these highly institutionalized travel forms.

In the years since 1956 when Wendall Smith first coined the phrase 'market segmentation,' the concept has come to be regarded as a fundamental pillar in marketing theory (Wind 1978) and a key strategic marketing tool (Doyle, 1987). Despite this widespread acceptance, however, segmentation is not without its critics. Most of the criticism revolves around the operationalisation and actionability of the segments identified (Young, Otto, & Feigin,1978; Yuspeh and Fein, 1982; Hoek, Gendall & Esslemont 1996). The segments detailed in this paper appear to fulfil–intuitively at least–Kotler's (1991) four criteria for useful segments; namely, they are (1) measurable (allowing marketers to evaluate their size and future potential), (2) substantial (large/profitable enough to warrant the firm's attention), (3) accessible (possible for marketers to focus marketing effort on) and (4) actionable (allowing marketers to develop effective programs to serve the segment). Empirical research is needed to test this assumption.

MANAGERIAL IMPLICATIONS

The Japan Travel Life Cycle can be an effective and useful segmentation method in a market in which consumer advertising and other marketing activities are prohibitively expensive for the great majority of tourism operators. The feature of the JTLC is that its segments are readily identifiable, stable and accessible. An understanding of the Japanese tourist through the study of the JTLC offers the tourism operator two distinct advantages. First, the operator is well placed to cater to the needs of particular segments in the Japanese market through his improved understanding of Japanese travel behavior. Just as importantly, he is able to market his product more effectively to Japanese intermediaries (such as outbound agents or inbound tour operators) by exhibiting an understanding of *their* customers that the competition is unlikely to possess. Trade marketing, rather than consumer marketing, becomes the critical marketing focus. Tourism suppliers who are therefore seriously intending to either enter, or expand their share in, the Japanese market, must craft efficient channel strategies. The JTLC also allows operators to better assess which customer segments best suit their product.

For tourism promotion bodies, the JTLC can be a strategic tool used to identify marketing opportunities. Figure 1 shows the relationship between a destination's market share of each segment (in this case the destination is Australia) relative to the growth of each segment of the TLC.

Certain segments of the TLC have strategic value beyond the immediate benefits of attracting customers in the short-term. As the hamburger chain McDonald's has shown, capture a customer in his or her early years and you may have that customer for life. The Japan Travel Life Cycle offers similar advice. For national tourism organizations, the Japan Travel Life Cycle suggests that the family and school excursions are the potential nurturing ground

FIGURE 1. Boston Matrix Applied to Travel Life Cycle: The Case of Australia

MARKET GROWTH

	High	Low
High	Overseas wedding Language study School excursions Family market	Honeymooners
Low	Silvers	Graduation trips In-company trips

DESTINATION'S MARKET SHARE

of future repeat customers when they shift to later travel patterns. Although the school market, for example, is not particularly high yielding, concentrated marketing efforts targeting this young group of Japanese customers may have medium- and long-term benefits in the form of repeat visitation.

The JTLC is offered as one, but not the only means, of segmenting a non-western travel market. As Kotler (1991) has argued, there is no single way to segment a market. Instead, marketers are obliged to seek out different segmentation variables that best fit their products and their organisational capabilities.

REFERENCES

Asahi Shimbun Newspaper, (1996). September 8.

Asahi Shimbun Newspaper, (1997). January 9.

Becker, G. S. (1965). "A Theory of the Allocation of Time," *Economic Journal*, 75, 493-517.

Bojanic, D. C. (1992). "A Look at a Modernized Family Life Cycle and Overseas Travel", *Journal of Travel & Tourism Marketing*, 1 (1), 61-77.

Butler, R. W. (1980). "The Concept of a Tourism Area Life Cycle of Evolution: Implications for the Management of Resources", *Canadian Geographer*, 24, 5-12.

Christopher, R. C. (1984) *The Japanese Mind*, Pan Books, London

Dibb, S. and Simkin, L. (1997). "A program for implementing market segmentation", *Journal of Business and Industrial Marketing*, 12 (1), 51-65.

Dimanche, F. (1994) "Cross-Cultural Tourism Marketing Research: An assessment and recommendations for future studies," *Journal of International Consumer Marketing*, 6, (3/4), 123-134.

Douglas, S. P. & Craig, C. S. (1992). "Advances in International Marketing," *International Journal of Research in Marketing*, 9, 291-318.

Douthitt, R. A. & Fedyk, J. (1988), "The Influence of Children on Family Life-Cycle Spending Behavior: Theory and Applications," *Journal of Consumer Affairs*, 22 (2), Winter, 220-248.

Doyle, P. (1987). "Managing the marketing mix", in Baker, M. (Ed.), *The Marketing Book*, Heinemann, London, Ch.12.

Fang, T. (1998). "Reflection on Hofstede's 5th Dimension", paper presented at Academy of Management Meetings, San Diego California, August 1998, also published by International Graduate School of Management and Industrial Engineering, Linköpings University, Sweden.

Fodness, D. (1992). "The Impact of Family Life Cycle on the Vacation Decision-making Process," *Journal of Travel Research*, 1 (Fall), 8-13.

Frank, R., Massy, W. & Wind, Y. (1972) *Market Segmentation*, Prentice-Hall, Englewood Cliffs, NJ.

Hoek, J. and Esslemont, D. (1989), "Limitations of use of cluster analysis in market segmentation studies," *New Zealand Journal of Business*, 11, 82-86.

Hoek, J., Gendall, P. & Esslemont, D. (1996). "Market segmentation: A search for the Holy Grail?", *Journal of Marketing Practice*: *Applied Marketing Science*, (2), 25-34.

Hofstede, G. (1980). *Culture's Consequences: International Differences in Work-Related Values*, Sage: Beverly Hills.

Hofstede, G. (1991). *Cultures and Consequences: Software of the Mind*, McGraw-Hill, London.

Japan Shugaku Ryokô [Japan Association of School Excursions] (1997). *"Kaigai Shugaku Ryokô no Jisshi Jôkyô"*[Situation of overseas school excursions], Tokyo.

Japan Travel Bureau (1993). *JTB News* September.

Japan Travel Bureau (1997). *JTB Report '97*, Japan Travel Bureau, Tokyo.

Japan Travel Bureau (1998). *JTB Report '98*, Japan Travel Bureau, Tokyo.

Japanese Ministry of Labor (1998). *Social Trends: 1997*, Japanese Government, Tokyo.

Jenkins, M. and McDonald, M. (1997). "Market segmentation: Organizational archetypes and research agendas," *European Journal of Marketing*, 31 (1), 17-32

Kanzaki, Noritake (1991). *Monomi Ensan to Nihonjin* [Sightseeing and the Japanese], Kodansha Gendai Shinpo, Tokyo.

Kotler, P. (1991) *Marketing Management: Analysis, Planning and Implementation*, Prentice-Hall, New York.

Kumagai, F. (1984). "The Life Cycle of the Japanese Family," *Journal of Marriage and the Family*, February, 191-204.

Lawson, R. (1991). "Patterns of Tourist Expenditure and Types of Vacation Across the Family Life Cycle," *Journal of Travel Research*, Spring, 12-18.

March, R. (1994) "Tourism Marketing Myopia," *Tourism Management*, 15 (6), December, 411-415.

March, R. (1997) "Diversity in Asian outbound markets: a comparison between Indonesia, Thailand, Taiwan, South Korea and Japan:, *International Journal of Hospitality Management*, 16 (2), 231-238.

Minagawa, Shingo (1991). *Ryokogyokai* [The Travel Industry], Kyoikusha, Tokyo.

Ministry of Labor (1997). *Report on Ageing*, Tokyo.

Miyauchi, Jun (1996). *Ryokôgyokai Hayawari mappu* [A Map of the Fast Changing Travel Industry], Kou Business, Tokyo.

Nihon Shugaku Ryokô Kyokai [Japan Shugaku Ryokô Association] (1997). *"Kaigai Shugaku Ryokô no Jisshi Jôkyô"*[Situation of overseas school excursions], Tokyo.

Nikkei Weekly (newspaper), February 14, 1997.

Oppermann, M. (1995). "Family Life Cycle and Cohort Effects: A Study of Travel Patterns of German Residents," *Journal of Travel & Tourism Marketing*, 4 (1), 23-44.

Schaninger, C. M. and Danko, W. D. (1993). "A conceptual and empirical comparison of alternative household life cycle models," *Journal of Consumer Research*, 19, March, 580-594.

Silvers, C. (1997). "Smashing old stereotypes of 50-plus America," *Journal of Consumer Marketing*, 14 (4), 303-309.

Smith, W. (1956). "Product differentiation and market segmentation as alternative marketing strategies," *Journal of Marketing*, 20, 3-8.

Travel Journal International (1996). *Travel Journal*, September 14.

Travel Journal International (1997). *Travel Journal*, March 21.

Travel Journal International (1997). *Travel Journal*, May 11.

Wells, W. D. and Gubar, G. (1966). "The Life Cycle Concept in Marketing Research", *Journal of Marketing Research*, November, 355-365.

Wilkes, R. E. (1995). "Household life-cycle stages, transitions, and product expenditures", *Journal of Consumer Research*, 22, June, 27-42.

Wind, Y. (1978) "Issues and advances in segmentation research," *Journal of Marketing Research*, 15, August, 317-337.

Young, S., Otto, L. and Feigin, B. (1978). "Some practical considerations in market segmentation," *Journal of Marketing Research*, 15, 405-412.

Yuspeh, S. and Fein, G. (1982). "Can segments be born again?" *Journal of Advertising Research*, 11, 3-10.

Meeting the Needs of Japanese Consumers: Hotels in Japan and the United States

Miwako Yamaguchi
Daniel A. Emenheiser
Johnny Sue Reynolds

SUMMARY. This paper describes the significance of Japanese consumers in today's global marketplace, as well as unique accommodations, amenities, products and services provided by hotels to Japanese consumers. The business and resort hotels included in this preliminary and descriptive study were located in the ten U.S. states most frequented by Japanese travelers. Sales managers of 50 prominent U.S. hotels located in major cities representing these destinations were surveyed. Twenty-six percent of the hotels represented are entirely owned by Japanese corporations, with 71% of the hotels offering Japanese staff in-room information and brochures written in Japanese. Forty percent of the respondents perceived the availability of appropriate shopping areas to be important to Japanese travelers. *[Article copies available for a fee from The Haworth Document Delivery Service: 1-800-342-9678. E-mail address: <getinfo@haworthpressinc. com> Website: <http://www.haworthpressinc.com>]*

KEYWORDS. Japanese tourists, Japanese hotels, consumer behavior

---

Miwako Yamaguchi is a graduate of the University of North Texas. Daniel A. Emenheiser is Equal Opportunity Officer, Office of Equity and Diversity, University of North Texas, P. O. Box 310937, Denton, TX 76203-0937 (E-mail: daniele @abn.unt.edu). Johnny Sue Reynolds is Associate Professor of Hotel and Restaurant Management, School of Merchandising and Hospitality Management, University of North Texas.

Please address all correspondence to Daniel A. Emenheiser.

[Haworth co-indexing entry note]: "Meeting the Needs of Japanese Consumers: Hotels in Japan and the United States." Yamaguchi, Miwako, Daniel A. Emenheiser, and Johnny Sue Reynolds. Co-published simultaneously in *Journal of Travel & Tourism Marketing* (The Haworth Hospitality Press, an imprint of The Haworth Press, Inc.) Vol. 9, No. 1/2, 2000, pp. 201-210; and: *Japanese Tourists: Socio-Economic, Marketing and Psychological Analysis* (ed: K. S. (Kaye) Chon, Tsutomu Inagaki, and Taiji Ohashi) The Haworth Hospitality Press, an imprint of The Haworth Press, Inc., 2000, pp. 201-210. Single or multiple copies of this article are available for a fee from The Haworth Document Delivery Service [1-800-342-9678, 9:00 a.m. - 5:00 p.m. (EST). E-mail address: getinfo@haworthpressinc.com].

In today's global business environment, it is paramount that hospitality professionals, educators and students gain an understanding of the impact and intricacies associated with international business. Likewise, it is important to understand the spending patterns of visitors traveling to the United States, including dollars spent on transportation, lodging, food service, retail items and other consumer goods and services. To best meet the needs of diverse consumers, hospitality operators are advised to understand priorities, customs and practices important within the cultures of international, as well as minority consumer segments.

In regard to international tourism-generated dollars spent in the U.S. in 1995, Japanese travelers accounted for 22% of the total ($16.8 billion), followed by travelers from the United Kingdom ($8.0 million) and Canada ($7.5 billion) ("Sources of U.S Tourism Receipts," 1997). The U.S. continues to be the most popular travel destination for Japanese consumers, while South Korea is the second most frequently visited destination, followed by Hong Kong ("More Japanese Travel," 1995).

From 1981 to 1994, the number of Japanese consumers traveling overseas increased every year, except in 1991, the year of the Gulf War. The steady increase in Japanese consumer travel was attributed to the growth in both the income level, and leisure time of Japanese citizens, as well as the annual appreciation of the yen ("More Japanese Travel," 1995). In recent years, one of the most significant reasons for an increase in outbound Japanese tourism stems from the government's tourism policy. In 1989, the Japanese Ministry of Transportation launched a "10 Million Program," aimed at increasing the number of outbound tourists to 10 million by 1992. In 1994, encouraged by strong currency and less expensive package tours and airfares, a record number of 13.58 million Japanese traveled abroad. Eighty percent of this travel was tourism based ("More Japanese Travel," 1995).

Japanese arrivals in the U.S. totaled 5,047,000 in 1996, and increased by 8.4% to 5,471,000 in 1997 ("International Visitors to the U.S," 1998). During the first quarter of 1998, Asian arrivals in the U.S. decreased by 12%. However, the largest source of international travel in the U.S. was Japan, with a decrease of 4% during the first three months of 1998 (Compart, 1998). As projected by the International Trade Administration of the U.S. Department of Commerce, Japan is expected to lead overseas arrivals in the U.S. with projections increasing from 6,138,000 in 1998, to 6,563,000 in 1999 ("Overseas Arrivals to the U.S.: Top 10 Countries," 1996).

In 1993, 1.52 million or 43% of all Japanese travelers to the U.S visited Hawaii. The second most frequently visited U.S. destination was California, with 508,000 Japanese travelers, and the third was Guam, with 363,000 visitors. Based on the location where Japanese tourists enter the country (first intended address), additional destinations in the U.S. are very popular, including New York, Florida, Washington, Nevada, Illinois, Massachusetts, Washington, D.C., and Texas (United States Travel and Tourism Administration, 1993).

According to a survey conducted by the Japanese Travel Bureau in 1994, destinations for honeymooners, the market segment spending the greatest amount of money, have changed. Hawaii, the leading destination in the past, had been replaced by Australia (Inoue, 1994). Sternberg (1993) noted that honeymooners continue to be a staple of the Japanese travel market, with an estimated 90% of all couples going abroad for their honeymoons.

Japanese travelers have been stereotyped as consumers or tourists who love to shop, spend money, speak little English, travel in groups, and who are concerned about travel safety and quality (Lang, O'Leary, & Morrison, 1993). When shopping, Japanese visitors buy souvenirs for their family, relatives, friends, and fellow workers. Japanese visitors to Hawaii are known to purchase clothing, jewelry, cosmetics and leather goods ("HVCB Reports Slight Increase in Spending," 1998).

The Japanese travel market represents diverse segments. There are more females (60%) than males traveling (40%) (Japan Prime Minister's Office [JPMO], 1994). Hotel operators should keep both single and married Japanese female travelers in mind, as females are influential when making decisions concerning family finances and travel (Lang, O'Leary, & Morrison, 1993). Fields (1992) noted that it is the bride who decides the destination for a honeymoon. Room amenities and services catering to female travelers are important considerations.

Approximately 30% of all Japanese travelers are in their twenties, while children under 15 years of age comprise another rapidly expanding market segment. Consequently, it is not uncommon for major hotels to provide activities for children supervised by Japanese-speaking staff (Sternberg, 1993).

Hotel personnel who are aware of international travelers' customs and needs can best meet their expectations. Younger Japanese travelers are less interested in traditional package tours (Radin, 1994). Less than 33% of Japanese travelers participate in group tours (Sternberg, 1993). As a result, travel agencies are offering less expensive package tours including just air fare and lodging (Ono, 1993). Visitors, who select tours without meals or guides, often depend upon their hotels for information about the city and for assistance when needed. Research by Pinhey and Iverson (1994) indicates that many Japanese travelers are not comfortable participating in activities away from their hotels, unless they feel confident in their communication skills.

Many Japanese visitors read, write, and speak English well, particularly the younger business and vacation travelers. In Japan, English is mandatory in school for six years, and students are now studying conversational English as well (Laab, 1994). Therefore, Japanese travelers are beginning to depend less on package tours than in the past, but are still appreciative of hotels where they feel very comfortable and welcome.

In 1997, Japanese visitors spent $3.2 billion in Hawaii (HVCB Reports Slight Increase in Spending," 1998). In the article entitled *Hotels Train to Help Japanese Guests,* Laab (1994) interviews Tomoko Yoshida, the training director for Japanese ITT Sheraton in Hawaii. Yoshida states that approximately 60% of Sheraton's guests in Waikiki come from Japan. Laab explains that "Yoshida's job is to teach Sheraton's guest contact employees about Japanese language and culture, and how to make guests feel comfortable and understood while enjoying the U.S. experience." Customer satisfaction is a strong generator of increased hotel business, particularly for Japanese visitors (Mathews, 1993).

Unique Accommodations and Amenities in Japanese Ryokans

Generally, there are two types of lodging found in Japan: western-style hotels, and traditional Japanese-style inns, which are called ryokans. Ryokans are small, family-operated hotels, which far outnumber Western-style hotels (Hara, Okamoto, & Inagaki, 1994).

The sparsely furnished ryokan guestrooms resemble the rooms of Japanese homes with tatami mats covering the floor. Ryokan room amenities include slippers, a toothbrush, a tea set including a bottle of hot water and green tea leaf, and a yukata, light cotton kimono. Dinner and breakfast are usually included in the room rate, and are often served in the room by the chambermaid. Check-out procedures may be completed in the guestroom with the assistance of the chambermaid.

Western-Style Hotels in Japan

The number of western-style hotels in Japan has greatly increased in number since the 1964 Tokyo Olympic Games. The number of rooms available has surpassed those of ryokans in metropolitan areas such as Tokyo and Osaka. The Japanese lifestyle has become increasingly westernized since the end of World War II, and travelers have become more comfortable with western-style facilities and services, particularly the privacy component and the room rate system which excludes meals (Hara, Okamoto, & Inagaki, 1994).

Japan's Western-style hotels are similar to U.S. hotels in terms of facilities, meals, room rates, amenities, room service, and check-in and check-out procedures. However, a green tea set, slippers, yukata, and toothbrush are found in each guestroom of both ryokans and western-style hotels in Japan.

METHODOLOGY

The purpose of this preliminary and descriptive study is to identify hotel products and services perceived to be important by Japanese travelers. The business and resort properties were selected to be representative of major cities, based on national ownership, chain affiliation, and hotel size. Marketing issues surveyed in this preliminary investigation included: availability of Japanese-speaking staff members, percentage of Japanese clientele, and local attractions and businesses important to Japanese visitors in the U.S. The hotels were located in the ten most popular U.S. destinations (excluding Guam) visited by Japanese travelers (United States Travel and Tourism Administration, 1993).

The professionals surveyed were sales managers or directors of 50 prominent U.S. hotels. A questionnaire and cover letter were mailed to the hotel contacts. Of the 50 hotel representatives contacted, 42 responded, yielding a response rate of 84%. Four of the hotels contacted did not have special services catering to Japanese travelers. Therefore, for the purpose of this investigation, usable surveys totaled 38. Of these 38 sales managers, eight were Japanese.

RESULTS AND DISCUSSION

At least two managers from each geographic destination surveyed responded to the questionnaire. U.S. corporations own 47% (18) of the hotels surveyed, and Japanese corporations own 26% (10). U.S. and Japanese corporations jointly own 5% (2) of the hotels.

Thirty-seven percent (14) of the sample hotels have between 300 and 499 guestrooms, while 26% (10) have between 500 to 999 guest rooms. Sixty-three percent (24) of the responding hotels have a minimum room rate between $150 and $350.

One to 5% of the clientele was Japanese for 47% (18) of the sample hotels. Thirteen hotels had a Japanese clientele between 6 to 10%. Thirteen percent (5) of the hotels had Japanese clientele of at least 11%.

Forty-nine percent (18) of the sample hotels, noted an increase in the number of Japanese guests since the implementation of the hotels' programs catering to this market segment. Thirty-five percent (13) of the hotels had offered special services for Japanese guests since their opening.

Hotel products and services offered to meet the needs of Japanese guests are illustrated in Table 1. Respondents presented numerous reasons for offering specialized products and services to Japanese customers who comprise a major international market. A New York hotel sales manager pointed out that it is imperative to offer special services because Japanese travelers often select hotels based on the type of services offered. More than 50% of the hotels surveyed, have language-related services such as: Japanese or Japanese-speaking staff, in-room information notices in Japanese, hotel brochures in Japanese, Japanese newspapers, AT&T Language Line, and translation services. This finding reflects the importance of providing communication services for Japanese travelers. Several sales managers mentioned that easy access to Japanese speaking hotel staff and Japanese written information is necessary because a significant percentage of Japanese guests do not speak or read English. Several hotels surveyed provide a Japanese guest service desk or a Japanese hotline. A hotel directory and information on using the telephone and area guide maps written in Japanese are additional examples of communication services. The availability of Japanese newspapers is important for business travelers because it is customary for businesspersons to read the newspaper daily in Japan, even on busy commuter trains. Two hotels surveyed offered Japanese cable TV, believing it is important for guests to quickly learn of news from Japan. Sixty-five percent (24) of the responding hotels offered a Japanese breakfast which includes steamed rice, miso soup, grilled salmon, egg dish, pickles, dried seaweed and green tea. In some hotels, tofu, boiled vegetables, tsukudani and/or fruit were also included on the menu, often written in Japanese. A few managers noted that the authenticity of food is important for Japanese visitors.

The participating hotels were located in major cities, including business districts and resort areas. Forty percent (15) of the managers believe that the availability of appropriate shopping areas is important to Japanese travelers. Twenty-nine percent (11) of the managers indicated that the availability of sightseeing opportunities is important to Japanese visitors, and 21% (8) of sales managers noted the importance of the hotel's location to the business district. Sixteen percent (6) of the respondents indicated that the availability of golf and tennis amenities was important.

Japanese consumers represent a substantial market segment when traveling both at home and abroad. Japanese vacationers and business travelers are an extremely important component of the U.S. travel industry, both in the number of visitors, and the dollars spent for transportation, lodging, food service, sightseeing and shopping. As an example, a sales director representing a hotel in Hawaii noted that Japanese visitors spend $345 per day, whereas mainland U.S. visitors spend an average of $129 per person per day.

TABLE 1. Hotel Products and Services Catering to Japanese Travelers (N = 38)

	Number of Responses	Percentage of Total Responses
Japanese staff	27	71%
In-room information notice in Japanese	27	71%
Hotel brochure in Japanese	27	71%
Japanese speaking staff (non-Japanese)	25	66%
Japanese breakfast	24	63%
Japanese newspaper	23	61%
AT&T language line	21	55%
Translation service	19	50%
Green tea in each guest room	13	34%
Slippers	10	26%
Yukata	9	24%
Toothbrush	6	16%
Japanese-style room	3	8%
Japanese cable TV	2	5%
Japanese voice mail	1	3%

Another respondent conferred that Japanese visitors are desired and profitable guests, and are able to afford the relatively high room rates.

A responding New York hotel sales manager indicated that the hotel's reputation, services, size of accommodations, and security features are extremely important to Japanese executives. Room rates and access to their head offices are important to regular business travelers from Japan. Hotel corporations often have a regional sales manager based in Tokyo to attract Japanese travelers.

A respondent from Washington, D.C., mentioned that attentiveness and timeliness of responses are very important services desired by Japanese visitors and tour operators. This is a reflection of complaints made by Japanese visitors and tour guides who describe the slow service of some U.S. hotels.

Efficient and correct service is usual and expected in Japan. Upon checking into the hotel after a long flight, the guest's first impression is important.

A responding Japanese sales manager from New York was concerned about a reverse effect of offering too many services reflecting the Japanese style. This hotel offers products and services characteristic of New York, thereby providing a "touch of New York" for travelers. This particular hotel seeks to attract business transient guests and technical visit/convention groups. A sales manager from a San Diego property emphasized the importance of technical or study groups as a profitable market segment to pursue.

A California hotel sales manager reported that the decrease in Japanese travel to California has resulted from disasters, such as earthquakes and riots. The manager further noted that Las Vegas is becoming an explicit substitute for California by many Japanese visitors. It cannot be denied that violence, fatal incidents, and disasters generate strong damage to tourism. It is necessary for hoteliers to provide safety and security for all hotel guests. This is a very important service for all travelers.

CONCLUSIONS AND RECOMMENDATIONS

This preliminary and descriptive study demonstrates the significance of Japanese consumers traveling to the U.S. as well as issues important to Japanese visitors when staying in U.S. hotels. Japanese corporations own 32% (12) of the hotels represented in this study either entirely or jointly. Forty-seven percent (18) of the hotels surveyed have a Japanese clientele of at least 6 percent. With respect to future prospects regarding the size of the Japanese market segment to the property, 90% (34) of the sales managers expected an increase in the number of Japanese guests.

A responding sales director at a hotel in Hawaii stated that without Japanese services, a hotel would not be competitive for this market segment in Waikiki. In today's competitive market, a substantial number of hotels are offering a variety of products and services perceived to be important by Japanese consumers. A Japanese breakfast is offered by 63% (24) of the hotels surveyed, substantiating the importance of a Japanese breakfast to Japanese travelers (Mathews, 1993). More than 50% of the hotels surveyed provide Japanese language-related services, including Japanese staff, in-room information notices, hotel brochures, newspapers, AT&T Language Line, and a translation service. Japanese communication services are particularly important for the increasing number of independent travelers from Japan.

As more international consumers make hotel reservations by themselves, central reservation agents need to be prepared to answer questions concerning the availability of products and services hotels offer, which cater to specific market segments. This is a most important consideration.

When traveling, it is most important for Japanese consumers to stay at hotels that are close to shopping, sightseeing, or business districts. The availability of golf and tennis is often an important consideration.

Hotels located in areas frequented by a substantial number of Japanese visitors, including vacationers and business travelers, are encouraged to understand the special needs of Japanese travelers who represent a sizable and profitable market to pursue. Japanese consumers select hotels, which provide outstanding service and comfort during their stay. Hotels that successfully cater to the Japanese market, are offering products and services important to Japanese travelers, with hotel marketers expecting the magnitude of this loyal market to increase in the future.

Through training, staff members of service businesses should be made aware of cultural differences of consumer groups, to ensure that the best service is provided. Hospitality educators and trainers are advised to incorporate diversity-related components into both management and marketing courses.

As part of today's educational process, it is imperative that educators incorporate international components within their courses, so that students have the opportunity to develop a realistic awareness of international business issues. It is important for both U.S. and international students to gain a global awareness, as U.S. corporations are aggressively expanding into other countries and international corporations are entering the U.S. market. It will continue to be beneficial for students to learn more about the cultural characteristics of others, including issues related to business, travel, lodging, food, communication, and recreation.

A recommendation for future research is to conduct a similar study on a broader basis, by surveying hotel operators located throughout the U.S., in order to better identify the diverse market segments and the unique needs of not only Japanese travelers, but other international and U.S. consumers, representing specific and diverse target groups. On a domestic basis, international and minority consumers could be surveyed to compare responses between managers and consumers.

REFERENCES

Compart, A. (1998). International arrivals dip 2.1% in first quarter. *Travel Weekly, 57* (70), p. 5.

Fields, G. (1992). Changes in overseas travel reflect changing social values. *Tokyo Business Today, 60*, p. 49.

Hara, T., Okamoto, N., & Inagaki, T. (1994). *Hoteru sangyokai [Hotel industry]*. Kyoikusha, Tokyo.

HVCB reports slight increase in spending. (1998, August 31). *Travel Weekly, 57* (69), p. H18.

Inoue, S. (1994, October 14). *Today's Japan*. Tokyo: NHK.

International Visitors to the U.S. (1998, January 22). *Travel Weekly, 57* (6), p. 17.

Japan Prime Minister's Office (JPMO). (1994). *Heisei 6 nen kanko hakusho: 1994 tourism official report*. Okura-sho Insatsu-kyoku, Tokyo.

Laab, J. (1994). Hotels train to help Japanese guests. *Personnel Journal, 73* (9), p. 28-35.

Lang, C., O'Leary, J., & Morrison, A. (1993). Activity segmentation of Japanese female overseas travelers. *Journal of Travel & Tourism Marketing, 2* (4), pp. 1-22.

Mathews, W. (1993). Marketing strategies for the international market: Make the connection. *Lodging, 18* (10), p. 15-16.

More Japanese travel. (1995, April 30). *The New York Times*, p. L13.

Ono, Y. (1993, July 21). Marketing: Focus on Japan. *The Wall Street Journal*, p. B1.

Overseas Arrivals to the U.S.: Top 10 Countries. (1996, December 12). *Travel Weekly, 55* (99), p. 21.

Pinhey, T., & Iverson, T. (1994). Safety concerns of Japanese visitors to Guam. *Journal of Travel & Tourism Marketing, 3* (2), pp. 87-94.

Radin, C. (1994, January). Low tide for Japan in Hawaii. *The Boston Globe*, p. 18.

Sources of U.S. tourism receipts. (1997, January 27). *Travel Weekly, 56* (7), p. 49.

Sternberg, R. (1993). Japanese go their own way. *Asian Business, 29* (10), p. 52.

United States Travel and Tourism Administration. (1993). *1993 summary and analysis of international travel to the United States*. Washington, DC: Author.

Index

[Numbers followed by an "f" indicate figure.]

ABS. *See* Australian Bureau of
     Statistics (ABS)
Adams, K.M., 117
Adelman, I., 155
Age and cohort effects, 21-42
Ahmed, S.A., 62
Ahmed, Z.U., 131,172,174f,177-180
Airlines
     Canadian Airlines, 120
     Delta Airlines, 120
     Japan Airlines (JAL), 1-2
     Korean Air, 120
Airports
     Chek Lap Kok, 75,77
     Hong Kong International Airport, 64
Alaska (as a destination)
     Denali National Park, 47
     Division of Tourism, 46
     Division of Tourism (Tokyo), 50
     Mt. McKinley, 47
     traveler demographics, peak and
          off-season, 43-56
Albers, P.C., 116-117,119
Andersen, V., 129,131,134
Anderson, B.B., 26
Anderson, J.R., 5,11
Andrews, S.B., 13
Anger, A., 43
Anterasian, C., 4
Anton, J., 62
Apasu, Y., 13
Armstrong, R.W., 61-62,64
Asahi Shimbun Newspaper
          (publication), 192-193
Asian Business (publication), 178
Athos, A.G., 2,4
AT&T (corporation) Language Line,
          206,208

Australia
     Australian Bureau of Statistics
          (ABS), 94-94
     BTR. *See* Bureau of Tourism
          Research (BTR)
     Great Barrier Reef (GBR), North
          Queensland (QLD). *See*
          Great Barrier Reef (GBR),
          North Queensland (QLD),
          Australia (as a destination)
     IVS. *See* International Visitor
          Survey (IVS)
Australian Bureau of Statistics (ABS),
          94-95

Bailey, A.C., 180
Bakan, D., 155
Bass, F.M., 10
Batzer, E., 11
Bavelas, A., 13
Becker, G.S., 186
Beeho, A.J., 131
Behaviors of Japanese travelers
     behavioral attributes, 174f
     introduction to, 171-173
     length of stays, 178-179
     literature reviews of, 173-184
     need for research about, 181-182
     preferred activities, 173-176,
          179-181
     preferred destinations, 173-176
     preferred shopping venues and
          items, 1-19,179-181. *See also*
          Shopping behaviors and
          preferences
     travel modes, 177-178

211

For Product Safety Concerns and Information please contact our EU
representative GPSR@taylorandfrancis.com Taylor & Francis Verlag GmbH,
Kaufingerstraße 24, 80331 München, Germany

Printed and bound by CPI Group (UK) Ltd, Croydon, CR0 4YY
12/05/2025
01867336-0001